PLATONIC PIETY

MICHAEL L. MORGAN

Platonic Piety

PHILOSOPHY AND RITUAL IN

FOURTH-CENTURY ATHENS

YALE UNIVERSITY PRESS New Haven & London

Published with assistance from the foundation established in memory of Philip Hamilton McMillan of the Class of 1894, Yale College.

Designed by Richard Hendel.
Set in Pilgrim type
by Brevis Press, Bethany, Connecticut.
Printed in the United States of America.

Morgan, Michael L., 1944–
    Platonic piety : philosophy and ritual in fourth-century Athens / Michael L. Morgan
        p.   cm.
    Includes bibliographical references.
    ISBN 0-300-04517-4 (alk. paper)
    1. Plato—Religion.   2. Athens (Greece)—Religion.   3. Socrates—Religion.   4. Mysteries, Religious.   5. Ecstasy.   I. Title.
    B398.R4M67   1990   89–38418
    184—dc20   CIP

The paper in this book meets the guidelines for permanence and durability of the Committee on Production Guidelines for Book Longevity of the Council on Library Resources.

10   9   8   7   6   5   4   3   2   1

In memory of

Lillian and Maurey Morgan

CONTENTS

ACKNOWLEDGMENTS

About a dozen years ago I decided that Plato's metaphysics and epistemology should be understood within the framework of his treatment of inquiry and learning. Some years later I came to think that historians of philosophy should not forget historical context, and the idea occurred to me that Greek ecstatic ritual and mystery cults might provide a helpful vehicle for understanding Plato's thought and its place in fourth-century Athenian life. I wrote a draft of the first chapter of this book, and the project was born.

Thanks to the helpful comments of Walter Burkert, Quentin Skinner, Robert Parker, Tony Long, Myles Burnyeat, James Beckman, and several others, I revised that initial chapter again and again until its treatment of Plato's conception of Socratic piety began to seem plausible and even captivating. Walter Burkert and Albert Henrichs kindly provided me with offprints or copies of many of their important essays; James Beckman sent me a copy of his out-of-print book on Socrates and religion. The remaining chapters followed—too long, too bulky, and with too many digressions. I want to thank Robert Parker, Richard Kraut, Giovanni Ferrari, Alexander Nehamas, David Reeve, and Quentin Skinner for reading the whole manuscript or large parts of it and for encouraging and guiding me, as I worked on revision after revision. I hope that the current product is more concise, clearer, and better; they tried to make it so, and I can only hope that I have succeeded. I would also like to thank Dan Richardson for his help with the proofreading and preparation of the index.

Throughout the process Quentin Skinner, Richard Kraut, and Alexander Nehamas have been good friends and provided reassurance when I had doubts. I owe old debts to Reg Allen, Alan Bowen, John Ackrill, David Gallop, Ken Seeskin, Paul Eisenberg, Julia Annas, and Nick White. Chuck Taylor and I enjoyed an excellent lunch together in Montreal a few years ago at a time when I desperately needed to try to explain to someone what I was doing; he was a patient, receptive, if critical audience. Over the years I have learned a great deal from books and articles of Nick White, Terry Irwin, and Gregory Vlastos. At times I conceive of this book as my attempt to do for the Plato of the middle dialogues what Quentin Skinner, Jim Tully, and others have done for early modern political thought; I would be pleased if they thought that I had succeeded, if only in a small way.

This book could certainly never have been written without the special friendship of Emil Fackenheim. It is a book about humility and aspiration, resignation and hope, despair and joy, the deep polarities of religious and philosophical life. Emil has taught me a great deal about these matters, as teacher, friend, and more. I shall never be able to thank him enough.

My greatest debts and deepest love go to Aud, Deb, and Sara. Together with our two cats, Tammy and Blaze, they remind me, when I am inclined to forget, that intellectual aspiration takes place in real life and flourishes best when the latter does.

Recent work on Plato's epistemology has proceeded by examining Plato's vocabulary for knowledge, belief, and inquiry, by considering carefully the arguments in which epistemological matters play a special role, by studying the linguistic and logical thinking that is relevant to understanding Platonic epistemology, and by trying to understand the relation between Plato's views on knowledge and belief and his metaphysics. The fruits of this work, nearly four decades of it, have been great, and we have learned much from it about the dialogues and how they might be interpreted, especially as they speak to issues within the context of recent philosophical inquiry.

Occasionally, however, there have been indications that other contexts may be better suited to illuminate Plato's thinking about knowledge and belief. Some commentators, for example, look back at Plato from the vantage point of Aristotelian interests, in knowledge, scientific understanding, and reasoning. They find indications in the dialogues that Plato was already aware of and attuned to distinctions that become important for Aristotle's treatment of scientific inquiry and understanding. Other commentators take an even broader view, placing Plato in a tradition of thinking about knowledge that stretches between Parmenides and Plotinus and that involves continuous reflection about the discursive and nondiscursive character of knowing. Unlike other recent attempts to clarify and understand Plato's thinking, both of these are historically sensitive, for their primary context of interpretation is not modern philosophical inquiry but rather an ancient tradition or development of which Plato was arguably an important part.

These historically sensitive interpretations are, I think, on the right track. They situate Platonic epistemology in a historically proximate context that is well suited to illuminate his vocabulary, thinking, and views. Rather than criticize such approaches, I would like to enrich them. In a sense, what I suggest is that we consider

two further contexts for examining and interpreting Plato's epistemology, contexts which take history even more seriously by seeking
to embed Plato's discussions of belief, knowledge, and their objects
not only in Greek intellectual history, as it were, but in Greek history itself.

The first context I have in mind is this: Plato generally does not
think of belief and knowledge independently of each other or of the
development called "learning" or "education." That is, for Plato
thinking about knowledge and the objects of knowledge is thinking
about how knowledge is gotten, who can get it, under what conditions, and to what degree. Plato's epistemological thinking is focused on a process and only on states such as belief and knowledge
insofar as they occur as stages in that process. This fact is significant, and if we consistently attend to Plato's epistemological thinking in this dynamic context, we have a better chance of clarifying
and understanding what he has in mind.

Second, Plato, at least in the dialogues of his middle period, is
not concerned with epistemology or metaphysics in any explicit,
thematic way. To say this, of course, may be to exaggerate a bit,
but only a bit. My point is that Plato's intellectual and human
interests are broad and embracing; only we, after the nineteenth
century, are so facile in separating out strands of thinking and la-
beling them as "metaphysical" or "linguistic" or "psychological" or
whatever. Plato would not have done so. This commonplace is too
frequently overlooked. Commentators notice but then forget that
Spinoza's primary interests are moral or that Descartes' are scientific. Similarly, commentators often do not bother even to ask what
Plato's primary and determinative interests are. What I would like
to suggest is that one grand or overarching interest of Plato's is
religious, in a broad sense. That is, Plato is interested in understanding the place of humankind in the cosmos, in relation to the polis,
its values, commitments, traditions, and self-image, and to the gods,
the divine. He comes to think that a certain kind of life, which
includes a particular primary type of activity, is better than any
other kind of life, precisely because of how it situates human beings
in history, the world, and the polis, and vis-à-vis the gods. Moreover, as I shall try to show, Plato's epistemological and metaphysical thinking, as we call them, are aspects of his appropriation and
development of a certain mode of piety, a mode of piety that in-

corporates and reflects an ongoing attitude to Athens, its values, traditions, and political decisions. I propose that we situate Plato's epistemological thinking in the history of early fourth-century Athens by focusing on the religious character of that thinking. Religion and especially ritual will thus become a bridge between Plato's developing account of what philosophy is and Athenian history.

This is a book, then, about one way in which religious terminology and religious life play a role in Plato's thought. The aspect of religion that I focus on, human aspiration to divine status, provides a valuable context in which developments in Plato's epistemology and metaphysics can be understood. This conception of human aspiration also expresses a critical attitude toward traditional Athenian piety and religious life and thereby toward the Athenian political and moral character. Put differently, Platonic piety provides an interpretive vehicle for understanding Plato's epistemology in its historical, political context. And if one is inclined to agree that such a context is necessary, or at least helpful, for understanding what Plato might have intended by his written dialogues and what his fourth-century readers might have understood them to mean, one will appreciate the results of this sort of study.

Throughout, then, this book attempts to do two things simultaneously. It tries to explore the dialogues of Plato's middle period—from the *Meno* to the *Phaedrus*—in terms of their religious portrayal of philosophical inquiry and their epistemological, political, and metaphysical treatment of issues relevant to that portrayal. Such a discussion has been infrequently undertaken in this century, especially during the past four or five decades.[1] But a great deal of exciting work on Greek religion and on Plato's philosophy is relevant to it. Substantively I draw on a very rich tradition or set of traditions, and my study could not have been written without the excellent results of many others.

The second task of the book is methodological. Plato's dialogues have been studied, during the past century, by many different types of readers—with a variety of interpretive strategies and a host of diverse goals. Some of Plato's readers are scholars—classical philologists, students of Greek law, religion, poetry, or education, and historians, especially social and political historians. Others are—for lack of a better term—literary readers, for example, students of classical literature and culture. Still others are critical—political theorists and philosophers of all kinds, historians of philosophy among them. Within this diversity, there is of course a great deal of overlap. The best of the critical readers will take classical scholarship very seriously, and many classical scholars will produce philosophically rich readings. At the same time, within the broad circle of philosophical readers, one tendency has become dominant, at least since the mid-1950s, and that is the tendency to approach Plato (and not only Plato) as if he were a contemporary philosopher dealing with current, indeed timeless philosophical problems, whose work can be translated into or at least interpreted by contemporary philosophical terminology, and whose arguments, distinctions, and claims can best be identified and assessed against the background of contemporary philosophical discussion. In its own way, moreover, this tendency is as prominent among philosophical readers who reflect scrupulously on the dialogues' literary character as it is among analytic readers, who read Plato in terms of Frege, Russell, Wittgenstein, and other analytic philosophers.[2]

It is simply false, of course, to charge the bulk of philosophical readers of Plato with complete neglect of historical context. Most attend to the nuances of the Greek language, the fifth-century context for moral and logical vocabulary, and more.[3] Few really good philosophical readers forget totally that Plato wrote Greek dialogues in fourth-century Athens. Nonetheless, it is true that attention to these "historical" matters plays a relatively minor role, for the point in studying Plato philosophically after all is one of relevance to current philosophical investigation, and hence the best reading is obtained by understanding the text in a way that is most interesting and revealing by our own standards of philosophical worth.

There are old, familiar problems lurking here—about interpretation in general and about the role and character of the history of philosophy in particular.[4] Let me set them to one side, with the single observation that if contemporary relevance is the final goal of all history of philosophy,[5] this does not conflict with a serious historical reading but in fact *requires* one.[6] And my point about the history of philosophy as it has been practiced during the past half-century is that often it disregards such a reading rather than demanding it, and in the study of Plato this is perhaps more common than not. There should be no mistake about what I am saying. Many excellent studies of Plato do utilize "historical" background, but most do not, or they do so minimally. And even the ones that do use such material do not treat the historical context as an important consideration that significantly shapes or directs an interpretation. In this book, I have tried to do just this. By focusing on the notion of religious aspiration and its total setting in regard to religious terminology and ritual, I have attempted to trace the development of a variety of themes in Plato's epistemology and metaphysics within the context of Athenian history, from Socrates' execution approximately to the Battle of Mantinea in 362 B.C.E.

In one sense, this book might be viewed as an attempt to revive an older mode of reading Plato, a mode of reading associated with such outstanding classicists as Burnet, Taylor, Cornford, Hackforth, Bluck, and Guthrie. In another sense, however, the present study could be conceived as a contribution to a recent movement, an attempt to treat Plato as others have treated Machiavelli, Hobbes, Locke, Hegel, and Bentham, among many great figures in the history of philosophy. Quentin Skinner's studies of Hobbes, J. G. A. Pocock's book on Machiavelli, John Dunn's and Richard Ashcraft's treatments of Locke—all these and more come to mind.[7] There is a contemporary "movement" toward rethinking great philosophers in their historical context, and my own work is an attempt to do something similar for an ancient philosopher—where problems of dating, historiographical accuracy, and so on are greatly increased.

Much of this historical-philosophical work has been encouraged either by the development of intellectual history that is a history of ideas *in* and *not detached from* context, or by the impact of interpretive theory on the study of literary works. And the latter movement is associated with developments in continental philosophy and questions about methodology in the social sciences.[8] The work of Skinner, Dunn, and others is the historical dimension of a pondering of the general historicization of the philosophical enterprise, the systematic side of which is represented by Rorty, MacIntyre, Cavell, and others.[9]

Some philosophical historians of philosophy, then, have come to this new attention to the historical context of philosophical writings and philosophical thinking out of a general commitment to historicism or relativism or a general worry about the possibility or necessity of either. Others come to it out of a particular concern with the changing character of political theory in the modern world. Nonetheless, by now anyone entering the fray can hardly avoid the influence of these predecessors, or be unaware of the compelling presence of Nietzsche, Heidegger, Gadamer, Foucault, and Ricoeur, of Kuhn, MacIntyre, Rorty, and many others. One might be motivated to avoid skepticism and seek a recovery of author's intentions, or one might be struggling with the question of the historicity of philosophy itself. One might be committed to the historical character of all interpretation, or one might be puzzled about the possibility of philosophical transcendence or the necessity of radical historicism. Or, more than likely, one might be moved by all of these considerations and others as well.

Without the work of others, this book could not have been written: Hammond, Hornblower, Sealey, and Cawkwell on fourth-century Greek history; Rohde, Wilamowitz, Nilsson, Dodds, Henrichs, Guthrie, Lloyd-Jones, Parker, and especially Burkert on Greek religion; Evans-Pritchard, Lienhardt, Douglas, and Thomas as well. Whatever novelty the book may have lies in its attempt to synthesize their results in order to try to situate historically investigation of the development of Plato's epistemology. This enterprise may well be foolhardy. But for all its boldness and seeming incaution, I hope that it impresses some readers as plausible and suggestive.[10]

CHAPTER ONE

SOCRATIC PIETY AS

PLATO SAW IT

In his book on Kant's life and thought Ernst Cassirer notes that in the years 1765 to 1770 Kant was significantly influenced by the recent publication of Leibniz' *New Essays*. This fact might lead the student to study Leibniz in preparation for studying Kant, but such a strategy is not correct. For the interpreter of Kant the issue of Leibniz' influence does not concern the

> actual historical meaning of Leibniz's system, but instead with how it presented itself to Kant's mind. Kant's interpretation of individual Leibnizian concepts and propositions is not free of misunderstanding and hardly could be, since, despite Dutens's collected edition [1768], the most important sources for Leibniz's philosophy which are available to us—especially the major part of the philosophical and mathematical correspondence—were still undiscovered in the eighteenth century. But this is of little importance for the history of Kant's intellectual revolution, since it is not a matter of what Leibniz was, but of how Kant understood and saw him.[1]

Here Cassirer suggests a principle of historical interpretation that is too seldom heeded, that important predecessors influence their descendants as those descendants see them, not as we do.

What is true of Kant and Leibniz is also true, if for different reasons, of Plato and Socrates. Even though Plato was thoroughly familiar with Socrates and doubtless knew much more about him than we do, still the influence that Socrates had on Plato's thinking is determined not by what Socrates "actually" said and taught but by what Plato took him to mean, how Plato understood him. In this chapter I want to consider how Plato understood Socratic piety, for his subsequent thinking on religious and epistemological matters is in important ways a revision and enrichment of that understanding.

This chapter attempts to clarify Socrates' religious life and his theological commitments as Plato perceived and portrayed them.[2] I base my account largely on the portrait of Socrates given to us by Plato in the *Apology* and several other dialogues. My treatment is not comprehensive. A complete account of Socratic piety as Plato saw it would require a book examining from the religious side much of what we know about Socrates from Plato's dialogues. In contrast, I focus on one feature of Socrates' theology, his understanding of the gap that separates the divine from the human and of the capacity and aspiration of human beings to overcome that gap. This theological issue is one of a cluster of issues involving the divine, the human, and their interrelationships. In this chapter I largely ignore questions about the nature and existence of the divine, about justice (providence, for example), about sacrifice (including propitiation), and about ritual veneration. Instead, because I think it is more central to Socratic theology as it came to influence Plato, I focus on human aspiration to divine status. What this means is that I shall be discussing the role of the soul's immortality in Socrates' thought.[3]

My strategy will be indirect. First, I shall look at passages from the *Apology* and set out alternatives for the Platonic picture of Socratic piety.[4] We shall see that although these texts involve rich discussion of religious issues, they do not fix precisely Socrates' theology, particularly his beliefs about the immortality of the soul. Second, I shall develop an account of Greek religious life and thought for the period 415–399 B.C.E. This period will emerge as one of increasing religious diversity and dramatic change in which possession cults, worship of foreign deities, and salvation-oriented initiation rites come to play a central role.[5] Third, I shall consider how the ritual conduct of different cults reflects alternative views of cosmic structure and especially the divine-human relationship. Finally, I shall propose an account of how Plato sees Socrates' place in this religious setting, calling upon texts that support my contention that—for Plato—Socrates viewed his goal as immortal tranquility[6] and his method as a "philosophical" version of ecstatic initiation rites.[7]

SOCRATES did have beliefs concerning the existence of the gods and the influence of divine beings on human affairs. The *Apology* contains a doctrine of particular divine providence cast in the form of Socrates' *daimonion*. This doctrine plays several roles in the speech, one of which is as evidence against the charge of impiety, or failure to believe in the existence of the city's gods.[8] Whether Socrates did revere the gods of Athens—Athena Polias, Zeus Meilichios, Apollo, Demeter, Dionysos, Artemis, and so on—is, I think, beyond serious question,[9] but I ignore the matter here. Suffice it to say that the impersonalization of the gods, if a historical phenomenon worthy of our assent, is not yet fully accomplished in Socratic thought. Rather than discuss these matters, I shall focus on the human soul and its aspiration to divine status.

The first passage that deserves our attention reviews the events that led to Socrates' practice of dialogical interrogation and ultimately to his indictment (20c2–24b2). It is the famous story of Chaerephon's visit to the Delphic oracle and his question, asking whether anyone was wiser than Socrates. The god responded that no one was wiser, and Socrates, bewildered because convinced of his own lack of wisdom, set out to inquire into what the enigmatic oracle meant (see 21e–22a). His conclusion is found in this statement:

> From this examination, Gentlemen of Athens, much enmity has risen against me, of a sort most harsh and heavy to endure, so that many slanders have arisen, and the name is put abroad that I am "wise." For on each occasion those present think I am wise in the things in which I test others. But very likely, Gentlemen, it is really the God who is wise, and by his oracle he means to say that, "Human nature is a thing of little worth, or none." It appears that he does not mean this fellow Socrates, but uses my name to offer an example, as if he were saying that, "He among you, Gentlemen, is wisest who, like Socrates, realizes that he is truly worth nothing in respect to wisdom." That is why I still go about even now on behalf of the God, searching and inquiring among both citizens and strangers, should I think some one of them is wise; and when it seems he is not, I help the God and prove it. Due to this pursuit, I have no leisure worth mentioning either for the affairs of the City or

for my own estate; I dwell in utter poverty because of my service to God. (22e8–23c2)

The traditional role of the Pythia was to endorse the decisive gap between divine power, knowledge, and immortality and human frailty.[10] This chasm between the divine and the human was at the heart of the Delphic maxim "Know thyself," which meant "Know that you are human and only that"—know your limits, the limits of finitude and mortality.[11] It is this belief that is voiced and adumbrated in Socrates' speech quoted above, especially where he interprets the oracle as meaning that "human nature is a thing of little worth, or none." If there is novelty or at least nuance in the Socratic version, it lies in the specification of wisdom as the core of the divine-human separation.[12] But even this feature has significant predecessors—Xenophanes, Heraclitus, Parmenides, to name but three.[13] And in light of this feature, that is, wisdom, the justification for the indictment against Socrates begins to take shape. Socrates appears to have wisdom because he seeks it in a way easily misunderstood. So he seems to be claiming divine status for himself and for others, including the physical thinkers, who gain the same ends. It is no wonder he is charged with "not acknowledging the city's gods," for the traditional gods exist only as utterly separated in status from humankind. His defense involves turning to Apollo and billing himself as his servant and defender. Indeed, Socrates portrays his life as an effort to ensure the Pythia's wisdom and thereby to save the divine-human separation. Unlike his enemies, Socrates sees himself as loyal rather than opposed to the traditional gods. Whatever initiative there is to span the divide that separates gods from men is the gods' alone. Providence but not presumption (hubris) is central to Socratic piety.[14]

If the tale of Chaerephon's visit to Delphi and its sequel are historically accurate, they portray a decidedly traditional Socrates. Parke, although uncertain about the most likely date for the visit, endorses its historicity.[15] Individual petitions were not unknown, and the story has a ring of biographical reminiscence that would have been hard to falsify. And if historical, the tale and Socrates' affinity with Delphi would establish Socrates' allegiance to the traditional gap between human achievement and divine status.[16]

But the *Apology* has more to say on this matter of divine-human separation. What at first glance seems clear and incontrovertible soon becomes imprecise and ambiguous. A short time later in his speech Socrates returns to discuss his mission, but this time he brings together three themes—his inquiry regarding the limits of human wisdom, the fear of death and our ignorance of what follows it, and the excellence of the soul and care for it (28a–32a). In so doing Socrates makes two crucial points: first, that his primary concern and what ought to be the primary concern of every Athenian is "doing what is best," which means developing "the greatest possible excellence of [the] soul" (29e); second, that fear of death is inappropriate to such a project because (1) it presumes a wisdom men do not have and (2) death is damage or harm to the body but not to the soul (30c–31a).

In the course of *Apology* 28a–31c Socrates makes these two points. Both, however, need to be developed and defended. This section of Socrates' speech takes off from the distinction between a traditional, honor- or prestige-oriented set of values and another set that includes what is right, just, or pious (28b). Dodds, following Ruth Benedict, notably dubbed this a difference between shame and guilt cultures.[17] The jury might charge Socrates with having put himself in danger of death by continued dialogue and inquiry, and surely Socrates would be ashamed of lacking the power to control his situation and avoid such danger. But, Socrates responds, the issue is not one of power; it is rather one of living as a good or bad man, and that involves doing what is just, which here means "disobedience to a superior, be he god or man" (29b). At times Socrates contrasts acquisitiveness, reputation, honor, and shame with being a good man and doing what is just (see 39d). As the speech develops, however, the contrast changes to one of reputation, honor, and acquisitiveness, on one side, and truth, understanding, and virtue, on the other (29d–30a). Finally, the contrast is drawn between money and other human goods on the one hand, and virtue on the other. The goal of these substitutions, it seems to me, is to associate wisdom, truth, and virtue, where a state of soul is what Socrates has in mind, and to oppose these to the body, its goods—admiration, wealth, and so forth—and its evils—disenfranchisement, exile, or execution (30c–d). The purpose of Socratic inquiry is the attainment of virtue or wisdom, as much as is humanly possible. The wiser Athenians are, the better they are as human beings and therefore the more like gods. The body is the center of physical desires and satisfactions and of physical damage—deprivation, dislocation, death. But these goods and evils have nothing to do with wisdom, for they concern the body and not the soul, whereas wisdom or virtue is a quality of soul alone. A good man has a wise or excellent soul—whether he is poor or even facing exile or execution.

Whereas Socrates' Delphic affiliation suggested a traditional fidelity to the virtually insurmountable gap between the divine and the human, the cleavage between wisdom as virtue of the soul and physical deprivation and harm encourages the rival view that the gap can be traversed, the separation overcome. Although he does not say so explicitly, Socrates seems to suggest that human wisdom is attainable to a degree worth aspiring to and that divine wisdom is superior but not incommensurable with it.[18] There is a continuum of wisdom, not a divide between all and nothing. And if this lifetime affords insufficient opportunity to do more than begin the quest, then we are bound to adopt a doctrine of the soul's immortality in order to ensure time for further stages.[19]

The current passage contains one further ingredient. Socrates makes the remarkable statement that if he had feared death so much as to abandon his divinely mandated pursuit of wisdom, then the charges would have been appropriate. For to shirk his charge out of fear of death would have been tantamount to (1) disobedience to the gods via the oracle and hence disobedience to a divine superior, a shameful act, and (2) a presumption of knowledge about death, where "to think one is wise when one is not" (29a) is equivalent to thinking that one is divine. Such hubris is de facto "not acknowledging the existence of gods" of the traditional sort. "No man knows death," Socrates says, implying that the gods do. Only they know whether it is a good to be desired or an evil to be feared. Socrates is distinctive because he neither has "satisfactory knowledge of things in the Place of the Dead" nor thinks that he has such knowledge. On one reading, this passage reinforces the Delphic Socrates' commitment to an intraversable chasm between gods and humankind. On another, however, the text reaffirms a separation that can be mitigated by a pursuit of knowledge. Perhaps no human knowledge is substantial enough to be considered divine; alternately, there might be stages of virtue and wisdom that stretch out between the ignorance of poets, craftsmen, and politicians, and the perfect, immutable wisdom of the gods. One who decodes the Delphic oracle is not Apollo, but neither need he be the Pythia herself.[20]

The *Apology* provides some encouragement for this alternative view. Although Socrates admits no "satisfactory knowledge" of death and the things that follow it, he does engage in discussion of these matters. And his discussion, aimed at talking about whether death is good or bad, is stimulated by an act of providence, a religious reason for discussing the post-mortem affairs of the soul. Before we leave the *Apology*, we must turn to 39e–41d and this discussion.

Convicted and condemned, Socrates turns at the end of his speech to those who voted for his acquittal, with words of consolation.[21] What he says concerns his impending death and his reasons for hoping that death is good. To summarize what Socrates has thus far led us to believe about death, he has no satisfactory knowledge of death and what follows it, and death is harm to the body but not to the soul. In addition, he has focused attention on two attributes that distinguish the gods from humankind: wisdom and power. Chastising his fellow Athenians, he charges them to exemplify their reputation for both of these qualities by attending to the cultivation of the soul's virtue (29d–e).[22] In essence he identifies genuine human power with wisdom, and wisdom becomes the fulcrum on which turns the whole issue of how divine a human being can become. One feature of this discussion, then, is a somewhat surprising disregard for the most prominent, traditional characteristic of divinity—immortality.[23] If there is a stage of human knowledge that can count in favor of the soul's divine status, surely it would be reinforced by the soul's immortality.

In his final words to those among the dicasts who supported him, Socrates makes several observations. He begins by noticing that his daimonion did not oppose his coming to court or his speech, and since it customarily appeared to protect him from error and evil, he can infer that its absence is a signal that death is not an evil for him. This absence, he says, is a "reason for high hope that death is good" (40c), and a suggestion that "to die now and be released from my affairs is better for me" (41d). The *Apology* ends with these words: "But it is already the horn of parting—I to die and you to live. Which of us goes to the better is unclear to all but the god"

(42a), whom I take to mean Apollo. These remarks make two points, one more ambiguous than the other. The first is that although knowledge of what death is and whether it is a benefit is ultimately only the prerogative of the divine, men can have reasons for holding beliefs about death.[24] This possibility is a further development of the idea that there are grades of knowledge—from presumption, to enlightened ignorance, to rational belief, to divine knowledge. The second point is less clear: Does Socrates have a rational belief about death being good *for him* or about death being a human good per se? The absence of his daimonion is clearly a signal that at least his death is not an evil for Socrates. But his final remark recalls his earlier suggestion that incarnate existence is an obstacle to genuine virtue and that death is never a real evil, meaning a real hindrance to excellence of the soul. Only if physical life were of uncertain worth in general and death a secure good would Socrates suggest—even obliquely—that from a divine vantage point his death may be better for him than the continued lives of his jury will be for them.[25]

Socrates' inference from the absence of his personal divinity, however, frames a more important passage, one that raises the question of Socrates' commitment to the soul's immortality in the most vivid way. The passage includes an argument which Socrates calls a "further reason for high hope that death is good" (40c). It is a simple argument by exhaustion of alternatives. Death is either nonexistence with no awareness, like a dreamless sleep, or it is a change of abode for the soul, from this to another world, peopled by true judges, demigods, heroes, poets, and victims. Socrates argues that death would be good in either case, but he commits himself to neither portrait. On the basis of this passage alone, we cannot conclude that Socrates takes death to be nonexistence or an altered state of soul. And if the condition of such a soul, like that of those in the other world, is immortality (41c), it is not certain that Socrates is committed to the immortality of the human soul. All that is certain is that he is familiar with stories of an afterlife, not that he believes that these stories are true.[26]

I am not persuaded that this passage can be satisfactorily illuminated by our discussion of earlier portions of Socrates' speech. The traditional portrait of the divine-human separation is qualified by the possibility of grades of knowledge, but only if Socrates is committed to the soul's immortality can we confidently take these grades as stages on the way to the attainment of fully divine status. The conception of Greek religiosity present in these stories of an afterlife is different from that present in the Delphic maxim. To be sure, although Plato does not have Socrates explicitly endorse these stories, he does have him appropriate them, in a sense, by noting that the greatest good would be gotten by the discarnate soul's testing and questioning the great men—Agamemnon, Odysseus, Palamades, Ajax, Sisyphus, and others—about their wisdom, both genuine and bogus.[27] In other words, even in a discarnate state, wisdom and any techniques for gaining it would be at a premium, and both can best be pursued without physical encumbrances. But Socrates surely could modify these stories in his own way without believing that they are true. We need more evidence than this to be persuaded that Plato's portrait includes a Socratic belief in the soul's immortality.[28]

The religious views represented in the *Apology*, if they express accurately Plato's perception of Socratic theology, did not develop in a historical vacuum. Greek religious life and thought underwent important changes during the final decades of the fifth century. Plato's interpretation of Socrates' beliefs and conduct should be understood within the context of the evolving character of Athenian religious life in these years.

This is not the occasion to attempt a comprehensive portrait of Greek religious life and thought during the decades of Plato's youth and the final years of Socrates' life. It is important, however, to sketch those features most relevant to the present purpose. Amid the diversity of religious cults and ideas current in the Athens of those years, there was a tendency toward possession cults, ecstatic rites, and salvation-oriented initiation rituals that expressed a widespread dissatisfaction with the traditional divine-human separation. This traditional attitude can be called "Delphic theology."[29] Within the broader parameters of Athenian religious life and thought, this tendency to ecstatic religiosity, I shall argue, forms the precise context for understanding Plato's conception of Socratic piety.

RELIGIOUS life and religious thought are not disconnected phenomena, and although either can occur without the other, one is more

likely to encounter a religiously active society that has neither the
desire nor the conceptual apparatus for religious self-reflection than
an articulated theology without any ceremonial or pragmatic foundation.[30] Athens, in the waning years of the fifth century (from 415
to 399), was active in both respects. We are fortunate to have rich
evidence regarding both ritual and theological activity.[31] Thanks to
the work of Dodds, Lloyd-Jones, and others, the evidence for theological diversity, its continuity and changes, is easily accessible,
although the interpretive conclusions about the most prominent
tendencies of the period have yet to be decisively drawn.[32] Recent
work on popular religion and morality[33] has added an important
dimension to our understanding of Greek religious thought, showing
how the latter occurs as a justification for, rejection of, or modification to ordinary religious conduct and belief. In short, we are in
an excellent position to isolate those strands of Greek religion that
will help us to place Plato's understanding of Socrates' revision of
the Delphic theology in its most appropriate and revealing context.

Socrates died at seventy. We cannot be certain how much his
thinking changed during the last thirty years of his life—the years
of the Peloponnesian War, the reign of the Thirty Tyrants, the democratic restoration, the heyday of Aristophanic comedy, the rise of
Cleon and the new politicians, the Sicilian expedition and the profanations surrounding it, and countless other events and trends to
which no sensitive thinker could have turned a deaf ear.[34] But rather
than presume a Socrates whose thinking was wholly shaped prior
to 429–428, I propose a man involved in the intellectual, political,
and religious affairs of his city. Clearly he was aware of and influenced by the physical thinkers of the fifth century (Archelaus, Anaxagoras, Empedocles, Diogenes, and Zeno) and by the methods,
themes, aims, and roles of the sophists. Aristophanes lampoons the
sophists through Socrates in 424. By then Socrates was intellectually
aware and practiced in interrogation through dialogue. He was also
familiar with Prodicus' philology and religious thought, Gorgias'
rhetoric, the natural philosophy of Anaxagoras, Empedocles, and
much else. If the sophists were the intellectual savants of the day,
then Socrates was one of them; this much of Aristophanes' assault
must be accurate. But it is by no means clear how much sophistic
thought he accepted, how much he rejected. One is hardly surprised
that Socrates could be tainted by association—as an opponent of

democracy, as a critic of traditional religion, as an enemy of the city. The criticism expressed most clearly in the famous fragment from Critias' satyr-play *Sisyphus* was in the air,[35] but we cannot be sure how fully Socrates endorsed it.

From what we can tell, the rational critique of the traditional gods—with Xenophanes as its ancestor and the sophists, together perhaps with Euripides,[36] its major spokesmen—was only one among many tides that rolled in upon Greek piety during the fifth century and especially during the Peloponnesian War. One thing is certain: traditional Greek piety was not swept away by such tides, either in life or in thought.[37]

Greek religion, as it developed in the sixth and fifth centuries, was a heterogeneous, comprehensive fabric of rituals (from the most casual and personal to the most primary and public), myths and stories, sacrifices, anointments, oracles, laws and institutions, festivals, and beliefs, some sophisticated but most unreflected upon and rarely articulated. It had no center, no Achilles' heel; it spread over the entire civilization of classical Greece in such a way that only the demise of that whole culture and society could have destroyed it. It was a religiosity of time and space, the sacred calendar filled with holy days, festivals, and rites,[38] and the living spaces filled with shrines, altars, and temples, architecturally blending the artificial and the natural into a single, multifaceted setting for sacrifice, petition, gratitude, and obeisance.[39] Greek religion was, to be sure, centralized: weakly at the international level through Delphi and the other oracles, through the common heritage of Homer and Hesiod, and through a sense of Hellenic kinship,[40] and more strongly through the particular conglomerations wrought in the major poleis and their spheres of influence. Each of these—Athens, Sparta, Thebes, Argos, Corinth, and so on—brought together gene, phratries, and families whose special cultic itinerary became, by agglomeration and compromise, the ritual affairs of demes and the polis.[41] Zeus, Artemis, Apollo, Demeter, and all the other native and incorporated deities were worshiped in countless ways, under a variety of guises, in diverse poleis throughout Greece and the colonies.

The enormous bulk of the acts of worship were sacrificial, offerings brought to ask divine favor or to show gratitude for it.[42] The Athenian in the final decades of the fifth century would have participated in hundreds of sacrifices and anointments in the course of a year, many small and private, involving an ancestral deity or a guardian divinity, but some performed by the Athenian demos as a whole, for example, the sacrifices conducted before the Sicilian expedition.[43] There can be no doubt that sacrificial rituals not only continued during and after the war but indeed proliferated. Andokides' On the Mysteries shows how much the citizens feared to undertake any project of significance without divine support.[44] The mutilation of the Hermes and the rumors of several profanations of the Eleusinian mysteries generated fear and anger; for different reasons, such acts were considered bad omens, events that would call forth divine punishment instead of care and aid.[45]

The theological superstructure of this cultic-sacrificial religious life—to the degree that we can identify and talk about a *single* theological framework—has been well discussed by Hugh Lloyd-Jones. It is what I have called the Delphic theology, which viewed the gods as distant and powerful, and men as frail and endangered.[46] Human affairs, voluntary action as much as its consequences, are under divine control, the guiding principle of which is the justice of Zeus—a retributive response to attention, fidelity, and kinship. Mary Douglas has shown how sacrificial rituals express in action a conception of god and man as radically separated in power and status.[47] This was the case for one dimension of Greek piety in Plato's and Socrates' Athens. For many of their contemporaries and at times for Athens as a whole, the sense of human worth paled before the dread of divine whim and divine power. It was ironic that the Pythia, which best expressed that theology and that piety both in act and in utterance, was held beyond Athenian reach during the years of the Peloponnesian War. It was both physically and prophetically estranged from Athens.[48]

No one expresses this traditional Greek piety better than Herodotus and Xenophon.[49] Both, in their own ways, follow the road of sacrificial cult, oracle, divination, and Delphic theology. And though what is haunting in Herodotus is glib in Xenophon, something deeply traditional underlies both.

But there is more to Greek religious life and thought in these years than traditionalism. In addition to the rational, critical view associated with the sophists and the traditionalism of so much of Greek life and conduct, another ingredient, itself variegated and

uneven, makes the final years of the fifth century especially exciting. I am referring of course to the introduction into Athens of new
cults, new rites, and new ideas, a stream that becomes a flood and
reaches its high-water mark during these years.[50]

If the prevalent Delphic attitude is submissive awe, an uncertain
caution in the face of divine power, it is not the only attitude current in Athens as the fifth century comes to a close. Athenian boldness and assertiveness mix with reserve and fearfulness to form a
frenetic atmosphere of highs and lows. It is during this period, for
example, that for the first time a Greek general is deified.[51] The idea
that flesh-and-blood heroes could attain divine status was long a
part of Greek religious culture.[52] But during the war years ideas such
as these stir emotion in a new, more urgent way.[53] In the midst of
a lengthy, debilitating war, they signal not inflated self-esteem as
much as an almost pathetic hopefulness, despair inventing its own
antidote. At the same time that the aristocracy is being breached
by a new class of nonlanded artisans and merchants, so the cosmic
structure is collapsing. What seemed a tight circle of traditional
deities is now being invaded—in part by deified human beings, more
prominently by imported divinities, and ultimately by worshipers
themselves.

Perhaps the single most significant religious phenomenon of the
final decades of the fifth century is the introduction of new cults
into Athens.[54] Access to Athens is provided, in mid- and late century, by its cosmopolitanism; Athens is the center of the empire,
the home of craftsmen, artists, poets, and so on. In addition, during
and after the war, it is a center for naval mercenaries, many of
whom are the vehicles for importing new cults and new deities into
the city. As ties to deme, phratry, and polis weaken, help is sought
outside the circle of conventional gods and rituals. New alternatives
invade Athens, ones not tied to the old, traditional social structure.
Among the most popular is Asclepius, an Epidauran import,[55] but
there are others—Bendis from Thrace, Ammon from Egypt, Kybele
from Phrygia, and others.[56] And there is, too, an increased interest
in charismatic religious leadership,[57] magic, and religious societies:[58]
Empedocles and Pythagoras, although foreigners and known only
by reputation in Athens, are the most famous figures of this type.[59]
If Lloyd-Jones persuasively charts the continuous course of the
traditional Delphic theology into this period, then Dodds just as

convincingly charts the era's ecstatic, nonrational dimensions. Euripides' *Bacchae* pinpoints the awful results when the two traditions collide.[60]

From 415 to 399 Athens was the scene of social and political upheaval. Overwhelmed by these traumatic changes, some Athenians doubtless turned to the security of the rituals and especially the sacrificial system of the past. Others, however, saw these rites as increasingly meaningless and began to doubt the reliability of the conventional piety. Not convinced of the justice of the traditional gods, not persuaded of the efficacy of traditional sacrifices or the benefits of divination, and not moved to accept the inferences drawn from suffering and hardship, these Athenians turned in a variety of directions, some to new cults of healing, others to ecstatic rites, still others to magic. Some also adopted or created forms of rational or intellectual religiosity. And some synthesized seemingly divergent modes of piety into a personal set of beliefs.

Among the rites and religious forms popular in these years, many involved practices in which the individual strove for a new, disengaged status or achieved such a status by means of divine possession. In other words, either through human endeavor or because of human accessibility to divine presence, man became divine, if only momentarily,[61] and in this way, the promise of salvation was understood to be the promise of periodic, perhaps permanent divinity.[62] Such rites and the cults that develop around them are not uncommon in Africa and elsewhere among traditional or primitive societies.[63] Where they occur, they reflect a belief in the continuity between human life and the divine. On the one hand, conventional ritual sacrifice, piacular and petitionary, expresses a cosmos in which man and the gods are radically separated and in which the distance between them is bridged, if at all, only by divine action according to divine rules or will. On the other hand, however, possession rites and ecstatic initiation ceremonies express belief in a different cosmic scheme, one in which the human can, in various ways, attain divine status.[64]

Perhaps we can say no more than that the Athens of Socrates' final years and of Plato's youth was the scene of extreme religious heterogeneity and of intense unresolved religious conflict. The old and the new mingled. Festivals were celebrated with new sincerity by some, with offhand perfunctoriness by others. So it was with sacrifices and anointments. Certain ritual events, such as the Eleusinian mysteries, gained in appeal and importance, but even these distinctive attempts to institutionalize ecstasy were not universally acclaimed.[65] Probably the traditional round of festivals and sacrifices had its most vigorous adherents among the relatively uneducated, while many of the intellectual elite were drawn to cultic societies and to ecstatic rites overlaid with intricate myths.[66] There was conflict and compromise, but it is impossible to identify a single dominant religious tendency of the age.[67]

PLATONIC dialogues are largely fictional, or so we today are inclined to think. But even so, certain features of the dialogues surely reflect impressionistic if not precise historical truths. As we try to place Plato's conception of Socrates in the religious context of the final years of the fifth century, and as we turn to the dialogues for guidance, the following bits of evidence stand out. Often in the dialogues Socrates is associated with new cults and divinities. At the outset of the Republic, Socrates is portrayed as attending a festival for the newly imported Bendis,[68] and at the end of the Phaedo, his last words to Crito remind his old friend of a debt owed to Asclepius.[69] Note that in the dialogues Protagoras and Parmenides are both treated as quasi-religious leaders,[70] and Socrates is portrayed as having affiliations with them both, as a sort of competitor. And in the Phaedo Socrates is attended in jail by, among others, two visiting Pythagoreans, whose dialogue with him concerns the immortality of the soul, death, and the philosophical life. There is evidence also that Socrates is familiar with Orpheus and Museus.[71] Even if this were the extent of such associations, it would be sufficient to suggest a general affiliation between Socrates and the new religious movements in Athens. But there is more.

Consider the Euthyphro, a dialogue invariably seen as a typical example of Socratic elenchos aimed at Euthyphro's purported confidence about what piety (to hosion) is. Rarely, however, has anyone tried to situate it amid the religious turmoil of the period. But if we do, Socrates' challenge to Euthyphro, an unreflective adherent of the traditional cultic and sacrificial system,[72] might be understood as a special example of the conflict between old and new piety.[73] The real content of Socratic religiosity is manifested both negatively, through his refutations of Euthyphro's proposals (that holiness is what is loved by the gods, or that holiness is service to them), and positively, through his methodical inquiry. It is this critical, structured inquiry aimed at gaining moral-religious knowledge—a divine prerogative—that is the means and end of Socratic ritual; it is his rational revision of ecstatic initiation rites that yields personal salvation. Euthyphro's concern, as one might expect, is with oaths, oracles, sacrifice, law, and ultimately pollution (*miasma*).[74] He takes knowledge for granted; power is the crucial dimension of divine-human distinctness. Euthyphro is Pentheus, although he comes to a different end, perhaps because Euripides is more fearful of hysterical, orgiastic cult than Socrates or Plato is sanguine about the future of rational inquiry.[75]

We fear being confused not with those most distinct from us but rather with those most like us, especially in a situation in which our common enemy, well entrenched and familiar, benefits from overlooking our differences.[76] In 424 Aristophanes could persuasively and unremarkably treat Socrates as a sophist; in 399 and thereafter, it was important for Socrates to be distinguished from lyric poets, rhapsodes, and mantics (corybantes).[77] Plato surely took this task quite seriously, for he felt that Socrates could easily be confused with them. There is evidence to support the conjecture that—in Plato's view—Socrates believed that inquiry and rational ecstasy complemented traditional Athenian piety.[78] The issue can be framed otherwise: conventionally gods and men are distinguished by power, wisdom, and eternity. All agree on the gods' immortality, but whereas others may focus on their power, Socrates focuses on their wisdom. If I am right, Plato sees him as taking some measure of divine knowledge to be humanly attainable and at the same time as treating the soul's immortality as a kind of metaphysical-theological postulate—for which Plato, among others, will later argue. The dialogues—as Kraut has shown[79]—give reason for thinking that Socrates was not a skeptic; he took knowledge to be achievable and to a degree achieved. The dialogues also, and this is my point, reveal how keenly Plato wanted to distinguish Socrates from poets and ecstatics. Like many of them, he held that the soul was immortal, but he replaced nonrational ecstasy with rational inquiry as a way to ascend to divinity, and substituted cognitive virtue and transcendence for pious displacement.[80]

The passages that support this proposal come from the *Ion*, the

Euthydemus, and the *Charmides*. Generally they are set aside as dramatic interludes. But I want to treat them more seriously, as historically, religiously, and philosophically revealing about Plato's way of understanding Socratic piety.

At *Charmides* 156d–e we find Socrates, near the outset of the dialogue, talking with Charmides, a young beauty noted for his philosophical and poetic skill, about a cure for the young man's headache. The conversation is an entrée to a discussion of the well-being of the soul and especially of the virtue *sophrosyne*. Socrates reports that a headache can be remedied by applying a certain leaf and uttering a charm (155e). The latter is a necessary element, and its special feature is that it is not restricted to curing the head; good doctors and good cures affect the whole, not merely the part (156b–c). Now we come to the passage of importance; Socrates says of the charm:

> I learned it while I was with the army, from one of the Thracian doctors of Zalmoxis, who are also said to make men immortal. And this Thracian said that the Greek doctors were right to say what I told you just now. "But our king Zalmoxis," he said, "who is a god, says that just as one should not attempt to cure the eyes apart from the head, nor the head apart from the body, so one should not attempt to cure the body apart from the soul. And this, he says, is the very reason why most diseases are beyond the Greek doctors, that they do not pay attention to the whole as they ought to do, since if the whole is not in good condition, it is impossible that the part should be. Because," he said, "the soul is the source both of bodily health and bodily disease for the whole man, and these flow from the soul in the same way that the eyes are affected by the head. So it is necessary first and foremost to cure the soul if the parts of the head and of the rest of the body are to be healthy. And the soul," he said, "my dear friend, is cured by means of certain charms, and these charms consist of beautiful words. It is a result of such words that temperance arises in the soul, and when the soul acquires and possesses temperance, it is easy to provide health both for the head and for the rest of the body." So when he taught me the remedy and the charms, he also said, "Don't let anyone persuade you to treat his head with this remedy who

does not first submit his soul to you for treatment with the
charm. Because nowadays," he said, "this is the mistake some
doctors make with their patients. They try to produce health
of body apart from health of soul." And he gave me very strict
instructions that I should be deaf to the entreaties of wealth,
position, and personal beauty. So I (for I have given him my
promise and must keep it) shall be obedient, and if you are
willing, in accordance with the stranger's instructions, to submit your soul to be charmed with the Thracian's charms first,
then I shall apply the remedy to your head. But if not, there is
nothing we can do for you, my dear Charmides. (156d–57c;
trans. Rosamond Kent Sprague)

On one level, this speech and its contents are a literary vehicle
whereby Plato has Socrates shift the topic of discussion from Charmides' headache to sophrosyne and the condition of his soul. The
shift is a typical example of what Cornford once called the "Socratic
revolution," from outer to inner, from the body to the soul, a transition we have already seen occur in the *Apology*.[81] The literary
maneuver makes a substantive point, but one we need not belabor.
On another level, however, the passage concerns Socrates' religious
commitments and what we might infer about Socrates from his possible association with the "Thracian doctors of Zalmoxis." These
are the issues I want to consider.

First, was Socrates ever in a position to learn directly from Thracian "doctors," worshipers of Zalmoxis? In the *Apology* (28e2), we
learn that Socrates fought in three battles—Potidaea, Amphipolis,
and Delium. Delium lies opposite Euboea in Boeotia, but both Amphipolis and Potidaea are in Macedonia, in the far north, just west
of Thrace. As Burnet argues, Socrates probably was stationed in
Amphipolis during the fighting accompanying its foundation in 437–
436;[82] he certainly fought at Potidaea, in the Chalcidice, in 432.[83]
Plato has Alcibiades describe Socrates' military conduct in a famous
passage in the *Symposium* (219e–20e). The *Charmides* is set upon
Socrates' return from Potidaea, indicating that Plato thought—or
at least wants the reader to think—that Socrates met the Thracian
doctors on his most recent tour of duty. This does not rule out the
possibility that he met them earlier, at Amphipolis. Plato might
have known the story of the encounter but confused its date and

location, or the events of Amphipolis and Potidaea may have merged in his mind. At least part of Alcibiades' famous description—Socrates' immunity to cold and drink, his trance-like state followed by a prayer to the sun[84]—smacks of the magical, ecstatic, and exotic,[85] once again suggesting contact with northern religious traditions, either in 432 or in 437–436. This much seems evident: Plato had reason to believe that during a military tour in Macedonia, in his thirties, Socrates was influenced by ecstatic, non-Greek religious traditions.

Second, what tradition did Socrates encounter, and what did he adopt from it? Who is Zalmoxis? What are the beliefs and practices of his adherents? In the *Charmides* Plato has Socrates report these features of the Thracian tradition: Zalmoxis is treated as god and king by his devotees; the soul is the focus of their attention; and the Thracian doctors engage in practices that involve or lead to the soul's immortality (156d–e). In a famous passage (4.94–96), Herodotus describes Zalmoxis as the divinity of a Thracian people, the Getae, who believe in the soul's immortality and conduct human sacrifices every five years, sending the victims to Zalmoxis as messengers.[86] Herodotus also records an alternate legend about Salmoxis, that "he was a man, and lived in Samos, where he was a slave in the household of Pythagoras, the son of Mnesarchus." He is said to have gained his freedom, returned to his native Thrace, preached a doctrine of life everlasting for the elite,[87] and conducted a ruse to garner support for his doctrine. Herodotus admits uncertainty about believing the details of this version, but he thinks that "Salmoxis lived long before Pythagoras' time" (4.94–96).[88] Dodds arranges the issues of Zalmoxis' divinity and his relation to Pythagoras this way:

> We know at any rate that Pythagoras founded a kind of religious order, a community of men and women whose rule of life was determined by the expectation of lives to come. Possibly there were precedents of a sort even for that: we may remember the Thracian Zalmoxis in Herodotus, who assembled "the best of the citizens" and announced to them, *not* that the human soul is immortal, but that *they and their descendants* were going to live for ever—they were apparently chosen persons, a sort of spiritual *elite*. That there was some analogy between Zalmoxis

and Pythagoras must have struck the Greek settlers in Thrace, from whom Herodotus heard the story, for they made Zalmoxis into Pythagoras' slave. That was absurd, as Herodotus saw: the real Zalmoxis was a daemon, possibly a heroised shaman of the distant past. But the analogy was not so absurd: did not Pythagoras promise his followers that they should live again, and become at least daemons or even gods?

Dodds draws this conclusion from Herodotus, who, he argues, "knows that Zalmoxis is a daemon (4.94.1), but leaves open the question whether he may once have been a man (96.2)."[89] I am less sanguine about his divinity, more convinced of his humanity. But this much is certain: Herodotus reports two traditions. To some, Zalmoxis was a god, to others, a man. To both he taught or was associated with a doctrine of life after death—whether it is immortality per se or something less precise.[90]

The gist of the Thracian message, then, as Herodotus reports it, is the same as the one taught to Socrates—that the soul is or can be made immortal and that in this doctrine and in Zalmoxis himself the human and the divine somehow merge. These elements are present both in Herodotus and in the *Charmides*. Let us keep them in mind as we turn to our second text.

In the *Euthydemus* Socrates tries to calm Cleinias, who is upset by the bantering of the elderly sophists, Euthydemus and Dionysodorus.[91] At 277d5–e3 he compares the sophists to the Corybantes at a Bacchic rite of initiation:

> For perhaps you do not discern what our two visitors are doing to you. They are acting just like the celebrants of the Corybantic rites, when they perform the enthronement of the person whom they are about to initiate. There, as you know, if you have been through it, they have dancing and merry-making: so here these two are merely dancing about you and performing their sportive gambols with a view to your subsequent initiation. So consider now that you are hearing the beginnings of the sophistic ritual (*ta prota ton hieron ton sophistikon*).

Dodds tells us that "the Corybantic rite [was] an offshoot from the Cybele-cult, which took over the goddess' healing function and gradually developed an independent existence."[92] The Dionysiac and Corybantic rites were similar in structure and purpose, as cures for anxiety by means of orgiastic dance with music.[93] Although both are primitive, Dodds notes, "we cannot dismiss [Corybantic rite] . . . either as a piece of backstreet atavism or as the morbid vagary of a few neurotics." Referring to the *Euthydemus* passage, Dodds continues, "A casual phrase of Plato's appears to imply that Socrates had personally taken part in the Corybantic rites; it certainly shows, as Linforth has pointed out, that intelligent young men of good family might take part in them."[94] Dodds is persuaded that Socrates himself was an initiate (*tetelesmenos*). Perhaps he is right.[95] My own point is slightly different, that Socrates was sufficiently acquainted with them, as were Cleinias and fourth-century readers, to use the Corybantic rites as a simile for sophistic examination. One is a rationalized version of the other; they are distinct but similar. Both are cures for maladies, either anxiety or ignorance.[96]

Just as Plato always distinguishes Socrates from ordinary sophists, so he distances him from Corybantics and participants in other orgiastic possession rites, both those that sought possession and those that sought to identify possession as a cause of malady.[97] If we turn to the *Ion*, we find Socrates sharply distinguishing men of art and knowledge (532c) from rhapsodes, reciters, and lyric poets. These latter are like worshiping Corybantes who are inspired or divinely possessed and not in their senses; "reason is no longer in [them]" (534b). All their utterances are not by *techne*, or knowledge, but rather by "divine power."[98] They are servants of the gods, like soothsayers and seers (534d), through whom the divine speaks to man (see also 534e). The Corybantes described in the *Ion* (534a, 536c) are people who, once possessed, draw milk and honey from rivers and dance, chanting, in response to certain music.[99] But the key feature of the rites is that like poets the Corybantes are inspired, possessed by the gods.[100] It is this characteristic that finally distinguishes poetry from *techne*; it is a matter of who is in control, human beings or the gods. Socrates' comparisons and his disclaimers leave untouched the truth common to all—to philosophy, poetry, and possession rite—that the gap between the divine and the human is bridged. The remaining issue is, under whose initiative and how.

Dodds associates Corybantic rites with Dionysiac cult in the following way.[101] Eventually, the cult is incorporated into the civic structure, but in the course of domestication, Bacchic ritual is also

civilized and muted.[102] Originally such rites included an element of
ritual madness, of collective hysteria manifested in mountain dancing and orgiastic live sacrifice and *sparagmos*.[103] As Dionysos is co-
opted by traditional religiosity, however, these elements do not die;
instead they pass over into other channels, among them the Corybantic rites. The purposes of these rites as they incorporate irrational features are cathartic and curative;[104] their strategies involve
a kind of psychic dislocation or immersion. Their guiding principle
is to identify a divine element in the sufferer that causes the malady
and to propitiate the responsible deity through sacrifice. In a sense,
the result was similar to that of divination and the consultation of
an oracle,[105] although the means differed dramatically. In an age
when Delphi was inaccessible for many, it is not surprising that
such rites flourished and grew.

But what does all of this have to do with Zalmoxis and immortality? The answer is a speculative but plausible one, derived in part
from Guthrie.[106] Dodds has shown that the wild, orgiastic descriptions in Euripides' *Bacchae* are not mere fancy; with the qualifica-
tions registered by Henrichs, we can accept Dodds' judgment that
these descriptions accurately reflect historical memory, renewed in
late fifth-century cultic life.[107]

How did this cult enter Greece? Guthrie's answer may not be
historically sound, but it certainly reflects the memory of fifth-
and fourth-century Athens: the cult came from the north, from
Thrace.[108] "Opposed at first, the new cult has proved irresistible,
and all Greece has become acquainted with the emotional experience of its ecstasies and the exaltation of union with the god."[109]
Guthrie makes a special point of the opposition that arose to the
entrance of the cult and the worship of Dionysos.[110] The story of
Pentheus, retold by Euripides, immortalizes this opposition and the
god's vengeance, "visiting with madness the women of the land
where he has been spurned [that] finally leads to their tearing a
victim to pieces" (165). Guthrie then shifts from the historical question to the psychological one, "Did [Dionysos] leave his mark on
[the Greeks]? In particular, what contribution did his impact make
to the Greek idea of the relations between man and god . . . ?" (174).
Guthrie turns to Herodotus' description of the Thracian worship of
Zalmoxis[111] as a reasonably accurate "account of purely Thracian
faith and ritual" (176). The belief in immortality is central, he says,

and it was this belief that was so "strange and foreign" to the Greeks. Guthrie clearly identifies Thracian immortality with Dionysiac ecstasy, where, in a sense, divine and human become one (174). By the late fifth century, this ecstatic practice had become domesticated, purged of its character as a possession cult, of its hysteria, and of its sense of transcendence. It remained only in the form of festivals of Dionysos, in which elements of the earlier worship persisted.[112] Guthrie then asks whether the belief in the soul's immortality was adopted by the Greeks as a result of the influence of the Dionysiac religion (180). His response is largely negative for ordinary worshipers, although he admits that several influences did lead "some of the best minds in fifth- and fourth-century Greece towards a new conception of the human soul in which its immortality played an essential role" (180). But these, he avers, were theologians or religious philosophers and not ordinary worshipers. In other words, Guthrie focuses on popular religiosity and not on sophisticated piety, ignoring the question of how, if at all, Thracian ecstasy influenced belief in immortality among the Athenian intelligentsia.

If Guthrie is right, however, the Corybantic rites, with which Socrates is so familiar,[113] are an affiliate of Dionysiac ritual, and a late fifth-century associate of the belief in immortality. At least it is reasonable to think that Plato and Socrates would have seen them this way. There is, in the tradition of Zalmoxis, a notion of malady and cure that compares with the palliative or cathartic role of Dionysiac and then Corybantic ecstatic or possession rites.[114] If there is no explicit reason to associate immortality with these rites, there is certainly reason to see all three—immortality, the tradition of Zalmoxis, and the Corybantic-Dionysiac rites—as related versions of the non-Delphic theology of divine-human union. For all three see the soul as potentially, if not partially, divine, although it is not clear how the doctors of Zalmoxis would manage the cure that results in a gain in status.[115]

WITH these pigments, then, Plato paints the following portrait. During his years in Macedonia, Socrates encountered Thracian religion, with its ecstatic features and its commitment to the soul's centrality and immortality.[116] In Athens, during the war years, he was once again exposed to ecstatic rites and a flood of imported cathartic traditions aimed at coping with the tensions of life in a beleaguered city. Socrates is both attracted to and repelled by these traditions: he is attracted by the lofty, central place given to the soul and the conception of a human struggle to cure it and seek its divinity,[117] repelled by the hysteria and the irrationality of the rites and the cults. Adapting these traditions, together with his unique method of sophistic examination and rational inquiry, Socrates develops a rational revision of ecstatic ritual based on the conviction that human beings can attain divine status.[118] Such a development has both religious and political dimensions, and it is radical, indeed revolutionary, in both regards.[119]

The *Apology* shows the tension between Delphic theology, with its commitment to a radical separation between gods and men, and a belief that human beings can, through cognitive enterprise, attain divine status. The dialogue leaves open the questions whether Socrates believes death to be good, and whether he believes the soul to be immortal. About the former, more must be said. About the latter, however, the evidence concerning the religious situation in Athens in the later fifth century supports the following answer. The Socrates whose portrait Plato has drawn adopted the belief that the soul is central to human well-being and seriously entertained—and perhaps also adopted—the beliefs that the soul is immortal[120] and that human striving to perfect its divine status should take the form of a disciplined search for knowledge.[121] Some may find this Socrates too Platonic for their liking, and in a sense he is similar to Plato.[122] But there is much left for Plato to do philosophically and theologically, and it does not detract from his stature to see him as having developed his conception of philosophy and religious aspirations on the basis of a picture of Socrates that he had already drawn.

In conclusion, let me say a word about my method in this chapter. A reader of the *Apology*, *Crito*, and other Socratic dialogues might doubt that Plato took Socrates to have entertained seriously and possibly believed in the soul's immortality. As Guthrie says, the belief in immortality "seemed a barbarous tenet to most of the Greeks, whom we know to have been brought up in the tradition of the aristocratic gods of Homer, with whom any infringement on their privileged position as the Immortals was a deadly sin and a courting of destruction."[123] At any rate, such a reader might reasonably withhold an interpretive conclusion based on the evidence of

the dialogues alone.[124] I have suggested that religious conduct and ideas can best be understood by looking at the historical situation in which they occur. In this case that means the religious situation in Athens from the onset of the war to Socrates' trial. My survey highlighted the religious options most likely to have been available to Socrates in the late fifth century. I proposed that according to Plato, Socrates developed a form of Greek piety akin to the ecstatic cults and to sophistic inquiry. The dialogues show evidence of Socrates' affiliation with imported, ecstatic rituals and in general with trends that endorsed the bridging of the divine-human gap. To Plato, Socrates was committed to the attainment of wisdom, acquired by disciplined inquiry and interrogation, and enabled by the soul's character and its immortality. Next, I examined the religious and historical context for an account of religious alternatives and of the situation which Socrates confronted and upon which he reflected. A new look at the dialogues—in this case the *Charmides, Euthydemus,* and *Ion*—helped to inform an understanding of how Plato conceived of Socrates' special place in Athenian religious life. In short, the fragments of dialogues became interpretively meaningful as mediated through an understanding of the historical context, and what they suggest is a Socratic piety that is both rational and ecstatic.

RELIGION, POLITICS, AND INQUIRY IN THE *MENO*

The influence of Socrates on Plato's thought can hardly be over-estimated. The dialogues, from outright portrayal to oblique reference,[1] bear witness to Plato's understanding of Socrates and his character. When Socrates was tried and executed, Plato was nearly thirty years old. He was an adult, a citizen, an aristocrat. Educated in poetry, gymnastics, historical memory, religion, and cult, Plato was drawn to the sophists and in particular to Socratic sophistry. In the early dialogues, written during the years of Plato's sadness and of Athens' revival—from 399 to 390, shall we suppose—Socrates is depicted with the reverence of a pupil. But at some point—there is no foolproof way to tell exactly when—the dialogical portraits acquire a new, nonrepresentational character. They no longer portray as much as they express problems, doctrines, and interrogations, and their "author" changes from the recollected teacher to the increasingly independent student.[2]

As we turn from Plato's conception of Socratic piety, a rational version of ecstatic ritual through elenctic inquiry, to genuine Platonic piety, we do find guidance in dialogues that are generally considered transitional, dialogues written some short time after 390, during or after Plato's first visit to Sicily in 388–387 and before the masterpieces of his middle period. The *Meno* is the first main source for a project whose goals are to identify the features of Socratic piety that dominate Plato, to watch how he struggles to accept and redeem them, and to investigate the religious resources that he uses to carry out his tasks. The results will be somewhat surprising and difficult, for him as well as for us. Aspiring to realize divine status by complementing the soul's indestructible status with intellectual

knowledge, Plato adopts Socratic inquiry only to find it embattled. He salvages inquiry but at rather steep expense. The *Meno* is no confident resting place, but instead a tentative stage on life's way.

The *Meno* was written, if we accept Bluck's persuasive case,[3] in 386–385, about a year after Plato's return from Sicily and roughly the same period after the "peace of Antalkidas."[4] The dramatic date of the dialogue between the aged Socrates and Meno, the relatively young aristocrat from Thessaly and friend of Anytus, Socrates' erstwhile accuser, is late January or early February 402, after the reign of the Thirty Tyrants, while Eleusis was independent of Athens and the laws of the renewed democracy were being revised.[5]

In the *Meno* Plato has Meno introduce, at a critical juncture, a sophistic paradox the point of which is that inquiry or learning is impossible. As I shall explain, the paradox is a serious one, for Socrates and for Plato; without a solution to it the ascent to knowledge by disciplined inquiry is sabotaged. To overcome this *aporia*, Plato has Socrates recall a "religious" doctrine about the soul's immortality and learning or inquiry as recollection. The background for this doctrine needs investigation, but we hardly know where to begin. For Plato, while associating the doctrine with unidentified "priests and priestesses" and with Pindar, says little more that is explicitly helpful about its nature and its origin.

One setting for the introduction of the famous doctrine of learning as recollection is the sophistic paradox of inquiry; another, however, is the religious and political world that looms behind the doctrine and the *Meno* as a whole. To illuminate that world we need to understand what Athens was like in 386, what thoughts dominated Plato's thinking at that time, and why he chose for the *Meno* the dramatic setting that he did—a setting of uncertainty, isolation, and instability.

The King's Peace of 387–386, negotiated by the Spartan navarch, Antalkidas, the Persian satrap of Sardis, and the king, Artaxerxes, surely dealt a severe blow to resurgent Athenian aspirations.[6] During the years preceding it, Athens had begun to reassert its "imperial ambitions" in Asia Minor under the guidance of Thrasybulus and Iphicrates.[7] But with the aid of Tiribazus, Antalkidas took possession of Athenian grain ships from the Black Sea and forced Athens into accepting the peace terms.[8] According to these terms the war was to end, Persia was to have hegemony over Asia, Clazomenai, and Cyprus, Athens over Lemnos, Imbos, and Scyros, and all other Greek cities were to be made autonomous.[9] But the provision of autonomy, at least politically and economically, could not assuage what was surely an Athenian sense of defeat. A hundred years after the Persian Wars, Athens was again subjected to Persian terms and, not two decades after the defeat of 404, to the Spartan yoke. Indeed, it is easy to see that "the Spartan position in European Greece was stronger after the Corinthian War than after the Peloponnesian War."[10]

The King's Peace was a shame to Athens. It is likely that a more detailed accounting of terms than that found in Xenophon included the dismantling of Athens' navy and the pulling down of the gates of the Piraeus.[11] These events, together with the strengthening of Sparta by a set of demands on Athens—made jointly by Sparta and Persia—would suggest that the Athenian mood in 386 should have been bitter and despondent. All at once Athens had been dealt a single blow by its traditionally worst enemies, Sparta and Persia, doubly damaging Athenian honor.[12]

If the *Meno* is in part a Platonic response—albeit oblique—to the shame of the King's Peace, it is not the only such Athenian response.[13] I think there is a tone of distress and bitterness in the *Meno*, a tone appropriate for that dialogue because it is expressly present in the minds of some of Plato's foremost contemporaries— Isocrates, Lysias, and Demosthenes. Isocrates refers often to the treaty,[14] noting that it was not so much a cooperative enterprise as an expression of Persian dominion and Spartan cowardice.[15] "No one could show that any peace treaty more shameful has ever been made, or more scornful of Greece, or more contrary to the reputation which Spartan courage has in many quarters. . . . Sparta betrayed many Greeks to the King."[16] The spirit of Isocrates' bitter condemnation recurs in Demosthenes' contrast between "two treaties between Greece and the King: one was made by our city [Athens] and everyone praises it; later the Spartans made the other, the one which everyone reproaches."[17] In 448 the Athenian treaty with Persia that had finally brought the Persian Wars to an end was received in Athens with a wholly different spirit from that which later greeted the King's Peace.[18] Surely this change was justified; in 448 Athens was at its pinnacle, full of self-confidence and self-esteem.[19] The mood of 386 was radically different. Thrasybulus and his dreams for a revived empire were smashed, and the specter of dependency, represented by the need for corn, cast a long shadow over Athenian hopes. In 386 Athens had been crushed not once but twice, and its sense of worldly self-control and independence, guaranteed de jure by the terms of the treaty, was smothered de facto by its situation and its memory.

Athenian attitudes toward foreign hegemony were harsh, and this harshness applies to all foreign powers, not solely to Persia. Simon Hornblower, for example, suggests that we read Lysias' *Olympic* oration, delivered in 384, as "a product of and reaction to the King's Peace."[20] In it, Hornblower notices, Dionysius, the tyrant of Syracuse, is yoked with Artaxerxes: "Both are barbarians against whom a crusade ought to be declared." To be sure, Lysias, a son of Cephalus,[21] was a Sicilian expatriate embittered against his former ruler. But Lysias' animosity was not misplaced, for Dionysius was in fact implicated in the Athenian defeat; he had contributed twenty ships to Antalkidas' fleet, which had hijacked the Athenian corn supply.[22] It was the act of a Spartan ally and hence of no special friend of Athens or of Lysias. It is not unreasonable, then, to assume that Athenian bitterness was directed at Dionysius as well as at Sparta and Persia, specifically the bitter feelings of such people as Lysias and Isocrates, loyal democrats or Panhellenists.[23]

Three ingredients must be added to our story before we can turn to the *Meno*. All concern Plato: first, the motivation, substance, and results of his visit to Syracuse in 388–387; second, the kind of reaction we might expect from Plato to the King's Peace within the context sketched; and finally, Plato's religious inheritance from Socrates and the religious climate in Sicily and Italy.

In the *Seventh Letter* Plato reflects on why he first traveled to Syracuse in 388–387 and how his early thinking had developed.[24] A careful reading should help us to understand how Plato might have responded to the King's Peace and the Athenian debacle. He begins the letter by identifying Dion's state of mind when Plato met him during his first visit. Dion, then about twenty—half Plato's age— thought that "Syracusans ought to be free and live under the best laws."[25] It was a view that Plato himself shared,[26] that citizens of a polis should be free (*eleutherous*) and live together under the best laws (*kata nomous tous aristous oikountas*). Plato describes first the waves of optimism and despair that came over him during the pe-

riods of the Thirty Tyrants and the restored democracy. The decay
was pervasive; all poleis had corrosive laws and practices and leaders without the capacity to stall the corruption. As Plato recalls it,
when he arrived in Italy and Sicily in 388–387, he had already come
to the conclusion that only one remedy for such corruption was
possible: since only the philosopher can see what public and personal just things are, the ills of the human race would come to an
end only when philosophers become political leaders or rulers become philosophers.[27] In 388, Plato had already conceived one of the
main theses of the *Republic*: that knowledge and not pleasure, rational order and not indulgent desire, would bring independence
and "the best *nomoi*"—that is, laws and practices conducive to the
best life.

If Morrow is right, then the *Seventh Letter*, written in 353 during
Plato's waning years, has a distinctly "apologetic purpose."[28] This
judgment is interesting because it points to a condition not only
present in 353 but already prominent in 388. Morrow reviews nicely
the evidence that Plato's relationship with Sicilian luxury and Dionysius' wealth was viewed in antiquity as corrupt and self-serving.
Even a contemporary of Plato's, Molon, is surprised by Plato's presence in Sicily. Diogenes Laertius reports an epigram of Molon: "The
surprising thing is not that Dionysius should be in Corinth, but that
Plato should be in Sicily."[29] Morrow builds on this explicit bit of
gossip, for events show how odious Dionysius was to the Athenians,
especially after the shame of the King's Peace. The Sicilian legation
at the Olympic festival in 388 was actually attacked, and the poems
of Dionysius I received jeers and hisses. Although the hostility to
the tyrant was doubtless rooted in democratic conviction, it was
also fueled by Lysias' "fiery speech," which associated Dionysius
with Artaxerxes.[30] One wonders twice about Plato's report in the
Seventh Letter, first about the accuracy of his "memory" of his own
views during his first visit to Sicily, and second about the motives
that led him to visit Italy and Sicily at such an inflammatory moment.

On the first score, Morrow is clearly right that Plato's connection
with Dion and Sicily would easily be misinterpreted by his fellow
Athenians, Plato's efforts to put Dion in a better light notwithstand-
ing.[31] But this fact does not explain why he originally established
such a relationship, nor does it confirm his report of his political

views at the time. Is there reason to think that Plato ventured to Sicily in 388, without invitation and at a moment of such anti-Sicilian feeling, in order to court Dionysius and to try to convert him to his political vision? And that he found Dion instead, the tyrant's brother-in-law, an accessible student? Or is it not more likely that the trip, made for other reasons altogether, brought Dion and Plato together, and that an enduring friendship eventually carried the political dividend of an invitation to teach the young Dionysius II about philosophy and political rule? As an apology, the *Seventh Letter* leaves open the questions of what Plato was really thinking in 388 and why he did go to Italy and Sicily.

This much, however, does seem reasonable: the reign of the Thirty Tyrants and the restoration of the democracy would have led to grave uncertainty on Plato's part. Morrow calls the early reflection a "sincere stocktaking" and the recollection of Socrates' plight a "simple but eloquent eulogy."[32] He is certainly right; both Plato's doubts and his fond allegiance to Socrates are indisputable, not distorted by the letter's "apologetic purpose."

So is it possible that Plato's primary reason for visiting Italy and Sicily was not political in nature? Perhaps we shall never know, but still we should recall that before 388 Plato visited Tarentum, where he seems to have made another lifelong friend, Archytas, a preeminent Pythagorean.[33] Whether this visit occurred on the same voyage is not clear, but it is reasonable to assume that it did. And, as Burkert reminds us, "later biographies of Plato agree that a principle motive of his first journey to Magna Graecia was to establish contact with the Pythagoreans there."[34] Indeed Cicero in the *De Re Publica* identifies both Archytas of Tarentum and Timaeus of Locri as people whom Plato met and notes that he also "acquired the papers of Philolaus." It is Cicero's judgment that Plato proceeded to "[interweave] the charm and argumentative skill of Socrates with the mysticism of Pythagoras and the well-known profundity of his varied lore."[35] Although this conclusion is certainly artificial, it may be true that Socrates and the Pythagoreans were early, strong influences on Plato's thinking and that the trip to Magna Graecia was motivated as much by desire to learn more about the one as it was to cope with the despair over the other.

The King's Peace had guaranteed autonomy to the Greek cities, but Athenians were shamed and dispirited at the Athenian plight.

In the *Seventh Letter* Plato recalls his conviction, at the age of forty, that people should be free and should live in a polis organized by nomoi for the best. The dissonance between promised and real autonomy at the city's level and desired and real freedom at the individual's could not have failed to move Plato. Nor could he have been unaware of a hidden dividend of the Socratic aspiration to knowledge and divinity—that unlike the Delphic or traditional model of dominion and subservience, it brings with it the hope for real independence and hence for real freedom, from exploitation, force, and tyranny.

In 386, moved by the new friendships and new ideas he gathered from the west and by the despair around him, Plato wrote the *Meno*. The human good is attainable; the soul, immortal in nature, can gain knowledge sufficient to lift it above worldly uncertainty and corruption. Socrates had tailored a dialectical strategy from sophistic threads, creating vestments for a new priesthood and a regimen for a new ritual. Plato accepts them both as vehicles to human fulfillment in the midst of despair. But he does not receive his Socratic inheritance uncritically. The same sense of aspiration is there, the same commitment to the soul's immortality, the same piety. But now they are under assault and in need of repair, and the resources for that repair come from Plato's recent explorations.

We are the beneficiaries of recent brilliant work on the Pythagorean and Orphic presence in Greece around the time of Socrates' execution.[36] In order to understand the author of the *Meno*, we must identify the Orphic texts, doctrines, and rites available to Socrates and Plato, in part through non-Pythagorean and in part through Pythagorean associations.[37]

Commenting on the famous passage in which Socrates introduces the doctrines of the soul's immortality and learning as recollection (*Meno* 81a10), Bluck notes that the origin of the doctrines, whether Pythagorean or Orphic, has been much disputed.[38] Thomas, Linforth, and others argue for a Pythagorean source, Guthrie for an Orphic one. Bluck reviews some of the arguments and concludes by recommending *epoche* (see 74–75, 276). He may be right; precision is doubtless beyond our reach. Nonetheless, we do know that Plato, in 386, had recently returned from Italy and Sicily, that he had there met Archytas and other Pythagoreans, perhaps even having sought them out, and that the doctrines are ascribed not only to "priests and priestesses" (81a10) but also to "Pindar and many other poets who are divinely inspired" (81b1). The mixing together of Pythagorean and Orphic doctrines, practices, and attitudes is commonplace in Plato's dialogues. There is no reason to see any sharp separation here, in such an imprecise passage. Hence, it seems reasonable to survey features of Orphic-Pythagorean religiosity at the turn of the century without attempting to separate interwoven strands.

Burkert, in a fascinating article, comes to a helpful conclusion: there are overlapping relationships among the practices at Eleusis, the variety of ways of worshiping Dionysos, Pythagorean belief and practice, and what is associated with Orpheus. These overlapping relationships are such that Orphic books, doctrines, and attitudes are absorbed and adapted by the other three domains of Greek piety.

> The characteristics of the "Orphic" field, apart from the reference to the name "Orpheus," are the use of books and some insistence on individual purification and afterlife. But there could be considerable variation and assimilation to changing environments and trends. The social reality behind the literature is not to be seen as that of a closed, self-propagating community . . . but as one of itinerant priests, *orpheotelestai*, meeting the (not always quite serious) needs of people no longer firmly enrooted in Polis tradition, but prepared to look out for new forms of experience and to seek remedies against new forms of anxiety. This seems to fit in well with the general situation of the 5th–4th century B.C.[39]

What Burkert is suggesting, I take it, is that there was an Orphic dimension to Pythagorean practice and doctrine in southern Italy, just as there was an Orphic dimension to Bacchic rites celebrated in Athens, and to the mysteries themselves, and that the evidence we have from Aristophanes, Euripides, Herodotus, Pindar, and others, refers to Orphic doctrines, rites, and motifs manifest in these various settings.[40] What these settings have in common is not only the use of texts but also an "insistence on individual purification and afterlife."[41] In the *Meno* Plato is interested in the soul, its nature as immortal, and its ultimate well-being, and to meet his goals he both draws on and rejects aspects of his religious situation. As Socrates had co-opted and revised the cathartic role of ecstatic,

Corybantic ritual, so Plato first ignores and then later denies the cathartic role of Orphic cosmologies, of dietary restrictions, and so on.[42] But the Orphic background of this conglomerate is undeniable. The availability of Orphic theogonical-cosmogonical poetry around 400 and the presence of Orphic priests are confirmed by new discoveries, among them the gold plate discovered in southern Italy and the Derveni papyrus unearthed near Thessalonike.[43] It is certain that both in Athens and in southern Italy Plato could have imbibed an Orphic wine that Socrates had only tasted and could have been excited by it.[44]

Is it hard to imagine Plato, accepting Socrates' rational version of Bacchic initiation, coming to the aid of Socratic elenchos with Orphic resources? By the end of the fifth century, it is well documented that there were those, especially in southern Italy, who performed salvific rites that could be described alternatively as Bacchic or Orphic.[45] Along with a confirmed interest in Pythagorean mathematics and a new appreciation for the Pythagorean way of life, Plato may very well have returned from Magna Graecia with another discovery—a new understanding of the Orphic dimension of Bacchic initiation rites and the ways in which both Bacchic and Orphic religiosity serve the quest for the good life of the soul. Susan Cole, in an illuminating article on the content of the new gold tablet discovered at Hipponion, a colony of Locri in southern Italy, confirms the existence of such eschatological rites at the turn of the century.[46] In her paper, Cole argues that the new tablet alludes to Bacchic or Dionysiac initiation rites and hence to a "religious context," "a cult wherein initiation ceremonies are a regular feature."[47] She recalls the dispute over whether the tablet and the rites involved are Orphic, Bacchic, or Pythagorean,[48] decides with Burkert that the rites are Dionysiac, but argues that the experience is one of initiation and hence presumes a cultic organization rather than mere "itinerant priests." For our purposes, however, the key point is not the social but rather the metaphysical one, that the tablets concern the soul's postcarnate blessedness and well-being, the rite of initiation whereby it can be attained, and the role of Memory (Mnemosyne) in that rite.[49]

If we combine Burkert's results with Cole's, we can conclude that what Plato encountered in southern Italy, in addition to Pythagoreanism, were Orphic texts, Orphic-Bacchic initiation rites, a much-heralded view that the soul is immortal, and the conviction that proper rites of passage could bring the soul to a better life than its worldly one. Some of this conglomerate would already have been available to Socrates and Plato in the writings and religious climate of late fifth-century Athens—from Empedocles, Pindar, Aristophanes, Euripides, Herodotus, and elsewhere. What the new discoveries confirm is their presence circa 400 throughout Magna Graecia, especially in southern Italy.

This sketch of what was available to Plato in Italy suffices to show that Plato, in his numerous references to Orpheus, Orphics, and Orphic writings and practices, is responding not to some rare exotic feature of Greek religious life but rather to ubiquitous tendencies in the religious life of fifth- and fourth-century Greece. He is attracted to these tendencies for a variety of reasons, not the least of which are their associations with rites and doctrines which he had already seen as appealing to Socrates—rites and doctrines about the soul, its immortality, and its aspiration to divine status. In later chapters, as we consider the *Phaedo*, *Symposium*, *Republic*, and *Phaedrus*, we shall see how extensively Plato draws on and incorporates these Orphic resources,[50] a practice that is already present in the *Meno*, with the introduction of the doctrines of the soul's immortality and learning as recollection.

But these Orphic-Bacchic tendencies include books or texts, and we should say something about their theogonical-cosmogonical content.[51] The key to the secret of inquiry and learning is that the truth sought is already had, that divinity is origin as well as goal, *arche* as well as telos. Is such a motif, in spirit if not in letter, present in the cosmogonies of fifth-century Orphic texts?[52] West, in his recent work on the Orphic poems, believes that the *Meno*'s doctrines (*Meno* 81a–b) need not reflect Plato's knowledge of extant Orphic cosmogonies,[53] but they might. West's reservations concern Plato's failure to cite the theogonies accurately or at all. But our interest in Plato's doctrines concerns man and the soul, and here the available Orphic motifs are more reliably identified and appropriated by Plato. The crucial text is the Derveni papyrus, discovered in a pass about eight miles northwest of Thessalonike and dating from the late fourth century.[54]

West discusses extensively the Derveni theogony-cosmogony, but we need focus only on one element of it, the birth of man and his destiny.[55] The papyrus has two components, an Orphic poem of sixth-century origin and a philosophical commentary dating from 400.[56] According to West, more than half of the commentary seems to be devoted to "an extended discussion of the Erinyes or Eumenides: their role in punishing sinners (?) after death (2), their supervision of the cosmic order generally according to Heraclitus, and their identity as souls."[57] Thus, the Orphic poem aside, the allegorical-philosophical commentary is concerned with postcarnate rewards and punishments and with divine or quasi-divine souls. There is, however, nothing in the extant fragments about mankind, the immortality of the soul, reincarnation, and so on, but if West is right, such a story—of a third race of men living under Zeus, with immortal souls, posthumous judgment, and so forth—was doubtless part of the myth but found on another, now destroyed scroll.[58] The story, West argues, is akin to hints of reincarnation in Empedocles,[59] and was certainly available to Plato both in Italy and in Athens, for Aristophanes and Pindar suggest mythic contexts for such doctrines.

Earlier we quoted a sober conclusion of Burkert's; we might usefully now return to two of its features. One was the ubiquity of Orphic tendencies throughout the Greek world, the other the social reality that stands behind their appropriation. Burkert's first point encourages us to think that on his visit to Italy and Sicily Plato encountered Orphic texts, myths, and practices that reinforced what already had been available to him in Athens since his younger days—and not only available but also attractive.[60] The second feature suggests why these sources were so appealing. Recall Burkert's words, stimulated by the work of Vernant and Detienne, that the Orphic literature and its itinerant, priestly bearers were responding to "the needs of people no longer firmly rooted in Polis tradition, but prepared to look out for new forms of experience and to seek remedies against new forms of anxiety."[61] Broadly, those attracted to Pythagoreanism and to Orphic texts, myths, and practices saw them as modes of dissent, as expressions of dissatisfaction with the sharp separation between the divine and the human that framed Delphic or (what we can now call, after Burkert) polis tradition and that formed the basis for its sacrificial system. To appropriate Orphic and/or Pythagorean resources was to nurture such dissent and thereby to respond to a sense of anxiety that polis piety could not assuage. In Detienne's words, "Orphism is a movement of religious protest that defines itself by an attitude of refusal, refusal of the whole politico-religious system organized around the Olympian gods and the distance that separates them from men."[62]

What, then, was Plato's state of mind in 386 as he wrote the *Meno*? Perhaps, like others, Plato felt the shame of Athens at her recent defeat. For him, an old discontent with Athenian democracy was confirmed. Real autonomy and all that it promised to bring in behalf of the human attainment of the best life possible—this was beyond the grip of the "polis tradition," Delphic theology, the sacrificial system, and civic piety. Socrates had been right; what was needed was a "new form of experience," a disciplined form of inquiry that would culminate in an act of initiation, an ascent to divine status, a rational version of ecstatic ritual. These convictions, confirmed by the new despair, were presented afresh to Plato on his recent visit to southern Italy and Sicily. There he became acquainted with Pythagoreanism firsthand and with Orphic overlays—doctrines, myths, and rites that incorporated doctrines such as the soul's immortality, reincarnation, and purification through knowledge.[63] Returning to Athens, Plato confronted directly his differences with the traditional piety concerning the best life and its attainment. At the same time, he began to wrestle with difficulties that beset his Socratic inheritance. He wrote the *Meno*, a dialogue intended to reaffirm and also to salvage the Socratic enterprise, and hence a drama set at an earlier moment of similar defeat with an interlocutor who symbolizes both the despair and the inadequacy to be overcome.[64]

Hence, the *Meno* is an expression of religious and moral dissent, but before we turn to that dialogue, it is possible to offer a further reason for Plato's decision to publicize his dissent in 386.[65] In 390 or thereabouts another student of Gorgias, Isocrates, had founded a competing school in Athens. In the *Panegyricus*, written around 380, Isocrates provides us with as full an Athenian response to the King's Peace and the defeat of Athens as we have.[66] If the views represented in this speech were already well known in 386, might we not treat the *Meno* as Plato's response both to the events of the preceding years and to Isocrates' understanding of them?

The central task of Isocrates' speech is the demonstration that Athens should lead the Greek states against non-Greek peoples.[67]

Athens, not Sparta, deserves the role of leadership. In addition to
providing lengthy reports of past Athenian triumphs, Isocrates notices the horrible effects of the King's Peace—piracy, violence,
internecine struggles, and revolt—and he attributes these harsh realities to the defeat of Athens, the rule of Sparta, and the impact
of Persia. He contrasts the debacle of the current treaty with the
aftermath of 448, following the Persian Wars.[68] The blame now,
Isocrates charges, belongs to Sparta.[69] The power and greatness of
Persia, moreover, are misplaced; the Persians are neither courageous
nor pious nor disciplined. Rather they are self-indulgent, "while
psychologically their monarchical constitution mocks(?) them de-
graded and cringing . . . prostrating themselves in adoration of a
man whom they address as a god, while it is gods rather than men
whom they treat with disdain."[70] Indeed, Isocrates portrays the Persians as having done battle not only against the Greeks but also
against their worship of the gods.[71] Vigorously and almost bitterly,
Isocrates rails against the Greek—especially the Athenian—leaders
who live with the treaty and treat the king as the author of freedom
and protector of the Greeks.[72] The true path is a militant one, to
become unified in opposition to Persia, to secure retribution and
return dignity and order to Greek life. Such a task, such a war,
would be in fact a "religious mission" for all Greece, an adventure
for true piety and a true future.[73]

It is not hard to read the *Meno* as a partial response to Isocrates'
platform. Plato, through the mouth of Socrates, chastens Athenian
pride. In a sense, Meno and Anytus[74] are surrogates for Isocrates,
preaching the wisdom of Athenian citizens, their capacity to exemplify and to teach human excellence, and their special role as
the servants of the gods. Both Plato and Isocrates feel the despair,
the anxiety of the peace, but whereas Isocrates camouflages Athenian weakness, ascribing blame to Sparta and malignancy to Persia,
Plato confronts Athenian disability and offers, through his portrayal
of Socrates and his defense of Socratic inquiry, a solution. And while
Isocrates is turbulent but supportive, Plato is calm but critical. For
Isocrates, hope lies in decisiveness, unity, and war, for Plato in a
disciplined effort to gain transforming knowledge. What Athens
lacks, for Isocrates, is self-confidence and boldness, for Plato, self-
discipline and knowledge—the recognition of its lack and the discipline to attain it. To Isocrates, the Persians err in worshiping a

man whom they call a god; to Plato, the Athenians err in not worshiping the desire and method for attaining divinity. Shortly after
his return from Sicily and just prior to writing the *Meno*, Plato
established a school or *thiasos*, a religious community in which to
study, learn, and worship with colleagues.[75] If the *Panegyricus* is
the charter of Isocrates' school, then perhaps the *Meno* is part of
the charter for the Academy—or possibly opening remarks by the
founder, remarks which set the tone for the Academy's political,
religious, and educational character.[76]

The *Panegyricus* is unabashedly traditional in its religious convictions. If the *Meno* dissents from its overall vision of Athenian
leadership, it would be encouraging to find evidence in the dialogue
itself for Plato's religious dissent.

The final pages of the *Meno* (87b–100b) employ a "hypothetical"
method to show that *arete* is not teachable. Plato's strategy is to
suppose that arete is teachable only if it is knowledge (87b–c) and
then to show what unacceptable consequences follow, for Meno,
from this assumption among others.[77] The precise structure and role
of the arguments are not our concern. What is of interest is a distinction drawn, in the course of the passage, between expert knowledge and something else, eventually called *orthe doxa*, correct or
true belief. The special importance of expertise is first introduced
in the exchange with Anytus (90b–95a) that derives the unteach-
ability of arete from the historical fact that even great statesmen
did not transmit it to their most dearly loved ones, their sons. Later,
at 96e–99c, Socrates introduces the distinction between *episteme* (or
phronesis) and orthe doxa (or *eudoxia*, *doxa alethes*) on his way
to showing that statesmen really have the latter, not the former.
But if such statesmen, including Themistocles, Pericles, and Aris-
tides, are good men who have arete, then the latter is not wisdom
or knowledge. And if so, it is not teachable. The dialogue ends in
aporia: the argument has led to the conclusion that arete in statesmen, as in prophets and oracles (*hoi chresmodoi te kai hoi theo-
manteis*, 99c2–3), is attained by divine dispensation (*theia moira*,
100b2–3; compare *enthusiontes*, 99c3; 99d2–4), that this unwitting
result is still provisional, and that the problem lies with not knowing what arete really is *auto kath' auto* (100b5–6).

Two features of this passage bear notice: the first is that the bur-
den seems to fall on the error of identifying arete with the kind of

wisdom that actual statesmen or experts have. This failure need not imply that arete is not any kind of knowledge but only that it is not the particular kind that statesmen have. In fact, the argument at 87d–89a, that wisdom is either the whole or part of arete, is never refuted. It is reasonable to think that for Plato arete is indeed a kind of knowledge but not *this* kind, and that it is teachable, but not the way that sophists or statesmen try to teach it.

Second, the passage seems to distinguish between two types of orthe doxa, where this means "believing truly or correctly," referring to the act and not the object of such belief. One kind is a believing, such as the slave boy's at the end of the initial dialogue with Socrates, which is a believing of what is true, a justified believing, and a stage of believing that can be transformed or strengthened into knowledge. The other kind is a believing, like that of prophets or oracles, which is wholly other than knowing, where the believer is possessed or inspired, a vehicle for publicizing a divine truth but not a real cognitive agent at all. Although Plato is rather slippery at times in these concluding pages of the *Meno*, he generally seems to draw this distinction between knowledge and true belief in this second way. It is what allows him to say at 99c that the relation of statesmen to knowledge is like that of oracles and prophets. They are "divine" or "inspired," passive receivers of truths that they cannot confirm or prove. Like the slave boy, they may grasp what is true and like him they may lack the *aitias logismo*, but unlike him they are not on the way to converting their beliefs into knowledge.[78]

One way of reading the *Meno*'s final pages is to take the attribution of "divinity," of possession or inspiration, of divine dispensation, as a Platonic slur—as irony. Some readers, that is, might think Plato is opposed to these phenomena as he is to a civic arete that cannot be transmitted. But this need not be so, of course, and if we are right about Plato's Socratic inheritance, it is not so. Plato has respect for knowledge and its attainment. To him, the knower and not the "oracle or prophet" is the person who is really and genuinely divine (99d7–9).[79] And the real and genuine *theia moira* is not a matter of revelation or possession;[80] it is instead a matter of disciplined inquiry, properly conducted and properly understood. Indeed, the *Meno* gives us both a clear example of such inquiry and a seminal defense of it. Just as Socrates has been contrasted in earlier dialogues with poets and rhetoricians,[81] and just as his commitment to the rational pursuit of truth is a kind of ecstatic rite for apprehending divinity and achieving divine status, so Plato contrasts real episteme with something else[82] and yet conceives of a genuine method for gaining knowledge as a religious rite of aspiration and ascent.

THE *Meno* is a paradigmatic portrayal of Socratic inquiry employed in behalf of a central Socratic concern: the nature of human arete. At the same time, it affords an early opportunity for Plato's special genius to express itself. For, in addition to some preliminary remarks about knowledge and definition, the *Meno* includes a remarkable stretch of dialogue in which the entire enterprise of Socratic inquiry is attacked and defended. Whereas the context and object of this encounter are Socratic, its features—the paradox of inquiry, the doctrine of learning as recollection, and much else—are distinctively Platonic. They are epistemological and metaphysical reflections set in a religious context.

In the *Meno*, Plato must confront two problems. One concerns Socratic inquiry and its possibility. It is a problem posed by the sophists or at least raised in a sophistical way and one that Plato takes with utmost seriousness. Second, Plato wants to understand exactly how inquiry is related to immortality and how it realizes the soul's ecstatic aspiration to divine status. In the *Meno*, Plato deals economically with both problems at once—by means of the doctrine of learning as recollection and the notion that the truths sought by inquiry exist always in the soul of the inquirer.[83] To be sure, Plato will in time see the shortcomings in this solution. In the *Phaedo* he will retain learning as recollection but with a dramatically revised estimate of its objects, their nature and status. Divine aspiration exerts a strong pull, and he continues to be devoted to it, even though the new objects cause even greater problems for the possibility of learning and the soul's ascent to transcendent knowledge. In the *Republic* we need a Socratic return to method, once again revised, but all because of the solution of the *Meno*.

At *Meno* 80d a frustrated Meno tries to stall his conversation with Socrates by setting up a roadblock.[84] If one does not know something, he asks, how can one search for it? For if one does not know it, either one cannot set it up as the object of one's search or, even if one could, one would not know that what one found is what one sought. Socrates acknowledges the gambit as a familiar one, though his own reformulation of the puzzle differs from Meno's version in an important way. To Meno, the puzzle about inquiry or searching is a dilemma about how, given an original ignorance, one can either begin or conclude a search. To Socrates, on the other hand, the puzzle is a dilemma about initiating such a search; to begin with knowledge of the object sought makes searching for it unnecessary (and perhaps impossible), and to begin without knowledge of it makes searching impossible to initiate. So for Meno the problem concerns the unacceptable consequences of initial ignorance; for Socrates it concerns, more radically, the impasse that results from either initial knowing or initial ignorance. Since it is Socrates' version that is addressed in the text that follows, we shall concern ourselves with it alone.

At 81a5–d5 Plato has Socrates present an initial reply to the paradox; it is an attempt to explain why the paradox fails. But the content of that explanation is a perennial difficulty. In order to clarify it we must proceed cautiously. First, Socrates' initial response has three components: (1) a statement of origin and advocacy (81a10–b2); (2) a report of the content of the teachings (b2–c4); and (3) a Platonic inference from this religious teaching (c5–d5). Although one cannot be certain that the third element is in fact a Platonic elaboration, I am inclined to agree with Bluck that it is "not simply a continuation of what the priests and priestesses said" but something "implicit" in their teaching.[85] The importance of the point may not be great, but if we are right, the Orphic-Pythagorean origin of the doctrine or teaching is more easily shown than if we were required to find evidence in these traditions of the epistemological thesis as well. There is also something attractive about taking Plato to have drawn the conclusion from the soul's immortality and thereby to have shaped the solution to the paradox. In the course of such reflection Plato reveals himself as an astute critic of his Socratic inheritance but also as a keen student of its resources.

What is the content of the doctrine which Socrates reports in the second stage? The text is subtly conceived and at the same time condensed and deceptive. "The soul of a man is immortal, at one time coming to an end—what is called 'dying'—and at another being born again, but never being destroyed" (b3–5). More precisely, of course, it is the person and not the soul which dies and is born, while it is the soul that leaves one body and then enters "once again" into another. The entire statement is too condensed, although Socrates makes his point. Immortality of the soul and its reincarnation, moreover, entail that "one must live his life as piously as possible" (b5–6). Plato realizes that the inference is not direct; he knits the two doctrines together with the moral-religious imperative by using poetic thread: those from whom

> Persephone receives requital for ancient grief,
> In the ninth year she restores again
> Their souls to the sun above,
> From whom arise noble kings,
> And men mighty in strength and greatest in wisdom;
> And for the rest of time
> They are called heroes and sanctified by men (b7–c4) [86]

Plato's point seems to be that if one wants to be known as a hero or as divine, one must be noble, strong, and wise while one is alive. The "ancient grief" is Persephone's distress over the human responsibility for the slaying of Dionysos, who was trapped by the Titans, torn to bits, boiled, roasted, and eaten. [87] Owing to his Titanic nature, man dies and goes to the underworld. But in time his soul returns to enliven a new person, whose character determines his reputation and fame.

The mythic background of the poetic fragment is doubtless Orphic and Pythagorean, [88] and the goal of the cycles of reincarnation is probably some kind of unification with the deity, an apotheosis that is the outcome of transmigration. [89] But in the *Meno* only a modest, vague attribution is provided—to "priests and priestesses who make it their business to be able to give an account concerning what they do," [90] to Pindar, and to other poets who are *theoi* (a10–b2). There is no conclusive way to track down the first attribution, but the substance of the doctrine—immortality, transmigration, reincarnation—makes it very likely, if we recall Plato's recent trip to Italy and Sicily, that these holy teachers and practitioners are Orphic Pythagoreans. If one is persuaded by my earlier sketch of Plato's situation in 386, his reasons for undertaking the journey west, and his attitude toward the King's Peace, Athens, and Isocrates, then

one has even more reason to ascribe the doctrine to Orphic-Pythag-
oreans and others, like Pindar, who are sympathetic to this Bacchic
tradition.[91] Plato finds it appealing, however, not just because of its
familiarity or the authority of its teachers. Indeed such considerations would doubtless have weighed little with him. What per-
suades him is the commitment to the soul's immortality, to the
possibility of attaining divine or quasi-divine status, and the fact
that the doctrines can be employed to solve the eristic paradox.
That these same teachings hold all these treasures is remarkable
and exciting to him.

Just as the Orphic-Pythagorean officiants or *telestai* not only conduct ecstatic rites but also provide accounts (logoi) of what they
do,[92] so a Socratic inquirer not only engages in dialectical inquiry
in pursuit of knowledge but also should give an account of what he
is doing.[93] This Plato has Socrates do by drawing out the implications of the mythic teachings and thereby solving the eristic paradox.

> Since the soul is immortal and has been born many times and
> has seen all things, both here and in Hades, there is nothing
> that it has not learned. So that it is not surprising that it can
> recall, about both *arete* and other things, what it once knew.
> For since all nature is akin, and the soul has learned all things,
> there is nothing to prevent one—who has recalled only one
> thing, which people call *mathesis*, from finding out all the rest,
> if he is courageous and does not grow weary of inquiring. For
> inquiring and learning are wholly recollecting (c5–d5).

The text here is difficult, if not simply imprecise. There is little
reason to think that Plato has thought through the difficulties raised
by this elaboration. Does he really believe that prior to any given
incarnation, the prenatal soul has seen "all things both here and in
Hades?"[94] What does he think this means, and does he take the
Orphic-Pythagorean teaching to entail or only to suggest it? To be
sure, one can recall only what one has known before, so that unlimited prior knowledge is required for unlimited recollection; but
why ought the recollection, and hence the learning, be unrestricted
in scope? Furthermore, why ought all things be akin? Why is it not
sufficient for unrestricted recall and therefore for unrestricted learning or inquiry that the soul have known and since forgotten all

things? Is it possible that Meno might find inquiry too imposing unless knowledge acquisition were somehow cumulative or perhaps self-propelling? Or does Plato think that knowledge somehow re- quires the kinship of its objects, namely, that knowledge is the result of following a path of connections or relations—perhaps even a deductive path—among its objects?[95]

Plato does not address these problems explicitly, nor does he worry about the threat of a regress of learning (is the paradox restricted to incarnate learning and inquiry?). Instead he turns immediately to an illustration of the doctrine that learning and inquiry—they are the same—are nothing but a process of recalling objects once known.[96] And then, at 86c, Socrates says, "We are agreed that it is right to inquire into something that one does not know." This statement shows that somewhere between 81a and 86c the paradox had been solved. But what is the solution, and how does it work?

Many recent interpretations of the doctrine of recollection and how it is intended to solve the paradox of inquiry rest on the same foundation. They agree that the doctrine must be about the epis- temological conditions necessary for inquiry and directed learning. These are present most vividly where the issue is taken to be one of reference and identity of reference, and hence how the learner's referential capacities at the outset of inquiry compare to his refer- ential successes at the end. But if, in a sense, Plato is interested in reference, in the learner's thinking of something, he is interested not in its epistemological conditions but rather in its metaphysical ones. He is concerned, that is, about the object of reference and not how the referring gets done. This mental referring, for Plato, is like any kind of grasping; without an object, it is just a matter of waving the hand. But if at the outset of inquiry, one has the object in one's grasp, then it is unnecessary and perhaps even impossible to look for it. And if not, then where does it come from? In Socrates' refor- mulation of the paradox, he says of the inquirer that if "he does not know, [then] he does not even know what he is to look for." This means that if he does have what is to be grasped, then how is he to grasp it—for all this mental grasping goes on in the soul.[97]

One of the keys that unlocks the paradox of inquiry and the doc- trine of recollection is the realization that for Plato the objects of true believing and knowing are truths. These truths he detaches from the world and places in the soul, and believing and knowing become grasping truths in one's soul. Inquiry or learning is a matter of searching for these truths, and the paradox of inquiry, to Plato, is a puzzle about how directed searching can succeed. The doctrine of recollection is the doctrine that having a truth does not imply grasping or knowing it but that knowing or grasping it implies and indeed requires having it. Beliefs do not solve the paradox, for true beliefs are already a matter of grasping truths, though tentatively, whereas false beliefs are no better than ignorance. Nor do sufficiently accurate specifications do the job, for the issue is not what directions one takes in getting the grasping or pointing started but rather what is there to be grasped or pointed at. The only thing that will solve the paradox is to show that the truths that are the objects of true believing and knowing are in the soul always, which is just what Plato shows at 85d–86b. The best Platonic image of how the doctrine of recollection is intended to solve the paradox of inquiry comes from Plato himself—the image of birds in the aviary of the soul and the distinction between having and holding.

In the passage immediately following the interrogation of Meno's slave boy (85b8–86b4), Plato indicates clearly that this is how he understands what he has written. If we look first at 85b8–c8, we see that in this passage Plato has incorporated an important transition, from a seemingly harmless description of the slave boy's behavior— the beliefs are "his own"—to a potentially serious epistemological and possibly metaphysical claim—they are "in him" (85c4). And what "in him" must mean at this stage of the dialogue is "not in another," for example, not in Socrates. The boy's beliefs, that is, are believings about things in him and not about things in another. Later Plato writes that among the beliefs in the boy are true ones (85c6–7), and that if this is so (86a6–7), then what is in him is *he aletheia ton onton* (the truth of things that exist). "In him" is explicitly said to mean "in the soul" (86b1–2), and so what Meno agrees to ultimately is that the objects of the boy's believing are truths in his soul.

At 85c9–d8 Plato has Socrates use this claim, that the objects of believing are in the soul, to generate the further conclusion that the boy's "recovering knowledge that is in him [is] recollecting"

(85d7). Meno casually accepts the proposal that beliefs, newly aroused like a dream, can be converted into knowledge, for he finds no difficulty in agreeing that once a truth is in the mind, the transition from believing it to knowing it is not insurmountable.[98] Hence, the boy can be said to "recover the knowledge out of himself" (85d3–4), where "knowledge" clearly refers to the object of the knowing, the truth about the diagonal on the given square. Meno so readily accepts the word "recover" that its meaning must be the most obvious. Prior to the boy's being asked a question, a given truth is in his soul but unattended to. When the question is asked, the boy responds by assenting to the truth, first as a belief, later as knowledge. And he does so by grasping again what he had grasped already but only in an unapprehended fashion, and such a grasping again is an act of recovery. This is how Socrates reasons: from belief to knowledge to recovery to recollection, with his attention always on the truths that are the objects of all four.

The final section of this sequel to the slave boy discussion (85d9–86b5) is difficult. Plato first describes the slave boy's behavior such that it can be seen as a case of recollection, and then he argues that what is recalled—the truths first believed and eventually known—are always in the soul to be recalled. Plato is concerned about getting inquiry started only insofar as he believes that *without* the truths present in the inquirer's soul it can neither start nor succeed. It is in this sense that his interest in inquiry is metaphysical and not epistemological; Plato's problem about reference is the referent and not the referring. Directed inquiry is possible only insofar as that referent is always in the soul and coming to know it is a matter of recollection.[99]

At 86b1–2 Socrates reports the additional inference, that "if the truth of things that are is always in our soul, then the soul must be immortal." Earlier Plato had elaborated the Orphic-Pythagorean teaching about immortality and reincarnation (transmigration) to identify the proposal that learning or inquiry is a kind of recollection. Here he shows that such recollection entails truths always in the soul and at 86b1–2 that this "always," this permanence, itself implies the soul's indestructible nature. In short, the teachings and doctrines that Plato endorses form an epistemological-religious network, one to which he is wholly committed.[100]

The *Meno*, therefore, marks a crucial stage in the emergence of

Plato's philosophical genius. He realizes that rational inquiry needs defense and that it is not yet securely bound together with the belief in the soul's immortal nature. Plato discovers that rational inquiry can serve the purposes of religious aspiration only if its objects, truths about all things, are permanently graspable by the soul and only if inquiry ultimately proceeds from true belief to knowledge about these same objects. Hence, the dialogue reveals Plato's allegiance both to Socratic inquiry and to the religious, ecstatic character we have found in it. In the *Meno*, responding to his opponents and to the despair of the moment, and drawing on the Orphic-Pythagorean resources available to him, Plato builds a defense of Socratic inquiry that satisfies nearly all his needs.

Nearly. But there is a flaw, and Plato soon comes to recognize it. For if Socratic inquiry is to respond to a desire for the attainment of divine or quasi-divine status, then the objects of inquiry or learning must not only be accessible, but they must also be—to a certain degree—inaccessible. The "truths always in the soul" are too immanent, too present. Plato has solved the paradox only to generate a new one. At the outset of inquiry, the objects are either present or absent. If present, they are human, all too human. But if absent and separate, they are divine but beyond our ken. With a firm grip on the soul's immortality, Plato turns—in the *Phaedo*—to the establishment of the conditions for this new threat to his religious and philosophical conception of the best life possible for humankind.[101]

CHAPTER THREE

PHILOSOPHY AND THE

LANGUAGE OF ECSTASY

IN THE *PHAEDO*

The *Phaedo* is written after the *Meno* and before the *Symposium* and hence can be dated around 385.[1] The political and religious setting is not, then, significantly different from that of the anti-sophistical trio—*Meno, Protagoras,* and *Gorgias*—and in many ways Plato uses the *Phaedo* to further the themes of these dialogues. The *Phaedo,* for example, takes off directly from the *Meno's* concern with immortality, inquiry, and arete and develops the *Gorgias'* eulogy to the philosophical life.

The first and most obvious of the *Phaedo's* themes is the immortality of the soul and its association with inquiry and the attainment of knowledge. But in the *Phaedo* Plato surpasses his earlier treatment. He actually employs the techniques of rational inquiry and dialectic in order to try to prove the soul's immortal and intellectual nature. This endeavor is a special departure, an effort to establish the rational connections between psychology and epistemology. What was a religious postulate or assumption for Socrates and a feature of myth for Bacchants and the Orphic-Pythagorean tradition here becomes an object of rational thought. Certainly, Plato here—as elsewhere in his attempts to prove immortality—draws on traditional elements, motifs, and arguments; what is novel, however, are the ways in which he synthesizes them into a rational search for truth about the soul and its nature. Philosophical inquiry manifests itself as an attempt to secure one of its own preconditions.

Second, Plato supersedes the *Meno* in terms of the object of inquiry and knowledge. In the *Meno,* Plato has acknowledged the threat of the eristic paradox and used the doctrine of recollection to disarm it. He took this doctrine to follow from an Orphic-Pythagorean teaching about immortality and transmigration, and both entailed that the "truths are always in the soul." But although this solution can be understood to thwart the paradox and develop Plato's religious commitments, it has important deficiencies. The most pressing religious weakness is that these objects are inappropriate to the aspiration to transcend the domain of nature and history in order to become divine. The most pressing epistemological weakness is that these truths lack the stability and purity appropriate to the objects of knowledge. In the *Phaedo* Plato confronts both of these problems and solves them in one swoop, with the introduction of unchanging, separate, and pure entities as the proper and exclusive objects of knowledge.[2] Moreover, those same entities which originally emerge as objects of religious, epistemic aspiration soon begin to flourish on their own, assimilating further characteristics often associated with divinity.[3] The discovery of the Forms, then, is the result in part of a deep religious need—for objects of inquiry and knowledge appropriate to the belief that inquiry is an ecstatic rite aiming at divine status and the cognitive complement to immortality. If inquiry is conceived as such a rite and the soul does indeed seek divinity, then the objects of knowledge must also be divine or at least akin to the divine.

Third, the *Phaedo*, like the *Meno*, betrays an indebtedness to Orphic-Pythagorean rites and teachings, but its debt is richer and less equivocal. The reason is apparent: the *Phaedo*, while a dialogue, is more homiletical than its predecessor and less exploratory—more rhetorical and less aporetic. And the purpose of its rhetoric is also apparent, to eulogize the philosophical life by displaying Socrates as its paradigm. Although Socrates himself was influenced by Bacchic and other ecstatic traditions and rituals, Plato uses a more distinctly identifiable religious profile as the frame for his portrait of Socrates—the Orphic-Pythagorean teachings and rites prominent in Sicily and Italy and indeed present throughout the Greece of the early fourth century.[4] This profile enables Plato to characterize with some precision the conception of the best life, the philosophical, inquiring life, in contrast to available alternate models, among them that committed to Delphic theology and the polis tradition, to the life of Protagoras or Isocrates.

Finally, since the soul's immortality is associated with myths of different origin and kind, it is not surprising to find Plato in the *Phaedo* constructing his own myth of the soul's posthumous possibilities. The *Phaedo*'s myth is neither his first nor his last excursion into creative mythology.[5] But whereas in other religious settings the soul's immortality is posited or assumed as a doctrine associated with an authoritative mythology, in the *Phaedo* the myth is a post-dialectical flourish—not a reason for accepting the soul's immortality, but rather a speculative revision of traditional imaginings, a fabulous attempt to push thinking where reason should not tread. Only later, in the *Republic* and the *Phaedrus*, is myth employed in a more integral way, as a surrogate for rational inquiry rather than an epilogue to it.[6] In the *Phaedo*, as in the *Gorgias*, the concluding myth is the beneficiary of and not the foundation for Plato's case for the philosophical life.

WRITING in the mid-380s, Plato locates his eulogy to philosophical or rational piety in Athens at the time of Socrates' imprisonment and execution. The setting, as background, bespeaks powerfully the failure of Athenian character, a message Plato repeats at the end of the *Phaedo* and in the *Seventh Letter*; it is a message recalled too in the *Meno*, the *Gorgias*, and the *Republic*.[7] The moment of Socrates' greatest nobility is also an Athenian nadir. Moreover, the conversation has the aura of a legend or myth itself, for it is being reported at some distance in time and place. The story of Socrates is the story of a new Pythagoras.

Socrates' story is retold in Phlius, a small Peloponnesian city; Socrates' main interlocutors are Cebes and Simmias, Pythagoreans from Thebes. As Hackforth notes, although Phlius was small, it was not insignificant; in fact it was one of the centers of mainland Pythagoreanism.[8] Echecrates was but one of four outstanding Pythagoreans who belonged to the town.[9] Indeed, one thing that Echecrates, Simmias, and Cebes have in common is that all three seem to have been students or associates of Philolaus, the important Pythagorean who had settled in Thebes after the sect was expelled from southern Italy.[10] Clearly, by 399 Philolaus had resided in Thebes for some time.[11] In the *Phaedo*, the relation between Philolaus and his "auditors"—especially Simmias and Cebes—portrays one aspect of the relation between Archytas and Plato; Socrates—the "new" Pythagoras—is the mediating figure. Socrates' Bacchic inclinations—the association between Dionysos and Thebes should not be forgotten[12]—are here recast in an Orphic-Pythagorean setting. The strains of Platonic dissent against Delphic theology and the polis tradition, which we have already introduced, are magnified. The *Phaedo* is blatantly revolutionary, a nearly seditious document.

Can there be any doubt that the *Phaedo*, seemingly an antihistorical document, is more properly understood as an anti-Athenian one?[13] Thebes, the devious and destructive political ally of Athens in the 390s,[14] turns out to harbor the real allies of the genuine Athens; Simmias and Cebes are Socratic confidants. But the story of their conversation is told neither in Athens nor in Boeotia but rather in a Peloponnesian town—not Sparta, nor Corinth or Argos, but in Phlius, a Pythagorean center. Indeed, it is this Pythagoreanism that unites in literary imagination Thebes and Phlius; Simmias, Cebes, and Echecrates, and—if Orphic-Pythagorean practices and teachings are as revolutionary as I have argued—opposition to the polis tradition and the Delphic theology.

SCHOLARS often excavate the *Phaedo* for Orphic and Pythagorean evidence, part of the chore of isolating pre-Platonic Pythagoreanism and of characterizing that elusive phenomenon, Orphism. As we turn to the dialogue, however, let us do so with a different purpose, not to mine it for evidence of something else but rather to try to understand the role Orphic Pythagoreanism and its vocabulary play in what Plato is doing in the dialogue itself. The proposal made earlier was that this context is relevant as four themes emerge— the Forms as objects of knowledge and religious aspiration, the application of Socratic inquiry to the problem of the soul's immortality, the use of Orphic-Pythagorean resources to eulogize the philosophical life, and the development of creative mythology as descriptive of posthumous reward.

Against the background of the Socratic dialogues and the early Platonic *Meno*, *Gorgias*, and *Protagoras*, the *Phaedo*'s powerful encomium to the philosophical life is not wholly surprising. But it is partially so, and its distinctiveness demands attention. One of the *Phaedo*'s dominant features is its emphasis on difference and separation. But unlike the traditional, Delphic theology, the central separations in the *Phaedo* are not along a line between the divine and the human but rather along a line between the physical or worldly, on the one hand, and the divine and psychic, on the other.[15] This separation influences centrally the apology for philosophy and the pursuit of knowledge, for it is the fulcrum on which turns the discovery of the Forms as the appropriate objects of knowledge and the denigration of the senses—together with physical desire, pleasure, emotion, and so on—and sense-bound beliefs.

Later I shall consider the motivation for and consequences of the identification of the separate Forms as the proper objects of inquiry and knowledge. For the moment, let us focus on the discrediting of the senses, the first result of which is that incarnate existence is also demeaned. Therefore, if the goal or one goal of human life is wisdom of a perfect and complete kind, this goal is primarily, if not exclusively, attainable in a postcarnate setting, when the soul is permanently and ideally separated from physical bodies and the distortions of sensation. But this result means that the aspiration to divinity via a wisdom that perfects the soul's immortal nature can really be satisfied only after death and not in life, a consequence that identifies inquiry and learning as at best propaedeutic to *eudaimonia*—in a rather dramatic sense. The *Phaedo*, in this way, severely constrains the possibilities of incarnate, worldly inquiry and elevates the status of postcarnate wisdom.[16]

This line of thinking, I believe, turns on the *Phaedo*'s negative view of the physical world and its denigration of physical states and faculties—sensation, pleasure, desire, and so on. It is not clear which of these states and faculties is more primary to Plato, but about Plato's attitude we can ask two questions. The historical one concerns which influences result in the *Phaedo*'s negativity, and here the possibilities range from Orphic and Pythagorean to Eleatic.[17] Of greater philosophical interest, however, is the question of how Plato discredits sensation and physical states. What are his reasons for thinking that the senses are incapable of apprehending the truth and yielding knowledge?

One way to discredit sensation, widely utilized in later stages of the philosophical tradition, is to use skeptical arguments to identify inconsistencies or contradictions in perceptual results, thus rendering those results suspect as the content of knowledge. In a way, Plato does just this in the *Phaedo*; later we shall consider how he does so. But whereas Descartes, for example, will take these inconsistencies to indicate that the senses cannot by themselves be trusted

as reliable witnesses to independently existing realities, Plato derives a different set of conclusions. He finds, first, that the senses
accurately reflect the nature of their proper objects; second, that
these physical objects are marked by change and compresence of
opposites; and third, that they are deficient and hence inappropriate
objects of genuine inquiry and knowledge. There is nothing wrong
with sensation by itself, as it were. What compromises sensation is
neither its relativity nor its dependence on context. What is wrong
with sensation are its objects, which are ontologically unsuitable
as objects of knowledge. Just as in the *Meno* Plato saves inquiry not
by examining and revising the mental activity of intellectual search
but rather by identifying its objects as always accessible, so in the
Phaedo he discredits the senses not by assailing features of the act
of sensing but rather by denigrating its objects.

The characterization of physical objects as the appropriate, albeit
deficient objects of sensation and sense-bound beliefs, the discrediting of sensation vis-à-vis knowledge, the introduction of appropriate, nondeficient objects of intellect and knowledge—these are
among the *Phaedo*'s most important philosophical contributions.
And one of the chief results of these contributions is the defense of
philosophy and the deferring of the possibility of real wisdom to an
otherworldly future.

The materials for building this account of the *Phaedo*'s defense of
philosophy, postcarnate wisdom, and the denigration of sensation
and the physical world can be found throughout the dialogue but
primarily in two stretches of text, 63e–69e and 77b–84b.[18] The first
passage incorporates Socrates' famous dialectical apology for the
philosophical life and the philosopher's welcoming of death. The
second includes the affinity argument for the soul's immortality.
For the present purposes, the second passage can be treated as a
supplement to the first, elaborating the features of the objects of
sensation and the distinction between the "lovers of knowledge"
and the "lovers of the body."[19]

The first text has as its goal support of the proposal that the philosopher is confident and optimistic as he approaches death, hopeful
that the philosophical life has adequately prepared him for posthumous reward.[20] Essentially the argument turns on the two theses:

(1) that the philosopher desires most of all the truth and the
knowledge of it, and

(2) that the truth is apprehended most clearly and efficiently once the soul is separated from the body.

The good life is led both in behalf of and in preparation for this outcome. Hence, the philosopher both readies himself for and even anticipates the state of ideal, uninterrupted postcarnate wisdom. The conversation that yields this result, moreover, seems to have three components: Socrates (1) portrays a contrast between philosophical desire and physical desires, (2) shows how the latter are an obstacle to the former, and (3) demonstrates how this conflict is reflected in a contrast between philosophical and slavish arete.

The difference between philosophical and physical desires is drawn sharply. The nonphilosopher desires the pleasures of food, drink, sex, and the prestige gotten from fine dress—the pleasures of the body.[21] To him, the body demands attention and nurture; physical desire is time-consuming and insatiable, leading to fears, fantasies, and ultimately to war and conflict. One central fact about physical desire is that it is overwhelming; it allows no moderation, is ever present, and permits no other desires to exist peacefully alongside it.[22] Its second central feature is that it is always a desire to accumulate pleasures and avoid pain.[23] Philosophical desire, on the other hand, is directed toward the soul,[24] to the truth, and to wisdom.[25] That is, whereas the nonphilosopher has an insatiable desire for pleasures of the body, the philosopher has an overriding desire to know the truth.[26]

In one sense these portraits can be viewed as a contrast of personal types, and to a certain degree Plato, even here in the *Phaedo*, intends such a contrast.[27] But in another sense, these desires can be seen to compete in each person, and surely one of Plato's central themes is the uncompromising way in which the desire for physical pleasures presents an obstacle to philosophical inquiry. Plato would surely not deny that all persons—all incarnate souls—have desires for a wide variety of physical pleasures, from food, drink, and sex to prestige and reputation. The problem for the philosopher is that these desires are insatiable, immoderate, and overwhelming. While incarnate, the soul of the philosopher must struggle to curb them in favor of its own desire for knowledge. Ultimately, in the *Phaedo*, Plato wavers on the body's utility as an aid to gaining knowledge.[28] At 65a9–66a10, however, he seems to be unequivocal: the senses are

said to be inaccurate and unclear.[29] Why? At 65b1–4 Plato ascribes
this judgment to unnamed poets and leaves at that both its character and origin.[30] Shortly, however, he chastises the body in general
as insatiable, demanding, competitive, disruptive—"It leaves us no
leisure for philosophy" (66b7–d7), and even when it permits a moment for inquiry (*dzetesis*, d5), it "once again intrudes everywhere
in our researches, setting up a clamor and disturbance, and striking
terror, so that the truth can't be discerned because of it." It is easy
to understand what Plato means when he criticizes physical desire
as demanding, insatiable, and so on. But it is harder to see what
effect such desires have, if any, on sensation. One might think that
Plato's two criticisms are distinct; the body is to be avoided for two
reasons, because physical desire leaves no time for inquiry and because sensation is too unclear and inaccurate as a means for achieving wisdom. But this complete separation of the two issues will not
do, for Plato seems adamant that physical desire disturbs inquiry
even when it allows time for it to occur.

The answer to this problem, the account of how physical desire
is implicated in the corruption of inquiry, is given later, at 82d9–
83e3. In this passage, Plato explains what occurs when a person first
becomes educated about having the philosophical desire for inquiry,
knowledge, and truth. Such a person's soul begins as "bound and
glued to the body," committed to inquiry through the senses and
riveted to the body by pleasure and pain. First, the individual is
persuaded that inquiry via the eyes, ears, and other senses is de-
ceitful. The reason, given earlier, is that because its objects are
never constant, it is confused by apprehending objects of a confusing
kind (79c2–8). But this correction is not sufficient; the philosophical
novice must also overcome his desire for physical pleasures, for each
person is forced to think that *whatever causes intense pleasure or
pain is the most clear and most real*. That is, as long as an individual
has an overriding desire for pleasure and the avoidance of pain, he
takes for most real what "the body declares to be so," that is, what
causes those pleasures and pains. Hence, such desires impede inquiry by misdirection, even when they allow time for inquiry to be
conducted. In short, such physical desires, when in control, direct
the inquiry into reality toward the objects of sensation. They may
not influence sensation ab initio, but they do confirm the results of
sensory investigation as the proper objects of inquiry into the real

and true. The body and the dominance of physical desire are corrupt systematically. For the incarnate philosopher, they pose a formidable and constant threat that must be overcome if genuine inquiry is to succeed.

The philosopher, then, anticipates death as the most desirable setting for attaining wisdom—without physical obstacles (66b–68b).[31] Moreover, the philosopher is the person of genuine excellence of character—temperate, just, brave—because he acts out of an abiding, dominant desire for wisdom. Only those who subordinate physical desire and pleasure to a desire for knowledge can be truly brave and self-disciplined.[32] Genuine arete, Socrates says, is a kind of purification (*katharsis tis*), and wisdom itself a kind of purifying rite (*katharmos tis*).

In the *Phaedo*, philosophy is defended as a mode of existence that exalts the desire for knowledge and truth, that encourages inquiry and the subordination of physical desires and pleasures, that rejects sensation in favor of intellect as a vehicle for inquiry, that treats postcarnate wisdom as the ultimate goal of human life, and that aspires to rational virtue and preparation for this posthumous achievement. Moreover, Plato's eulogy—still to be completed by the myth at the dialogue's end and by the clarification of the role of the Forms for philosophy—is developed in a richly religious vocabulary that sets high standards for the objects of philosophical desire and rational inquiry.[33]

We begin with the passage at 69b8–13, in which Socrates speaks of the aretai as a kind of purification and of *phronesis* as the vehicle for purification.[34] He then acknowledges a saying regarding the initiations at Eleusis (*tas teletas hemin*, c3), that whoever dies uninitiated will lie in the mud, while those who arrive in Hades purified and initiated will dwell with the gods. Quoting—or slightly misquoting—a popular doctrine, Socrates says, there are "'many who bear the wand but few who are devotees [*bacchoi*]'; now these latter . . . are none other than those who have practiced philosophy aright" (69c8–d2). As Parker has pointed out, the background of these notions of purification and initiation is Eleusinian and Orphic.[35] Moreover, Burkert has argued that there are no clear boundaries in this period between Orphic teachings and rites and those associated with Eleusis, the Pythagoreans, and the Bacchic devo-

tees, the Corybantes for example. The resources for Plato's synthesis—of Eleusinian initiation and purification, the Pythagorean
reverence for philosophy, the Orphic doctrine that the soul is imprisoned in the body,[36] and the Socratic use of rational inquiry as
an ecstatic rite—pervade the religious life of early fourth-century
Greece. Pythagorean elements doubtless emerge when, for example,
Socrates calls philosophy "a very high art form" (*megistes mou-
sikes*, 61a4–5),[37] Orphic elements when Plato notes that the soul is
imprisoned in the body (62b2–5 and throughout), and Eleusinian
elements with the reference to philosophy as a purificatory rite of
initiation. Plato sought to graft all of this onto a Socratic root stock
and to define philosophical inquiry as a religious rite, the goal of
which is a "communion with the divine," passing the rest of time
with the gods.[38] He was well supported by generous materials at
hand.[39]

Armed in this way, then, Plato attempted to deepen the Socratic
strategy by using Orphic, Pythagorean, Eleusinian, and Bacchic motifs to underscore the therapeutic role of philosophy and rational
inquiry. Compared with the Socratic conception of philosophy, his
conception serves a more otherworldly goal; for Plato physical incarnation is a debility, and ideal wisdom is posthumous. In the
Phaedo, philosophy is a form of initiatory purification rite, the
philosophical inquirer an officiant of such rites,[40] and the denigration of the body and sensory experience the proper vehicle for inquiry.

Philosophy, therefore, is a strategy of transcendence facilitated
by the unusual character of its objects. But what, we might ask, are
its appropriate objects? The *Phaedo*'s outstanding philosophical novelty is the introduction of the Forms as the proper objects of rational
inquiry and ultimately of knowledge. For lack of an alternative, it
is best to treat the Forms and their characterization as Platonic
achievements—the results of reflection on the deficiencies of sense
perception and of the divine status which wisdom or knowledge was
intended to attain.

Often in the *Phaedo* Plato says that the soul is divine,[41] but although Orphic teachings tell us that it is divine in one sense, we
can see that in another it is only potentially so. And that potentiality can be realized only by proper conduct and achievement, by
rational inquiry and knowledge. But in the *Phaedo* this conduct or

inquiry involves turning away from the senses to reason and thereby rejecting the physical world in favor of a different domain of objects altogether. Indeed, as we have seen, the deficiency of sensation and the advantage of reason turn on just this, their different objects. With the Forms come divinity, purity, clarity, and much else, including a radical discontinuity that restores the problem of inquiry or learning in an unexpected way.

Much has been said about the Forms in the *Phaedo*. Fortunately, we can focus briefly on what is, relatively speaking, uncontroversial. First, although other functions do enter the picture even in the *Phaedo*,[42] the epistemological function of the Forms, as the proper and exclusive objects of genuine knowledge, that is, knowledge of the real or knowledge of what each thing is,[43] provides the primary motivation for their introduction. Inquiry is properly directed toward the knowledge of these entities and succeeds only when it has achieved that knowledge. Second, these entities have properties that distinguish them from the objects of sight, hearing, and so on. They are incorporeal, invisible, incomposite; they are constant and unvarying, uniform, pure, divine; they are always existing, immortal, and intelligible.[44] We need not explore in detail these properties. Some are not all that clear and precise; others seem honorary at best. For Plato the divinity of these entities concerns their purity and eternality and derives from the fact that real knowledge requires such divine, stable entities as its only suitable objects.[45]

We may never know which Plato realized first: the need for divine, separately existing objects of inquiry, aspiration, and knowledge, or the deficiency of sensory experience as a vehicle for inquiry conceived as an ecstatic rite. We shall never know whether Plato's primary motivations were epistemological or religious. In one sense, the two are coordinate needs and discoveries. The realization of what makes physical things inappropriate objects of knowledge is closely related to the realization of what suitable objects of inquiry and knowledge must be like. In the *Phaedo*, the central features of this joint realization concern stability, permanence, and clarity. The senses are neither accurate nor clear, for their objects "vary and are never constant."[46] Some commentators take as radical the change that characterizes physical things, such that nothing is stable at any time in any respect; others have argued that the sort of change or instability Plato has in mind involves relativity, comparison, and in the end the compresence of opposites.[47] Whether or not instability as a feature of sensible objects ultimately reduces to the compresence of opposite properties, it is clearly this instability that demeans the objects of sensory experience, making it impossible for them to be objects of inquiry. Inquiry into what is real and knowledge of it are the objects of the philosopher's life and his desire. By discrediting sensory objects, Plato requires a set of nonsensible objects that have precisely the opposite properties. They are stable, always the same, ungenerated and incorruptible, and never qualified by their opposites.[48] Unlike sensible properties that occur together with other properties, including their opposites, and are found in things, these objects, the Forms, exist separately.[49] No matter how much we might be inclined to reduce the force of this separation, by arguing for example that the compresence of opposites constitutes this separation in toto, Plato's treatment will resist such reduction. His portrayal of separation is graphic, vivid, and bold.[50]

The transcendence of the Forms—the "discovery" of a domain of pure, stable, divine, eternal entities—is not an unmitigated achievement. There are clues in the *Phaedo* that Plato does not delay long in appreciating both the power and the problematic of his discovery. In the *Meno* true belief about some objects of inquiry, for example a diagonal and a square, can be converted, by repeated questioning and the process of working out the reason for the truth, into knowledge about those same objects. In slightly different and more accurate terms, both true belief and knowledge can be of the same truth. But once the *Phaedo* displays a domain of knowable entities separate from the sensible world and inaccessible to sensory experience and to sense-bound beliefs about what is real, the continuity is shattered and with it the possibility of inquiry or learning as a transition from belief to knowledge. What is needed in order to rectify the problem is a more fine-grained analysis of the acts of believing and knowing than Plato has thus far provided.[51] Belief is not even prominent in the *Phaedo*, and Plato uses the vocabulary for knowing indiscriminately throughout the dialogue. To be sure, there is conclusive evidence that Plato distinguishes between knowing as a mental grasping or seeing of its objects, the Forms, and knowing as providing (or being able to provide) logoi of them.[52] But there is only a hint that Plato recognizes the further refinements that need to be made. Knowing what x really is involves both knowing or identifying x and understanding what it is that x really is. These are not two kinds of knowledge but rather two aspects of knowing. Furthermore, there are degrees of both: one can know or identify x strongly or weakly, directly or indirectly; and one can understand what is the true account of x completely or incompletely.[53] But in the *Phaedo*, imprecision in the use of the terms for knowledge in the anamnesis argument and the unclarity about the type of sensory experience involved[54] suggest uncertainty on Plato's part. The solution to the discontinuity problem and a further elaboration of these issues must wait for the *Republic*.[55]

THE *Phaedo* is clearly the *Meno*'s successor in terms of the importance of inquiry and the specification of its genuine objects. It also distinguishes why rational rather than sense-bound inquiry is the only path to knowledge. But these are not its only debts to the *Meno*, for like its predecessor, the *Phaedo* also appreciates the connection between inquiry and immortality, although it does so in a rather different way.

Doubtless there existed various arguments in Plato's day for the soul's immortality, but the *Phaedo* is surely the earliest comprehensive and systematic treatment. Proofs of the soul's immortality henceforth become part of Plato's continuing effort to develop his understanding of inquiry, knowledge, and eudaimonia.[56] For our purposes the importance of the arguments lies not in their often subtle structure but rather in their presence at all, for they show Plato's employment of Socratic techniques of rational, dialectical inquiry with a different goal, not the nature of moral or mathematical properties but rather the soul's everlastingness.[57] Moreover, in seeking to demonstrate the soul's immortality, the proofs also reveal something about what Plato takes "immortality" to mean.[58]

Affirmation of immortality extends far back into Greek history, to Tyrtaeus, the Spartan poet, and continues forward to the fourth century and beyond. Only as the notion of the soul takes shape in the fifth century, however, especially under the influence of the *physikoi*, the Pythagoreans, and Orphic writers, does the conception of the soul's immortality crystallize. Associated with reincarnation, transmigration, and metempsychosis, immortality may best be thought of not as a property of individual personality but rather as a generic property of the soul per se. For a particular soul to be immortal amounts to its being ungenerated and indestructible. The soul neither comes into being nor goes out of being; persons are born and die but the soul, like the gods, does neither.[59] Against these general views Plato's treatment in the *Phaedo* seems generally uncontroversial. The anamnesis argument shows that the soul must have existed prior to any given incarnation and, together with the earlier cyclical argument, that it will still exist after death.[60] Plato is clear: if the soul is immortal, then before and after any period of incarnation it must exist. But although it must exist for all time, it is something called psyche that exists and not the personality or character of any particular incarnate individual.

Plato's treatment, however, is not uncontroversial, and he seems to realize this. What Plato wants for the soul is divinity, provisional at least, and while the religious and literary tradition associates immortality with divinity, it does not make clear in what immortality consists. Plato's Eleatic sensitivity tells him that it should mean that the gods, if they are ultimate and divine reality, should undergo neither generation nor corruption. An immortal soul, however, even if it exists prior and subsequent to each incarnation, still might not continue to exist without interruption. For it is still possible that during the period of discarnate existence the soul might cease to exist and then be reconstituted. In short, immortality by itself does not entail everlasting, continuous existence. These problems are left open by the cyclical and recollection arguments. Plato seems to recognize this, for he immediately supplements the recollection argument with one aimed at showing that after death, the separation of soul from body, the soul cannot be dispersed because, like the Forms, it is incorporeal, incomposite, and hence imperishable. In effect, this argument, if persuasive, makes the soul's immortality a matter of indestructibility so that its existence is everlasting and continuous.[61]

In the *Phaedo*, then, Plato clarifies that immortality involves everlasting, continuous existence and tries to argue that the soul has such existence, for immortality is a presupposition of the philosophical enterprise. But it is not the only such presupposition; much depends on the prospective philosopher's abilities and character. In the *Phaedo*, Plato has only a little to say about these matters, but there are hints concerning a dimension of the philosopher's quest which will occupy Plato more and more in the years to come. This dimension involves what might be called Plato's "cognitive psychology."

ALTHOUGH wisdom and abiding communion with the Forms is the goal of human life, it is not wholly clear why someone with other strong desires, most notably for riches and prestige, would be moved to turn his attention to knowledge and the rational inquiry that leads to it.[62] This is a problem of motivation or of cognitive desire. Is there reason to think that some persons always have an overwhelming desire for knowledge? Or is it not more likely that "purification" requires not only training in inquiry but also, and more fundamentally, a cultivation of the desire for knowledge? Thus it would seem that philosophers are not born but educated. If so, how can Plato in the *Phaedo* salvage inquiry as philosophical purification without attending to its psychological, motivational dimension?[63]

In the *Meno*, inquiry and Plato's doctrine of recollection are associated with the enterprise of Socratic questioning and elenchos. How does the process of recollection influence one's desire to learn? The role of desire in recollection and learning is not clarified very thoroughly in the *Meno*. In certain cases, the initial stages of the elenchos may dissolve one's self-deceptions and thereby release one's desire to learn the truth.[64] In other cases, perhaps the majority of them, that process may stimulate or generate a new desire to learn. About the operation of desire at the later stages of recollection, Plato has nothing to say. In the slave-boy dialogue, he simply takes it for granted that once the learner's false answers are revealed, he will want to discover the truth and that once he has come to believe what is true, he will want to proceed to the level of knowledge.[65]

Recollection, a process requiring elenctic preparation in the *Meno*, appears virtually automatic in the *Phaedo*.[66] The comparative reflection, whereby one's current object of experience is checked against an earlier object that is recalled, is spontaneous and not voluntary. The mere resemblance between the current object and the prior object "triggers" a reflective comparison that tests the accuracy of the current perception. There seems to be no appreciation on Plato's part that this process—of learning what *y* is via recalling *y* in order to check our seeing-*x*-as-identical-with-*y*—requires desire or psychological motivation. Plato does not explain why the soul becomes "dissatisfied" with its sense experience and why that dissatisfaction should issue in a desire to apprehend a Form, an entity ontologically separated and distinguished in kind from the objects of observation.[67]

The argument for the soul's prenatal existence requires that such reflective experiences occur virtually at birth, with the onset of perceptual experience itself. But this in turn means that the acts of perceiving that issue in recollection must be nondeliberative, not raised by doubt or reflective consideration of what one knows or does not know. Hence, the argument in the *Phaedo* seems to require that the process be virtually automatic.

At the same time that the recollection argument leaves little room for a desire to know, and does not even seem to appreciate the momentous redirection of desire accompanying the recognition that Forms exist and that questions about what x is are really questions about the nature of these transcendent entities, other passages in the *Phaedo* portray Plato's awareness of both of these facts. In a famous argument, the soul is shown to be similar to the divine Forms (see 80a–b), and it is only a small step to the conclusion that the soul loves the Forms and indeed seeks to imitate them.[68] Earlier Plato delivers his first encomium to philosophy, in the course of which he speaks of the soul as fleeing the body, seeking to be by itself, striving for that which is, and loving wisdom.[69] For Plato the philosophical soul, for some unidentified reason, aspires to knowledge of the Forms and to that release from the body which will facilitate its goal. Plato actually calls this aspiration a desire for knowledge, an eros or *epithumia*.[70] It is an aspiration that Plato identifies, names, and eulogizes, but does not explain.[71]

In neither the *Meno* nor the *Phaedo*, then, does Plato raise any doubts about the possibility of cognitive desire, of the love of knowledge. It is, as it were, given in the character of some and not in the character of others. There are lovers of knowledge and lovers of the body, those who are initiated and those who are not. "Many are those who bear the wand, but few who are devotees."[72] However, we should hardly be surprised by this outcome, for a sharp distinction between those with an overriding desire for knowledge and those without it parallels the separation between the physical world and the Forms. Just as the second distinction threatens to sabotage the continuity between belief and knowledge, wrecking inquiry and learning, so the first distinction does the same by making it impossible for a nonphilosophical believer to come to *want* overwhelmingly to abandon his physical desires to seek knowledge. Plato recognizes neither the psychological nor the epistemic conditions for learning, inquiry, and hence for rational aspiration. The world of the *Phaedo* is a rigid class world, with no appreciation of the opportunity or desire for upward mobility.

IN the *Phaedo* what proceeds via logos ends finally in mythos.[73] Plato venerates posthumous wisdom and the rewards of the philosophical life, but when it comes to describing those rewards, he turns to a literary genre of ancient and revered provenance. The *Phaedo* begins with a reference to Socrates' fondness for Aesop's fables and his own efforts at poetry; it ends with an early example of Plato's mythic art. And indeed Plato is a great storyteller. His dialogues are products of his narrative skill, although in them action gives way to a movement of thought, and within those dialogues there are fragmentary products of a similar skill, from recollected metaphors—the statues of Daedalus, the song of the dying swans— to didactic narratives and full-scale fables and myths. One might be tempted to treat these products uniformly, calling them all mythoi and locating their status in juxtaposition to the logoi of rational inquiry. But especially given our historical interest it is wiser to treat each case as it occurs, to consider it along with similar writing of the same period, and to assess its role in each dialogue and at the precise stage of Plato's development. Such a strategy will lead us, I think, to treat the myth in the *Phaedo* as a creative attempt to conclude Plato's eulogy to the rites of philosophical inquiry by portraying the results of philosophical life in the most natural way, via constructive mythology.[74]

The eschatological myth in the *Phaedo* should be read alongside that of the *Gorgias*, for they are composed by the same man in a similar spirit in similar circumstances.[75] They are two attempts to do roughly the same thing, to culminate an apology for philosophy by sketching its ultimate rewards.

The two myths do differ; they are introduced for different reasons and in different ways. In the *Gorgias*, Socrates' final encounter with Callicles has articulated a view of philosophy in contrast to rhetoric

and tyranny, among other things, and Socrates concludes that portrait by affirming the philosopher's genuine fear. Unlike his opponents, the philosopher fears not dying but rather doing injustice. In
part, much of the dialogue has been taken up with the question of
justice and the defense of the just life. The idea of dying was
introduced only late in the dialogue as part of an allusion to Socrates' trial and his defense. Socrates admits that he would be an-
noyed if put to death because he was unable to defend himself
except by saying and doing what is unjust. If he lacked flattering
rhetoric, he would confront death easily and with no fear. But why?
Because one's worldly conduct determines one's final reward; injustice here leads to the greatest ultimate evils, but justice brings
its rewards.[76] The myth is "an account (logos) of how this is so"
(522e6).

The *Gorgias* treats death as ancillary; the just and the unjust
ought to approach it differently because posthumous reward or punishment is a function of incarnate conduct. In the *Phaedo*, death—
from the dialogue's outset—lies at the center of Plato's attention.
The soul's immortality is proven; it is clear that once separated, the
soul will survive in some fashion. The soul needs care, Socrates says,
not only for its present state but also for its condition "for the whole
of time" (107c4). Posthumous reward and punishment are explicitly
introduced as a motivation for incarnate virtue. If the soul disintegrated at death, it would be a boon to the wicked. But once immortality has been proven, the only way to avoid subsequent ills
and to attain salvation is "to become as good and wise as possible"
(107d2). So in a sense our earlier question about motivation is answered in an unremarkable way: the wicked are moved to desire to
learn and hence to become virtuous by the prospect of posthumous
judgment and reprisal.[77] The myth is the tale that describes this
process.

Whereas the *Gorgias* myth is intended to comfort the just, the
Phaedo myth is meant to frighten the wicked. Death and immortality, both central to the *Phaedo* and its movement from rational
inquiry in this life to divine knowledge in the next, are only afterthoughts in the *Gorgias*.[78] They are compatible with this dialogue's
rich and antagonistic confrontation between philosophy and hedonistic politics, but they are not part of it. One reason is that the
Gorgias is less personal and more public than the *Phaedo*. Its attack

on the Athenian heritage is less dramatic than the *Phaedo*'s but more explicit; this is because it is more straightforwardly political and moral, rather than religious and epistemological.[79]

Still the *Gorgias* myth, with its emphasis on justice rather than wisdom, is indebted to the *Phaedo*'s convictions about immortality and the distinction between the body and the soul.[80] The myth in the *Gorgias* could not occur without these doctrines.[81] The result is a portrait of posthumous judgment in which the soul's incarnate conduct constitutes the testimony in terms of which its future is decided.[82] The *Gorgias* considers the wicked, the tyrants and the unjust, more extensively than the philosopher, a "soul that had lived piously and with truth" and who had been just (526c1–4). The *Phaedo* reverses the focus, precisely because its myth is intended as motivation for the wicked to convert and as a culmination of the defense of philosophy.

Both, nonetheless, are only myths; one wonders how seriously Plato intended them. He introduces the tale in the *Gorgias* by having Socrates call it an account (logos, 522e5), indeed a "very fine account" (*mala kalou logou*, 523a1),[83] and note to Callicles, "I suppose you'll think it's a tale (mython), but I think it's an account (logon), for I will tell you what I'm about to tell you believing that it is true" (523a2–3). Later, Socrates reiterates that he believes the account to be true[84] and will draw inferences from it, both theoretical and practical. It is hard to avoid the conclusion that in the *Gorgias*, where Plato first tries his hand at constructing such an eschatological myth and with the figure of such a powerful, uncompromising opponent before him, Plato exaggerates his commitment to the tale he tells.

Plato emphasizes that it is a logos, not a mythos, and that he believes it to be true. Dodds asks what Plato means by these twin claims and answers this way: the myths are true because "they are the imaginative expression of an insight which could not be expressed save in symbolic terms," and it "is called a logos because it expresses in imaginative terms a 'truth of religion'."[85] This solution, if it is one, is hardly clear, although Dodds is surely correct to suggest that mythos and logos do not differ as false and true. In a sense, what he seems to be saying is that Plato appreciates the need to communicate truths that are simply beyond didactic boundaries. With this I agree; it is a logos because it is not a *mere* myth, a fantasy or fable that is simply a story and does not reveal any truth at all. But at the same time, it *is* a myth and not a logos—a statement or argument or theory—for it is a purportedly true picture of a religious-moral-epistemological goal that is beyond finite powers to describe even with the use of Orphic-Pythagorean and mythic devices.

Irwin worries that Plato might be using the myth to support his view that the just life is best. After all, the traditional religious stories should be accepted only when they fit our moral convictions; faith is judged by moral right and is not needed to vindicate the latter.[86] But we can read the myths and Plato's intention more charitably than this, not as the unnecessary trappings of a posttheological moral philosopher but rather as the imaginative expression of a religious conception of human attainment that recognizes worldly justice and rational inquiry as goods in themselves but also as paths to posthumous wisdom and blessedness. As a goad to Callicles, the myth is a warning and hence, as in the *Phaedo*, a source of motivation. The value of justice and philosophy does not lie exclusively in their rewards, but there *are* such rewards for Plato and displaying them in the most natural, mythic way can only serve to motivate those resistant to the Platonic vision.

In interpreting the *Gorgias* myth and what Plato means by claiming that it is true, Dodds wisely refers us to the *Phaedo*, where Socrates, referring to the tale (mythos, 114d7) he has just told, says: "Now to insist that these things are just as I've related them would not be fitting for a man of intelligence; but that either this or something like it is true about our souls and their dwellings, given that the soul evidently is immortal, this, I think, *is* fitting and worth risking . . . for a noble risk it is" (114d1–6). There is wise counsel here, that the tale is worth believing to be true, though not as an exact picture but rather as an impressionistic one. And the reason is not formal but substantive; there is nothing intrinsically about tales like this that recommends for or against acceptance. What does so here, in this case, is the fact that "the soul evidently is immortal" and hence that some story, whether this one or another like it, is bound to be true—or at least worth the risk of believing it to be true. There is something natural about assuming that the outlines of eschatological judgment and bliss, sketched in Orphic-Pythagorean mythology and elsewhere, when filled out by a rationally discovered conception of virtue and goodness, are worth believing. For if one is persuaded by the *Phaedo*'s arguments, then to disregard such pictures is to risk eternal ill, while to accept them and be moved by them is possibly to gain salvation.[87]

In the *Gorgias* and *Phaedo*, then, there is no tension between Plato's commitment to logos and rational inquiry, on the one hand, and his use of mythos, on the other. In the *Phaedo* especially, the latter naturally grows out of his arguments for the soul's immortality. The myth accounts for a motivational factor required by inquiry and extends our thinking in a way that is at once demanded by the certainty of immortality and yet prohibited by its detachment from living persons. In a sense, rational inquiry and philosophy *demand* the completion of myth; once wisdom is ideally placed at a time when the soul is separated from the body and is most akin to the divine, the most appropriate mode of discourse available to portray that outcome is imaginative and symbolic. The mythological tradition—from Homer and Hesiod to Orphic and Pythagorean and other contemporary lore—was the natural vehicle for Plato's philosophical creativity.[88]

The core of the *Phaedo* myth is Plato's portrayal of the philosophical wisdom that is the goal of human life. Guthrie has noted how these accounts are descriptions of telestic initiations, mysteries, Orphic, Bacchic, and Pythagorean rites, revised and transformed to suit a goal that is at once religious and cognitive.[89] While Plato advances beyond Socrates by identifying eudaimonia with a state of discarnate wisdom and with communion with the divine, it is his mythological accounts that describe that state by means of a revision of religious vocabulary.[90] Although Plato, following Socrates, turns religious rite into rational discipline, he nonetheless returns to religious myth for his description of the good for humankind.[91]

Early in the *Phaedo* Plato signals his strategy: he will use the language of Bacchic rites and the Eleusinian mysteries,[92] the language of purity and purification, of love and initiation to describe divine wisdom. The same terms recur in the affinity argument with its description of the Forms, of the soul, and of the results of philosophical inquiry.[93] But their fullest and richest employment comes only here, in the course of the eschatological myth that speaks of the soul's entrance into Hades with nothing but its "education and nurture"[94] and its subsequent judgment and rewards. Here we see exactly how Plato employs the terminology of initiation, purification, and ecstatic ritual to shape a conception of the human good in opposition to that of the polis tradition and Delphic theology.[95] If logos is the process of Platonic-Socratic ritual, then mythos signals its outcome.

As Hackforth explains, the extensive account of the earth and the hollows where we live enables "Plato graphically to contrast the world of ordinary experience with another, a better world which is literally nowhere, but which we can only conceive as a 'place' (*topos*), the abode of such discarnate souls as have deserved, by a good life on earth, to reach this abode of bliss."[96] The 'true earth,' he continues, is the Isles of the Blessed of the *Gorgias* and Homer, the destination of the philosopher. At 114b6–c8 Plato tells us that those who have lived exceptionally holy lives leave the hollows, like prisons, for the pure (*katharan*) dwelling above the earth. Hackforth identifies the final destination of the philosopher with this 'true earth.' In fact Plato does not.[97] For him the philosophers, who are among the holy and have been "sufficiently purified by philosophy" (114c2–3), "live bodiless for the whole of time to come and attain to dwelling places fairer even than these, which it is not easy to reveal, nor is the time sufficient at present" (c2–6). When Socrates says that the prize is fair and the hope great, he is referring to this final destination, beyond the true earth.

The description of the true earth, a mythos according to Socrates, then, is not a description of the philosopher's ultimate dwelling place.[98] Instead it is an interim abode, between the world of the Greek polis and the domain of permanent discarnate, divine existence. Taking a clue from Burkert's discussion of Philolaus, we can appreciate that the thrust of Plato's account of the true earth (110b5–11c3) is Pythagorean and Ionian with Philolaun features.

The centrality of the earth, which harks back to Anaximander,[99] is canonized by Plato and inherited by Eudoxus and Aristotle, among others. Together with its sphericity, the earth's centrality can, based on Aristotelian evidence, be ascribed to Pythagoras or to early Pythagoreans, and although Burkert doubts this hypothesis, it is possible that Archytas if not Philolaus held such views.[100] The sun and the moon are the Isles of the Blessed to the Pythagoreans,[101] and Plato, at the end of his account, notes that the inhabitants of the true earth, directly aware of the gods, also see the "sun and moon and stars . . . as they really are" (111c2–3).[102] Moreover, Philolaus taught that the moon is inhabited by creatures and plants larger and more beautiful than ours,[103] a view that Plato might well be elaborating when he says that the trees, flowers, and fruit exceed ours by proportion, while the people there "surpass us in sight, hearing, wisdom, and all such faculties."[104] Burkert treats these themes as the outcome of shamanistic myths, information conveyed by individuals on their return from a "journey through the skies," the results of ecstatic experience.[105] If he is right, then what we have in the *Phaedo* is a Platonic appropriation of Pythagorean ecstatic myths, used to eulogize the interim results of rational, philosophical inquiry.

Some may read the account of the true earth and see clearly its Pythagorean and Ionian roots, but remain dubious of its connection with initiation rites and ecstatic ritual. But we can, as a final point, make this connection too. Earlier we noticed Plato's identification of wisdom as a purifying rite,[106] and we followed Parker in taking the sources of this ascription to be Orphic *teletai* and the mysteries at Eleusis, both with their Bacchic dimensions. *Phaedo* 69c–d seems to confirm that conjecture. It also contains an early use of a pair of opposites, versions of which come to pervade the entire dialogue. That is the opposition of purity and impurity, and its associates are those of clean and dirty, clear and confused, brilliant and murky.[107] This opposition is rooted in the very notion of purification itself and has its impact on posthumous reward, for the teaching of Eleusis and Orphic rites is that while the initiated and purified will go on to dwell with the gods, the uninitiated will lie in the mud.[108] Not only does impurity require cleansing; a failure to cleanse consigns the victim to further impurity.

These same oppositions—between purity and impurity, clarity and obscurity—are present in the eschatological myth and the account of the earth. The true earth, Plato says, is "purer and fairer" than life in the hollows (109d3–4); our earth is "corrupted and eaten away, as are things in the sea by brine . . . there are eroded rocks and sand and unimaginable mud and mire" (110a1–6). In the true earth, on the other hand, there are brilliant colors—purple, gold, white—and mountains of stones that are "pure, and not corroded or corrupted, like those here, by mildew and brine . . . bringing ugliness and disease to stones and earth and to plants and animals as well" (110b5–11a3). In short, the earth we live in, the hollows, is contrasted with the true earth in terms of impurity and purity. Indeed, the gods actually dwell in their groves, and the inhabitants commune with the gods face to face (111b6–c1; compare 84a7–b4). From the *Phaedo* to the *Republic* and then to the *Phaedrus*, these oppositions will continue to have a powerful grip on Plato's religious and philosophical imagination.

For all its achievements, the *Phaedo* leaves Plato with significant problems. First, there is the well-known observation that the *Phaedo* is "wholly individualistic," as Hackforth puts it.[109] Plato's portrait of religious-philosophical piety lacks a political, social dimension, and whether this lack is consistent with Socratic arete or that of Plato in the *Meno* is not as relevant as the observation that in later works Plato himself recognizes the deficiency. Second, as an Orphic-Pythagorean version of philosophical piety, the *Phaedo* exhibits a severe one-sidedness fostered by an overly rigid set of dichotomies. It is the negativity that stands out, the aversion to the body and all the desires and abilities, especially sense perception, associated with it.

Third, there is the introduction of the Forms and all the problems that beset Plato's commitment to them—their nature, their relation to the physical world, and so on. What begins as an ingenious solution to a religious-epistemological problem about the proper status of the objects of inquiry and knowledge soon takes on a life of its own. And that life, adumbrated especially in the anamnesis and final arguments in the *Phaedo*, is not unproblematic—from the problems about Forms as universals and *paradeigmata* in the earlier argument, to the problems about the compresence of opposites and about Form interrelations generated in the later one.

Finally, however, and perhaps most shocking, is the unwanted implication for the nature of inquiry itself. For if the Forms are separated and pure, objects of a different ontological order from the objects of sensation and sense-bound belief, then how can inquiry ever occur? How can the continuity between the objects of true belief and those of knowledge in the *Meno* be maintained in the rigidly dichotomous world of the *Phaedo*? How can the human become divine? Having solved one paradox of inquiry in the earlier dialogue, has Plato now damaged learning and inquiry with an even severer blow? Is divine knowledge now a matter of all or nothing? The Forms may be pure and perfect enough to be akin to the divine, but perhaps they are too separated to be accessible at all.

CHAPTER FOUR

PHILOSOPHY, DESIRE,

AND THE MYSTERIES

IN THE *SYMPOSIUM*

The date of composition of the *Symposium* is a matter of some scholarly controversy. I side with those, like Guthrie, who believe the
dialogue was composed after the *Phaedo* and shortly after 385.[1] We
shall have to look, of course, at its treatment of immortality, which
plays an important role in such calculations, but there are abundant
other philosophical reasons for treating the *Symposium* as subsequent to the *Phaedo*. Indeed, if the dialogue *rejects* the soul's immortality, as some commentators seem to think, no early date is
possible, and although it could not have been written before 385,
no date after the *Republic* and *Phaedrus* makes any sense. So it is
better to leave it at 385–384 or thereabouts and to interpret the
discussion of immortality in that context.

Like many of the dialogues written in the 380s, the *Symposium* is
a eulogy to Socrates, a further attempt at a new apology for Socrates
and the Socratic way of life. Some commentators believe that
among Plato's aims are "to round off his portrait of Socrates by
showing him in a relaxed and convivial mood, and through the
mouth of the disreputable Alcibiades himself to refute the charge
that Socrates had been his evil genius."[2] There is surely some truth
in this twin judgment, as there is in the claim that here, as in the
Phaedrus, Plato shows that he can write rhetorical set speeches as
well as dialogue.[3] But for our purposes, the central features of the
Symposium concern its contribution to the religious conception of
philosophical inquiry as ecstatic rite—a conception we have seen
emerging from Plato's earlier works. What exactly does the *Symposium* add to this conception?

There is virtual unanimity concerning the dialogue's dramatic setting. "The scene of the main narrative is the dinner given to his friends by the tragic poet Agathon when he won the prize with his first tragedy, in 416 B.C."[4] But, as in the *Phaedo*, the events reported are not the dialogue's direct setting. There Phaedo tells of the conversation to Echecrates in Phlius at an unknown time, probably in the late 390s. Here Apollodorus tells the story of the victory dinner to a group of rich businessmen, but unlike Phaedo, Apollodorus was not himself present at the original banquet. Indeed, his account is the result of further reports. Apollodorus had already told the story once, to his friend Glaucon, and he himself was told the tale by Aristodemus from Cydathenaeum. In short, the current conversation includes a secondhand report, told some years after the event itself but while Socrates is still alive.[5] The reader of the dialogue, Plato presumes, knows that the dialogue is set between 416 and 399 and that it reports events that took place in 416.[6] But the time of the telling, the place, and the recipient are anonymous, and this anonymity focuses attention on the tale, its own time and setting, and its direct importance for those alive in Athens shortly after 385. It is hard to imagine that the Athenian reader could ignore the juxtaposition of the year, 416, with the presence of Alcibiades and the prominent use of the terminology of Bacchic rites and the Eleusinian mysteries. The dialogue will leave the reader with a transformed understanding of the relations among Socrates, Alcibiades, philosophy, eros, and Eleusis, an understanding that takes shape against the background of the profanations of the summer of 415[7] and of the antipathy between Alcibiades and Anytus and Thrasybulus. The *Symposium* seems to fit the profile of the other dialogues of the 380s. It is antitraditional, critical of attacks on Socrates' name or person, and it is an attempt to revise the understanding of Socrates and the philosophical way of life.

Since our concern is with the relation among inquiry, knowledge, immortality, and ecstatic ritual in Plato's thought, we need not attempt a comprehensive analysis of the dialogue. Three issues require discussion: (1) Plato's account of the education of desire and its role in moral-religious inquiry; (2) the treatment of immortality in the *Symposium*; and (3) Plato's employment of religious vocabulary from the mysteries and Bacchic worship. We shall concentrate on Socrates' speech on Eros (199c3–212c3) and Alcibiades' encomium to Socrates (215a4–22b7).[8]

THE *Phaedo* raised a problem: If one is a lover of the body, of wealth, and of fame, then how can one learn not only to use the method of inquiry necessary for gaining wisdom but also to *want* that wisdom at all? That is, philosophy is a desire for knowledge—and indeed an overriding desire, without which inquiry would be unappealing and irrelevant. But if one does not simply have that desire, how does one gain it? How is it cultivated? What motivates the nonphilosopher to want to learn?[9]

In order to answer these questions, let us consider Socrates' speech on love.[10] Socrates begins with an elenchos directed at Agathon's concluding praise of love as most supreme in beauty and goodness (197c1–3). Socrates' refutation turns on the twin claims that love is always love of something, which means that it is the desire for something, and that its object is something love now lacks (200e8–9). If love or desire (epithumia) is always of what is beautiful and good, then Love must not be the most beautiful and best of things but rather that which lacks both of these qualities. This elenchos is effective against Agathon, who fails to see any error in it,[11] but what is important is not its success but rather this: in the course of the argument Socrates makes three points to which he seems to adhere throughout—(1) that epithumia is a synonym for eros;[12] (2) that good things are also beautiful (201c2); and (3) that love or desire is always for what is good and beautiful.

In place of a speech on Love, Socrates continues with a report of a conversation between himself and Diotima, a woman and a diviner from Mantinea; the product is to be her account (*ton logon*, 201d1) of Love. The report follows the order of a typical Socratic inquiry, investigating first what Love is and thereafter its effects (*erga*, 201e1–2).[13] The method is dialectical (201e2–7).

What, then, is love? Diotima gets Socrates to agree that contraries are not contradictories. Holding a true belief without being able to give an account, for example, is an intermediate stage between knowledge and ignorance.[14] Such a belief is not knowledge, for the latter requires a logos, but neither is it ignorance, because its object is the truth. Hence, it must lie between them. The same need for an intermediate applies to beautiful and ugly, to mortal and immortal. Love, Diotima claims, is not merely ugly, because after all it desires what is beautiful, but it is not beautiful because it has yet to possess its object. Similarly, love is not merely mortal, presumably, because it *desires* to be immortal; but it is not yet immortal because the desire has yet to be satisfied. In short, love is a "great *daimon* . . . half-way between divine and mortal" (202d13–e1). Love or desire, which aims at the good and beautiful, that is, divinity, is the bridge in man between mere mortality and possible divinity. Its capacity is to interpret and convey messages between the divine and the human, to bridge the gap and to "prevent the universe from splitting apart" (202e3–7).

At this point Plato's dissent from the traditional polis system and the Delphic theology becomes explicit. The existence of daimones makes possible all the features of traditional piety—divination, sacrifices, spells, magic. The divine is not present in man, but through these intermediate beings the gods communicate with men, and a person wise in these matters is called a "daimonic man," to distinguish him from a mere artisan. Love, moreover, is such a daimon, but, as Plato already hints, it is a daimon present *within each one of us*. The desire for the good, for beauty and divinity, is not a matter of privileged access; it is a universal possibility. As we shall see, this universality does not obviate the need for training and education, but it does make both possible. Plato is taking a stand against the prerogatives of Delphic polis religion in favor of a universal capacity for and a common aspiration to divinity.

Love is the offspring of Poverty and Contrivance, born on Aphrodite's birthday.[15] This means that desire is always in need and scheming to satisfy itself, to get what is beautiful and good, that is, wisdom. It arises, flourishes, and dies, only to return—hence its status between mortal and immortal; it is neither rich nor poor, neither wise nor ignorant. The gods are wise already and hence do not, like Eros, desire wisdom; neither do the wholly ignorant, who are satisfied with themselves. It is only those in between, aware of their lack and with a sense of aspiration, who desire wisdom. For love is always love of the beautiful, and wisdom is one of the most beautiful things (204b1–5). Hence, love is philosophy and an encomium to love is praise of philosophical inquiry. The person with true belief is the philosopher, neither ignorant and self-satisfied nor wise and self-sufficient. The truth is that love is not the object of desire but rather the loving of it. The object of love, that is, wisdom, is supremely beautiful and perfect, but love itself surely is not perfect, for it implies a lack and is the force for overcoming it. And if the good and beautiful is eudaimonia, then love, properly speaking, is the desire to live well and flourish, a goal which is not different from the attainment of wisdom and divine status.[16]

There is in human beings, then, a quasi-divine constituent, an aspiration or desire uniformly directed at the good, the beautiful, at immortality, divinity, eudaimonia. That human characteristic—given to all—defines the place of human beings as halfway between mere mortal creatures and the divine. Desire for transcendence is a common human potentiality. To be sure, Plato wonders why it is not recognized as such, since love or desire for the good is common to all.[17] Why, if all human beings share this desire, do we not call everyone "lovers"? The answer lies in the appropriation of the term *love* to mean one kind of love—heterosexual love—and the failure to use it to designate desires for other types of goods, such as money, wisdom, or fame. Love for the permanent possession of what is good may be common to all, and wisdom and divinity may be that good, but not all realize this. It is no wonder that the term *lover* commonly refers to one form of the desire for the good—physical wholeness and intimacy. Nor is it remarkable that so few recognize desire's genuine, primary object.

According to Diotima, this account clarifies the nature of Love; what remains is to show its effect on human conduct. What is its work (*to ergon*, 206b3)? What role does the desire for wisdom and divinity play in human affairs? The most interesting feature of Diotima's response (206b1–7a4) is that love or desire does not have the beautiful as its object; rather its object is its function, that is, desire is desire to do something, and this action is not a mere having or possessing. According to Diotima's account, to be more precise, desire or love has divinity or immortality as its object; the soul in love wants to exist always, to be immortal, and this is the good at which it aims.[18] But although incarnate and mortal, a person cannot be immortal in a perfect or complete sense; what it can do is desire to do something that increases its immortality or approximates it.[19] This activity Plato calls "procreation in beauty" (*tokos en kalo*, 206b7–8); all men have a natural desire to procreate, both physically and spiritually (compare 206e5), and this is the immediate object of love or desire. Since the beautiful is akin to the divine, moreover, the procreation must be done in beauty and not in ugliness, that is, in a beautiful way or with a beautiful result.

What, then, is Diotima saying? First, that while the *ultimate* object of desire is to be immortal, the *immediate* object is to generate or produce in a way that is beautiful and continuing. Having children is only the most picturesque example of such actions; others would doubtless include the creation of beautiful objects and institutions, and the performance of beautiful acts. Second, although the ultimate goal of desire is to be immortal or to realize one's immortality, this is not incompatible with doing worldly things in the meantime, things that approximate such a goal or help to facilitate it. Finally, desire of this kind is common to all people and indeed, as Diotima goes on to claim, to all beasts. In a sense, therefore, generation of all kinds—procreative, cultural, moral, and so on—is the *immediate* result of the presence of love or desire in animate creatures, and the ultimate reason for this function or effect lies in the final goal toward which such love or desire always aims, namely immortality.

Socrates is surprised by the implications of this account, first because it seems to mean that animals and human beings do not differ with regard to the goals of their overriding desires, and second because it means that human action is or can be more automatic and less rational or deliberative than one might have thought.[20] Love or desire now appears as a psychic force or drive that leads to certain forms of behavior without reflection or deliberation. But Socrates is naturally bewildered by this outcome, for Diotima has already taught him that the final object of love or desire is at once beautiful, good, and divine. It is, in short, wisdom; for love is not any desire but philosophy. But how can the ultimate goal of a "blind" drive, which is primary and basic, be wisdom? How can one be led unreflectively and thoughtlessly to perform actions that further one's quest for divine wisdom? How can beasts be philosophical? Surely, Socrates cannot be wrong that the path from true belief to knowledge, the path of desire, must also be a path of reason, of rational inquiry and cognitive progress.

Diotima appreciates Socrates' bewilderment. She explains that their conversation has been preliminary; it has progressed on the assumption that Socrates was but a novice, only able to understand the nature and function of desire within limits. But Socrates' dismay indicates his desire to proceed further, to explore the functioning of desire in a deeper, more profound way. Dialectical inquiry in conversational style ceases, and Diotima, like Plato in his myths at the end of the *Gorgias* and *Phaedo*, turns to soliloquy and description couched in a richly religious idiom.

Just as the prospective initiate into the mysteries of Eleusis begins the rites together with hundreds or thousands of others in Athens and proceeds with them on the trek to Eleusis, so Socrates—an initiate—joins Diotima in the early stages of his education. But now Diotima wonders whether Socrates can follow further and be initiated into the concluding revelation (*ta telea kai epoptika*, 210a1). Surely the issue is not whether Socrates can hear the words; it is whether he can really "follow" and understand what the words mean. And because such understanding is a private or personal matter, the recitation of the revelation is not public but rather "private"; it is a private showing in soliloquy of a deeply religious truth about love and the progress to its ultimate goal. To teach it, Socrates tells his friends what Diotima once said, but he cannot do more than display her words. And far from a profanation, Socrates' original hearing and subsequent retelling constitute acts of pious reverence—if not for the mysteries of Eleusis, then surely for Diotima's rational revision of them.

Commentators have recognized that the "ascent passage" (210a4–12a7) is the heart of the *Symposium*, the core of Diotima's and Plato's teaching about love or desire.[21] But they do not always see why. First, it is a soliloquy—a showing—to be grasped or not, depending on the listener's receptivity. Unlike the preceding conversation, the speech is not based on what Socrates believes and accepts but rather it confronts him with an account which he can either understand and accept as a whole or fail to understand at all. Second, the speech is about desire and inquiry and wisdom, their roles and structure and interrelations. It is, in other words, a speech about philosophy, how it proceeds and how it ends. The "ascent passage" stands between the *Phaedo*, on the one hand, and the *Republic* and *Phaedrus*, on the other, as Plato's great attempt to understand the relations among desire, rational inquiry, and wisdom and to portray this process in religious and mythological language. Finally, I suggest that these few pages are Plato's attempt to vindicate Socrates from an old charge and to underscore his own indictment of Athenian piety, by portraying Socrates as a devoted initiate into mysteries even deeper than those celebrated at Eleusis.

In the *Phaedo*, Plato had contrasted the "lover of the body" with the "lover of wisdom," and earlier in the *Symposium* he had pointed out how diverse are the things—wealth, gymnastic fame, money, and so on—that people take to be good and hence to be the proper objects of love or desire.[22] Clearly, since all people have a dominant desire for the good and beautiful, what distinguishes them is their assessment of what that good is. So one central question about desire is how it is directed and what its scope is. Another is whether a change of specification or belief about what the good is suffices by itself to effect a redirection of desire. A third is whether one form of inquiry can be viewed as a sequential reassessment of what the good is, a reassessment that involves both rational deliberation and the redirection of desire, culminating in knowledge of the Forms and especially the Form of the Beautiful.

In her speech to Socrates, Diotima describes the ascent of desire, from the love of one particular beautiful person to the vision of the Form of the Beautiful itself, the knowledge of which is knowledge of what beautiful is. The end of love or desire, then, marks its own dissolution, for all the stages of redirected desire finally disappear in a permanent knowledge of and response to Beauty and Goodness themselves, in an existence of true knowledge and virtue.[23]

The first step in this process is from the love of one particular beautiful person to the love of all physical beauty. Then the initiate comes to realize that beauty in the soul is worthier than that in the body, that there is beauty in conduct and in laws too, and that physical beauty is less desirable than moral-spiritual beauty. Next the initiate turns from this moral-spiritual setting to forms of knowledge, and he comes to find the beauty of such enterprises even more attractive, leading him to "give birth" to many beautiful logoi (statements) and *megalopropeis* (magnificent things) and finally to catch sight of that "one particular form of knowledge, which is knowledge of the Beautiful itself" (210d7–e1). Diotima describes this ascent as "seeing beautiful things in an orderly and correct way," which suggests that the order, if not necessary, is at least sufficient to generate the desired result. This result is the vision of what has been desired all along—not a temporal beautiful thing, nor one that changes or goes out of existence, nor a qualified one, but rather an eternal Beauty that is incorruptible, pure, uniform, in which all other beautiful things partake.[24] In short, the final goal

of genuine desire is the Form of the Beautiful, which must mean
that such desire is (at least in part) desire for knowledge of what
Beauty itself is. The object of inquiry, the Form, is also the object
of desire, for desire is desire for immortality, and that means wisdom, which is the end of inquiry. And just as inquiry is an orderly
process of discarding false beliefs, identifying true ones, acknowledging the Forms as the proper objects of one's search, and finally
coming to know them fully, so desire undergoes a process of redirection until it is finally dissolved in knowledge of the Forms. If
knowledge is a kind of satisfaction, then the real goal of genuine
desire is its own demise, an end that is a sign of divinity, immortality, goodness, and beauty.

Regarding this orderly process that is both rational inquiry about
the good and the beautiful and a redirection of desire toward these
ends, Diotima shows—although she does not state—that the one
process is both rational and affective. That is, the initiate will think
about what he is doing, recognize what he desires and why, and
reidentify what he takes to be most beautiful and hence desirable.
Then he will redirect his love or desire to the new object. He will,
for example, come to think that spiritual beauty is more honorable
than physical beauty, and as a result he will attend with greater
sensitivity to fine persons whose physical appearance may be plain
or ugly.[25] This appreciation, moreover, will compel him to realize
how beautiful certain conduct and practices can be and hence how
little value really resides in physical beauty.[26] In short, at each
transition, the initiate thinks about what is beautiful and what
should be the object of his love and concern, directs his desire to it,
adjusts his thinking, redirects his love, and so on. Plato is not wholly
clear whether or not the desire follows the new estimate automatically.

But why is this particular order a correct one? Did not Diotima
say[27] that desire is ultimately desire for immortality and divinity?
How does this order of inquiry and desire lead to that end?

First, this end, as Diotima describes it, is constituted by a vision
of the Form of the Beautiful, a supreme knowledge of what Beauty
is; the object is called "the divine Beauty itself" and the initiate
gazes on it and "is together with it" (*synontos auto*, 212a2). Also,
such a person "begets not images of virtue, because he is not in
touch with images, but rather [he begets] true [virtue], because he

is in touch with the truth" (212a3–5). Having brought forth and nurtured true virtue, he will be loved by god (*theophilei*, 212a6) and become as immortal as a man can be. In other words, Diotima sees this state as the highest result of the human desire for immortality. Men do not become more immortal than they are once they have gained the highest form of knowledge. Ideal knowledge is divine knowledge, of the Forms and ultimately of the Form of Beauty itself. The knower and the known draw together and yet remain distinct; man becomes god-beloved but not actually divine, truly virtuous but not wholly and completely immortal.

Second, if Diotima had earlier made the relation between the desire for immortality and human conduct seem too automatic, here she qualifies that immediacy. Men desire the good, and they desire immortality. But they do not, automatically and unreflectively, recognize how closely associated the two are with each other and with wisdom. So man identifies some thing as good, only to revise his estimate, redirect his desire, and so on. All along he desires immortality, doing what he thinks is good and what he thinks will advance his goal. But the process is deliberative and controlled until the end arrives—if it does—and the initiate sees that wisdom, immortality, the good, and the beautiful are nearly identical. Then philosophy— if the state is attained after death—becomes wisdom.

As we read the "ascent passage," it is hard not to treat the object of the initiate's final vision and kinship as a Form. The language is so characteristic of the *Phaedo* and so similar to it, moreover, that it is surely right to do so. But there are difficulties in so doing. Is the Form of Beauty and the ascent to it an example of the highest wisdom, or is it the one and only content of such wisdom? Is the ascent passage a model for the joint processes of rational inquiry and the education of desire? Or is it the single correct account of that process? Or how is this process related to the rational inquiry that leads to knowledge of the other Forms? And finally, how does Plato, in the *Symposium*, deal with the problem of inquiry raised by the *Phaedo*'s introduction of the Forms as the proper and exclusive objects of knowledge?

First, it is not clear that Plato even addresses the discontinuity issue in the *Symposium*. To be sure, the elaborate vocabulary that he uses to describe the Form of the Beautiful does show that he recognizes the radical difference between Forms and physical exemplifications. But he never stops to ask how the assessment of beautiful things actually turns from activities and forms of knowledge to the Form of Beauty itself. He simply assumes that such a turning of attention can occur without obstacle or complication. Second, in the *Symposium* there is no mention of other inquiries—into the nature of justice, piety, equality, unity, and so on. The role of such inquiries and the aspiration to know these Forms are never noticed or discussed. To be sure, we could speculate that the general coordination of rational deliberation about what x is with the desire to know what x is and the cooperative readjustment of the two in *this* case mirrors what ought to go on in other inquiries, and it is probably reasonable to do so. But Plato is not particularly encouraging, and some might be reluctant to generalize without Plato's explicit imprimatur. Third, one can be confident that the Form of Beauty is here meant to be the exclusive object of *this* desire, for Diotima's account is intended to build on her earlier conversation with Socrates in which she explicitly said that the ultimate object of love or desire is the good, the beautiful, immortality.[28] To be sure, people have other desires, although one might hold that in one sense or another all are desires for what is good. But the subject of Diotima's teaching is desire or love of a preeminent kind, not desire for some good or other but rather desire for *the* human good, a life of wisdom, near-divinity, true virtue, ecstatic success, eudaimonia. Finally, the *Symposium* does not raise the interesting possibility that inquiry into and love for the Beautiful may be not the whole of wisdom but nonetheless somehow necessary for the successful attainment of complete wisdom, that is, necessary for and indeed antecedent to such wisdom. In other words, the *Symposium* leaves open the possibility that while one may have to be receptive to Forms prior to knowledge of any of them, it may be possible to know the other Forms fully only once one has a prior knowledge of the Beautiful or the Good or some other preeminent Form.

COMMENTATORS have sometimes doubted that the *Symposium* follows the *Phaedo* on the grounds that its view of immortality is different from and indeed incompatible with that of the *Phaedo*, and from the *Phaedrus* and the *Republic* as well.[29] Since the immortality of the soul plays such an important role in our interpretation of Plato, we must at least consider what Plato says about it in the *Symposium*, why he says it, and what he means.

First, the *Phaedo* and the *Symposium* differ dramatically in this regard: in the former, but not in the latter, Plato's primary concern is posthumous knowledge and hence that kind of immortal, even everlasting existence that makes man as divine as possible. In Plato we must appreciate the difference between incarnate knowledge and posthumous wisdom, between the soul's *status* as immortal and indestructible and its *ultimate goal* of everlasting, discarnate existence.[30] The *Symposium* is much more this-worldly, in substance and in tone, than is the *Phaedo*.[31]

Nonetheless, there are places in the *Symposium* where Plato has Diotima describe a state of wisdom and near-divinity that some commentators are convinced is intended to be identical to that described in the *Phaedo*.[32] But the description at 211e4–12a7 need not be read this way—and if it need not, then it should not. The expression "dwells with it" (*synontos auto*, 212a2) need not be taken literally or, for that matter, exclusively, as if one who has preeminent knowledge of the Beautiful could not then exemplify that knowledge in acts and works of beauty, for instance, in leading a philosophical life.[33] One is hard put to imagine what kind of true arete is possible for the soul, discarnate and existing (literally) among the Forms. If the *Phaedo* is to be our guide, the notion of arete subsequent to perfect, everlasting, discarnate knowledge really does not make sense.

Still, the absence in the *Symposium* of an explicit description of posthumous immortality does not show that Plato has jettisoned the notion.[34] Diotima first introduces the idea of immortality to explain what gives rise to love or desire. The genuine object of love, she had said, is to "procreate and bring forth in beauty" (206e5). This is so because "procreation is perpetuity (*aeigenes*) and immortality (*athanaton*) as it is in a mortal being" (206e7–8), and love is love of immortality. Clearly, "immortality" here means "continued existence after death." That is, in the case of divine beings, each one exists forever; in the case of mortals, the most each individual can hope for is to exist continuously after death and hence to contribute to the everlasting existence of the species (aeigenes). This desire is what accounts for the desire to procreate, both in men and in animals. "Mortal nature seeks, so far as it is able, to exist always and be immortal" (207c9–d2). Diotima, then, shows that this mechanism in behalf of immortality is the same as that used by men in daily life, whereby their physical and mental identity is maintained. Both the body and the soul undergo constant change, losing parts and gaining new ones,[35] and this is true of beliefs, desires, pleasures, and fears, as well as of hair, flesh, and bones. Only the divine is always the same at all times; through this process of loss and repair, "a mortal being partakes of immortality, while an immortal being is so in a different way" (208b2–4). Diotima follows this account with a lengthy defense by example of ways in which the human desire for immortality leads men to do such things as seek fame and glory, die for their children,[36] write poetry, make laws, and so on.[37]

One solution to the problem about immortality, posed by this discussion, is to distinguish between everlastingness and eternal life, that is, lasting for all time and existing atemporally.[38] As I showed, however, in discussing the *Phaedo*, Plato identifies immortality as everlasting, continuous existence. In such a case we have no clear notion of timeless eternality, and although such a view does emerge in the *Timaeus*,[39] there is no good reason to read it back into these dialogues. There just does not seem to be clear evidence in the *Symposium* for a notion of immortality other than existing-for-all-time.

Two related solutions, however, do seem appropriate. The first amounts to the suggestion that whereas the *Phaedo* ascribes immortality to the soul, the *Symposium* ascribes it to the person as a whole, that is, to the mortal being.[40] Both person and soul strive to attain immortality: mortal beings seek to become as immortal as they can, despite change and death, whereas the soul seeks to "perfect" or "complete" its immortality with incarnate knowledge and ultimately with permanent discarnate existence and wisdom.

The second solution involves the wise caution that the above passage and the notion of "vicarious immortality" are contained only in the dialogue between Diotima and Socrates that is preliminary to the "final revelation" and the "ascent" passage.[41] Indeed, in that earlier passage, the *aition* of love or desire, the overriding desire for immortality as the good, is presented as common to men and animals, a point at which Socrates is surprised. Among other things, the further revelation distinguishes human beings and animals by noticing the rational or deliberative element in human desire and the ordered hierarchy of desires and desirables that culminates in knowledge of the Beautiful. It is not impossible that while the earlier stage points to vicarious replacement as the mechanism for achieving "limited" everlastingness, the later one conceives of the same goal—which is required for the account of the aition to make sense[42]—but now with a new mechanism and greater achievement. These center on increased knowledge and not on "procreation." Now—to combine this proposal with the earlier one—it may also be that in these passages Diotima shifts the subject from the mortal person to the soul.

I am not persuaded, however, that the shift is this explicit and complete. It may be that while the *Phaedo*'s dualism is reflected at certain points in the text,[43] the focus on the soul as personal subject is not.[44] All along Diotima treats the mortal person, that is, the incarnate person, as the proper subject of the aspiration to immortality. Hence, Plato is correct not to call this conglomerate immortal, and he is right to see it as using two different sorts of strategies for attaining whatever immortality a person can attain (see 212a6–7 for the key text). But because Socrates is addressed at two distinct stages of initiation, Diotima treats him in two ways, and the result is not a limitation to "vicarious" rather than "personal" immortality, but rather two different methods for a person's attaining immortality. That the soul is itself immortal in nature and capable of permanent posthumous wisdom is not incompatible with but simply beyond this revelation.[45]

Thus, immortality is not equivocal in name; it is equivocal in fact. When attributed to the soul, immortality is a property *and* a goal; the soul, stuck in the circle of physical incarnations, is immortal but not completely or perfectly so. When attributed to the mortal person, on the other hand, immortality is a goal that can only be imperfectly attained. The *Phaedo* focuses on death and the prospects of posthumous bliss for the philosopher; the *Symposium* attends primarily to incarnate life itself and the role of the desire for eudaimonia within it.

In order to describe the philosopher's life and his "ascent," Plato employs a religious vocabulary reflecting his commitment to human transcendence and his strong sympathies with ecstatic ritual. But, as in the *Phaedo*, Plato's religious resources are varied, and one must be cautious about what this diversity means to him.

Although the god, or better, the daimon at the center of discussion is Eros, there is another god in the not too distant background—Dionysos, whose presence significantly influences the language of the *Symposium*. The Lenaia, a kind of primitive city Dionysia, is devoted to him, and despite our dearth of resources we can surmise that in the late fifth and fourth centuries the festival included dramatic contests, a procession, and possibly maenadic, ecstatic dancing.[46] Agathon's victory banquet, then, occurs as part of a celebration of Dionysos,[47] a dimension of the dialogue's atmosphere underscored no doubt by Alcibiades' drunken entrance.[48]

From the Lenaia, moreover, and its Dionysiac character, our thinking might proceed in two directions. One leads to the shamanistic, charismatic portrait of Socrates that receives full form in Alcibiades' speech but is already prefigured at the dialogue's outset.[49] The other path is more complicated. It develops from the twin facts (1) that the *archon basileus*, organizer of the Lenaia, was by the fourth century joined by the Eleusinian priests[50] and (2) that the lesser mysteries occur shortly after the Lenaia in the month of Anthesterion,[51] and it proceeds to the fact that the "ascent passage" and Diotima's references to her teaching and Socrates' role as student or initiate are couched in Eleusinian language. At first glance, then, the religious backdrop for Plato's treatment of inquiry, desire, and immortality, and the terminological vehicle for his expressions of praise for Socrates and dissent from the Athenian tradition are twofold—Bacchic and Eleusinian—and the Lenaia, the occasion for Agathon's celebration, reflects their interpenetration.

We begin by looking at Alcibiades' portrait of Socrates. Early in Aristodemus' recounting of the banquet, he tells Apollodorus that he has met Socrates, who invited him to accompany him to the celebration. But Socrates drifts into deep thought, and Aristodemus must proceed alone. Eventually Socrates appears, trance-like and completely oblivious, standing alone on a neighbor's porch, deep in thought. While this embarrasses Aristodemus, Agathon recognizes it as standard practice for Socrates.[52] One function of the episode is to anticipate Alcibiades' portrait of Socrates as a charismatic of sorts. And this, when viewed against the background we sketched in chapter 1, recalls Socrates' association with Bacchic-Corybantic rites and ecstatic religious practice.

Alcibiades begins his inebriated reminiscence by comparing Socrates to Silenus and Marsyas, the first a constant companion and even a teacher of Dionysos and a prophet, the second a satyr associated with Dionysos.[53] Both appeared mean but alluring—charmers, divinities, or magical figures who used the flute to overcome their victims. Each could be thought, Alcibiades implies, to hide within his unappealing exterior a divine core.[54] The songs of Marsyas, for example, "are capable, by reason of their divine origin, of throwing men into a trance and thus distinguishing those who yearn to enter by initiation into union with the gods." Socrates, Alcibiades says, "produce[s] the same effect by mere words without any instrument."[55] Alcibiades admits that when he listens to Socrates, "his heart beats more than that of Corybantes" and "tears run down his face from his words."[56] Socrates forces Alcibiades to agree that he is full of deficiencies and that he is neglecting himself by "serving the needs of Athens."[57]

In the end, Socrates makes Alcibiades so ashamed that he flees, not knowing what to do about him. And Alcibiades is not alone; "the piping of this satyr" has affected many this way. Socrates seems enthralled, even intoxicated with young, good-looking men, but inside, like Silenus, he has no concern for physical looks or fame or wealth. Rarely does he expose his core, which is self-disciplined, divine, precious, and marvelous.[58] But Alcibiades saw it once, and he tells a story of Socrates' commitment to the "madness and frenzy of philosophy" (*tes philosophou manias te kai baccheias*, 218b3–4), a story that will make sense to Socrates' friends but not, Alcibiades says, to the "vulgar and uninitiated" (218b6).

There is more to Alcibiades' speech, but even here we must stop to notice his imagery and vocabulary. Plato is painting a portrait of Socrates that may be exaggerated but that is nonetheless consistent with his view of Socrates' convictions and character. The Orphic and Pythagorean features of philosophy are set aside in favor of others, which I shall call Bacchic or Dionysiac. Socrates is himself divine;[59] he is a charmer, a celebrant at Bacchic initiations,[60] but his implements are words and argument, not a flute, and his vehicle is not physical ecstasy or dance but rather philosophical transcendence. What he urges is an attention to one's self and not one's image, fame, wealth; he advocates philosophical probing rather than political participation. The consistency between this characterization and the Platonic portrait of Socrates which we constructed earlier is remarkable.[61]

It is, moreover, a portrait not inconsistent with what we know of Dionysiac cult and rite in the period. As we have noted, there is no single practice that we might call the "Bacchic mystery rite," but we can nonetheless collect a set of features that were probably characteristic of such rites in Plato's day.[62] The rites are practiced by a Dionysiac or Bacchic cult, although they are private,[63] and the participants, when successfully present in the other world, are called *mystai* and *bacchoi*.[64] Since there were separate paths for the initiated and uninitiated in Hades, those mystai had been properly prepared for the soul's postcarnate journey. Mystai is a generic term for initiates;[65] mysteia are any secret initiation ceremonies.[66] The Bacchic preparation, if Cole is right, involves special knowledge and enabled the initiate to become like the gods. If the gold tablet is a guide, the final blessed state—as in the *Phaedo*—occurs after death,[67] and the preparation takes place in teletai of Dionysiac devotees, a kind of purification rite, performed in private, to enable posthumous bliss. All of this is appropriate, for in addition to wine and maenadism, the domain of Dionysos was thought to include the afterlife and preparation for it.[68] While maenadism is restricted to women, "beginning in the fifth century B.C.E. at the latest, men too 'went mad' (*mainesthai* used in combination with *bakheuein*) for Dionysus and enrolled in private congregations which admitted both sexes, met in secret, and required initiation ceremonies (teletai)."[69] And while there is growing evidence in the fourth century and later for Dionysiac associations, private rituals were also prominent.[70]

As was generally the case in the Greece of these centuries, there was no single "religion of Zeus" or "religion of Dionysos." Maenadism, for example, is often associated with Delphi and Boeotia but is present elsewhere, whereas Dionysiac worship at the Anthesteria and at other times in Athens is by no means uniform. Our special interests, however, are ecstatic ritual and Bacchic initiations, and as we have already noticed, these were prominent in southern Italy, Athens, and beyond.[71] Unlike Dionysiac festivals, maenadism, and wine celebrations, the "so-called private mysteries of Dionysos" moved quickly and rapidly throughout greater Greece[72] and became the dominant form of Dionysiac worship by the Hellenistic period.[73] Overall, the geographic spread of such practices in striving for a blissful afterlife was remarkable—from Hipponion to southern Italy, from Thessaly to Crete.[74] In drawing on the imagery and terminology of such practices, then, Plato in the *Symposium*, was identifying Socratic inquiry, genuine desire, and wisdom as parts of, or akin to, a religious pattern with increasing prominence and impact on Greek life.

We can now turn to the second dimension of Plato's use of religious vocabulary. In the dialogue, Diotima sees the ascent to knowledge of the Beautiful as an ascent to immortality and divinity, and something like this end is affirmed often throughout the *Phaedo*. How indebted is this conception to the religious movements we have just sketched? What is the ultimate goal of the Dionysiac mysteries? Unsurprisingly, "the essence of the Dionysiac experience apparently culminated in visible *imitatio Dionysi*, accomplished through external and mechanical means."[75] Some scholars take these means to be omophagy or drinking of wine, a Dionysiac sacramentalism as it were, with a this-worldly result. But some take the ultimate identification with the deity to occur not on earth and temporally but rather after death and permanently, although the gold plates—together with the Platonic dialogues—are our only evidence for this interpretation. In this regard, moreover, as Henrichs and others have noted, the promise of a happy afterlife is not unlike the expectations associated with the Eleusinian mysteries.[76]

Diotima's speech and the language of Eleusis, however, should be understood within the framework of Alcibiades' portrait of Socrates. Having described Socrates' sexual restraint—another Dionysiac motif but expressed in reverse—Alcibiades remembers Socrates' military performance at Potidaea and Delium. Socrates, Alcibiades notes, is never seen to be drunk, and seems immune to the effects of ice and cold.[77] No one resembles him; he is extraordinary, so far beyond human beings that only a comparison with sileni and satyrs begins to do him justice. There is no better indication of Socrates' special status than Alcibiades' description of his day-long trance, engaging in inquiry in silence from early one day through the night until the next dawn.[78] Now Alcibiades is surely trying to portray Socratic arete—courage, sophrosyne, and intense commitment to wisdom. But at the same time his portrait of Socrates' immunity to drink, like his sexual restraint, are a studied counterpoint to Bacchic frenzy, whereas Socrates' ability to withstand cold and ice and his capacity to engage trance-like in thought all day are the characteristics of a magician or sorcerer. In the background of Alcibiades' account are Bacchic practices that encompass activities from frenzied dance to ecstatic trance.[79] Socrates is someone both like and unlike such figures.

The Dionysiac features of this description are a frame, as it were, for the central picture of philosophical eros, which is given to us through Diotima's dialogue with the young Socrates and then through her speech to him. Commentators generally refer to these as the "lesser mysteries" and the "greater mysteries" of Love, perhaps comparing the two components of Diotima's teaching to the two separate occasions when the mysteries of Eleusis were celebrated in Athens.[80] The evidence that Plato is referring specifically or exclusively to the mysteries at Eleusis is not conclusive. Burkert points out that the language of the passage—*myesis, epopteia,* and *orgiazein*—is that of the mysteries, but he does not refer explicitly to Eleusis.[81] In fact, terms such as these appear very rarely in Diotima's speech.[82] To be sure, the presence of Alcibiades and the dialogue's dramatic date, 416, do hint that the final revelation which the ascent reaches is like the epopteia at Eleusis. But these are at best indirect hints.

What is more significant than any direct allusion to Eleusis, I think, is the fact that Diotima's teaching involves two stages—one that occurs through a dialectical inquiry, the other including a description of an ascent of desire that culminates with knowledge of the Beautiful and virtual immortality. Although we have little detailed knowledge of Bacchic mysteries, we have extensive information about the mysteries celebrated in Boedromion.[83] One might reasonably take the dialogue's early speeches to be analogues of the *pompe* from Athens to Eleusis along the Sacred Way and the dialogue between Socrates and Diotima to parallel the first entry of the *mystes,* escorted by his *mystagogos.* The "final revelation" (*ta telea kai epoptika,* 210a1), then, would correspond to what is shown to the epoptai on their second visit.[84] What I am suggesting is that even though the terminology is general, the structure of the *Symposium* and other features, such as its dramatic date, recommend that the mysteries alluded to are in fact the Eleusinian.[85]

This interpretation is not incompatible with our earlier proposal that the dominant religious background for the *Symposium* is that of the Bacchic or Dionysiac mysteries. Not only is there some evidence that Dionysos was associated with Eleusis in the fourth century, but there is also a sense in which these mysteries, widely attractive and participated in almost universally by Athenians, are one domesticated version of the more individualized and radical Bacchic mystery rites. Hence, at the core of the *Symposium*'s encomium to Socrates lies this portrait of institutionalized ecstasy, the Athenian expression of the Socratic and Platonic commitment to disciplined initiation and ascent. The mysteries of Eleusis mediate between Bacchic frenzy and philosophy—the desire for the good, for knowledge, for immortality and the rational inquiry that serves that goal. In the end, then, Plato does not so much appropriate the vocabulary of the mysteries as he replaces the mysteries with philosophical inquiry and the joint desire for this-worldly and otherworldly immortality. Eleusis represents the capacity of the polis tradition and Delphic theology to co-opt its ecstatic opponents. Philosophy, the new Eleusis, is the Platonic reinstatement of that opposition and thereby a Platonic response to the Athenian tradition.

CHAPTER FIVE

EDUCATION, PHILOSOPHY, AND HISTORY IN THE *REPUBLIC*

Very early the *Republic* announces a cluster of metaphors—emigration, sojourning, temporary citizenship—that symbolize the dialogue's persistent attempts to overcome apparently rigid, unbridgeable dichotomies.[1] Cephalus is a famous metic, wealthy, powerful, and respected. In a sense, the soul too is a "metic," for while the soul lives temporarily in the world of history, politics, and moral conduct, it is a sojourner, always anticipating its future and the possibility of permanent citizenship among the divine. But these hopes, ever present and prominent in the *Phaedo*, muted in the *Symposium*, are carefully orchestrated in the *Republic*, while their force is only really felt at the dialogue's conclusion in Book X and in the myth of Er. Although the *Republic* does not reject immortality or ignore the afterlife, it focuses its primary attention elsewhere, on incarnate, worldly, historical life and the problems that beset the philosopher there. The *Republic*'s religious posture is one of deferred hope and honest resignation.[2]

What does Plato accomplish in the *Republic*? First, he develops his Socratic conviction that the proper vehicle for religious aspiration is a rational ecstatic rite, or inquiry and education as initiation, and he emphasizes how this rite—and especially mathematical *paideia*—transcends and replaces the traditional system of sacrificial ritual and Delphic theology embedded in Homer, Hesiod, and others. Plato continues to exploit the language of initiation rites, for example, the Bacchic mysteries and those of Eleusis, and shows both his indebtedness to and differences with traditional Greek education. At the core of the *Republic*, then, is an integration of religious ritual and political paideia.

Second, Plato mitigates his dissent from the polis tradition—but only slightly. The account of philosophy in the *Meno*, *Phaedo*, and *Symposium* is anti-Athenian and to a great degree antipolitical. Here Plato returns to realize that worldly existence is naturally social and political. Whereas the ultimate goal of philosophical ecstasy is a blissful afterlife, life in this world is the setting for inquiry and conduct, both of which are preparation for, indeed a search for that goal. Therefore, the religious and philosophical life must be lived in a polis, and hence there must be political rule. And so, Plato asks, what role should the philosophical inquirer play in the life of the polis? Should he or she rule? If so, when? And how? And if not, why not? And who should rule, if not the philosopher? To be sure, Plato could have treated philosophy as a private and isolated enterprise to be practiced alone for private goals, but he does not. Why?

Third, in the *Republic* Plato confronts and solves the most pressing epistemological problem inherited from the *Meno* and *Phaedo*: how to make the cognitive transition from worldly beliefs to knowledge of the Forms. The central epistemological gains of the *Republic* are concerned with that solution, and they include the recognition of the complexity of believing, inquiring, and knowing, and the introduction of mathematics as the device for solving the problem of inquiry. As we have seen, Socratic inquiry as rational ecstasy cannot succeed once the Forms are introduced as the proper objects of inquiry and knowledge. It cannot endure the gap between sense-bound beliefs and knowledge of the Forms. The traditions of mystery rites and initiations required a bridge that would span that gap. Orphic teachings connect immortality with prior knowledge, and Plato has argued that learning is recollection. But the process is still obscure. The Pythagorean tradition will provide the key, a notion of mathematical thinking that weaves together recollection, immortality, and knowledge of the Forms. The mathematical thinker is the genuine philosopher, who becomes the political ruler and creates and nourishes a polis that encourages ascent from the cave to the divine world of the Forms.

In place of the old sacrificial system, the old Delphic theology with its roots in Homer, Hesiod, and traditional mythology, and the old and modified educational systems—including the innovations of the sophists and Isocrates, among others—Plato gives us a revolutionary new synthesis of Socratic, Orphic, Pythagorean, and Bacchic elements, and more. In the *Republic* the heavens are invaded by an intellectual attainment made possible by mathematics and realized in dialectic. The old Apollo, the god of Delphi, is replaced by the Sun, the light of wisdom.[3]

SCHOLARLY opinion suggests that the *Republic* was completed around 374–370, long after Plato's first Sicilian visit and before the second, a work that doubtless took the better part of a decade to write.[4] Hence, although we cannot be sure whether the *Republic* was completed before or after the battle of Leuctra and the great defeat suffered by Sparta, we can be reasonably confident that the bulk of the dialogue was written during the decade preceding the peace of 375.

The decade was one of turmoil for Greece, and it is hard to imagine that Plato was unmoved by the events of those years and their fatal consequences. Torn between Sparta and Thebes, Athens gained a renewed ascendancy in these years, albeit a short-lived one, and Sparta traveled the road from powerful bully to defeated victim.[5] The issues of the period are political, moral, and religious: the *Republic* is deeply engaged in reflection on all three subjects.

The period from 382 to 371 was an eventful one, and its culmination—the final defeat of Sparta—was arguably the single most important event in the fourth century. "It was to bring to an end Sparta's pre-eminence of three centuries, . . . and so deprive Greece of the only power which could have provided both the hoplite strength (unlike Athens), and the ideological magnetism (unlike Thebes), to lead the fight against Philip—and win."[6] For our purposes, the central features of the period are Athens' ambivalent relationship with Sparta, the reestablishment of the Athenian Confederacy, and the peace of 375, an agreement initiated by Athens with an eye to Theban ascendancy. Although the *Republic* does not much discuss the foreign relations of its ideal polis, its admiration for Spartan character is well known, and the account of *dikaiosune* points a finger at the greedy, the grasping, and those who have no commitment to alliances.

A brief glance at one actual alliance—the Second Athenian Confederacy—will be useful here. Plato does not explicitly refer to it. But it is likely that he knew of it and had it in mind as he reflected

on dikaiosune, freedom, autonomy, and the Athenian future.[7] Moreover, its provisions or "charter" are preserved in a stunning epigraphical treasure, the stele of Aristoteles of 378–377.[8]

The purpose of the confederacy is to ensure that Sparta "allow
the Greeks to have freedom, autonomy, tranquility, and security in
the possession of their lands." All—except those countries under
Persian rule—are invited to become Athenian allies while retaining
their "freedom and autonomy." Athens will not interfere with their
governments, nor will it impose "garrison, governor, or tribute."
Basically, the alliance was a defense league guided by a commitment to guaranteed aid and governed by a twofold body—the Athenian Assembly and an allied *synhedroi*, with the latter bringing
matters such as the fixing of contributions (*syntaxeis*) before the
former.[9] As Hornblower emphasizes, the "charter" contained or im-
plied non-interference and mutual support. Public possessions in
allied territory were to revert to their owners; constitutional freedom and autonomy were secured; tribute, governors, and garrisons
were forbidden. On paper, then, Athens' fear of Sparta expressed
itself in an arrangement of enormous self-restraint and collegial
commitment, more than it would ever manifest. What Athens
promised its partners was autonomy and security, from itself as well
as from Sparta.[10] If dikaiosune is expressed through the honoring of
such an alliance,[11] then any breach would be *adikos*, as would be a
fortiori entering into such an arrangement with the expectation of
nonperformance.

Inflated by the growth of the alliance and by the success of its
own sea power, Athens overtaxed its financial resources and those
of its allies.[12] Needing time to replenish its resources and fearing
Theban willfulness, it opened peace negotiations with Sparta. An
agreement was made in which the alliance was to be recognized
but with Thebes as only a member of it. As Hammond puts it, when
the peace was concluded, "Athens was jubilant. A statue of Timotheus was set up, and an annual sacrifice on the anniversary of this
peace was decreed in perpetuity."[13] Athens, however, continued its
policy of escalation, with disastrous consequences. Timotheus was
prosecuted and replaced in Corcyra by Iphicrates. But even Iphicrates had to hire out his sailors as laborers in order to obtain food.
The problems of financial overextension and strains between allies
were evident to everyone. In 371 Callistratus persuaded the Athe-

nians to negotiate with Sparta once again for peace. But this time
Thebes was not so easily controlled. Withdrawing from the treaty
negotiations, the Theban delegates, headed by Epaminondas, returned to Thebes. Shortly thereafter, Theban forces routed the Spartan army at Leuctra. Athens, shamed by financial disorder into
repeated pandering to Sparta, now tried to capitalize on the Spartan
defeat. The truth was doubtless evident to many leading Athenians;
power had shifted away from Sparta, but Thebes and Jason of
Pherai—not Athens—were its new possessors.[14]

Within this historical context, Plato wrote the *Republic*. The *Gorgias, Phaedo, Symposium*, and *Republic* all eulogize the philosophical life, with the *Republic* as the fitting culmination to the group.
In it Plato confronts directly the challenge of Callicles, who claimed
that the best and most flourishing life is one of power, greed, and
dominance—in short, the life of a tyrant. At the same time, Plato
acknowledges that the defense of philosophy must be fought on a
this-worldly battleground. Posthumous reward, though not irrelevant, must be temporarily set aside if there is to be a genuine dialectical encounter with the tyrant. And the requirement is not *only*
dialectical; focusing on the life, the incarnate experience, of the
philosopher is not required only by the interlocutor's beliefs and
attitudes. It is also required by the very nature of philosophical
living. For the philosopher, like all others, must live in society and
in a polis,[15] and hence the nature of that polis and of the philosopher's role in it are crucially relevant to the question whether the
philosophical life is the best possible life for humankind.

The *Republic*, then, advances far beyond the *Phaedo* and *Symposium*, for it not only elaborates the virtues of a philosophical life,
but it also appreciates fully the social and political dimensions of
such a life. It is hard not to believe that the events of the 370s,
recalling old failures and giving rise to new ones, helped Plato to
focus on the worldly situation of philosophical virtue. In those
years, as Plato watched Callistratus, Timotheus, and Iphicrates of
Athens, Cleombrotus of Sparta, and Epaminondas of Thebes, all
vying for control—with Dionysius and Jason in the wings—is it
surprising that for him the central political issue was that of rule,
both the type of rule and the type of ruler? The *Republic* has as one
of its primary themes whether the philosopher should rule and if so,
why. The training and education of a ruler, given Plato's final an-

swer to this question, become a matter of philosophical study. The road from politics to epistemology is torturous but direct.

The religious dimension of the *Republic* is both different from and more complex than that of the *Phaedo*. Discussion of the soul's immortality and posthumous reward comes only at the end, and the use of ritual vocabulary, less prominent than in other dialogues, is more muted. Yet, at the same time that Plato is less strident in appropriating ecstatic language, he intensifies his critique of traditional religious ritual and beliefs. He criticizes traditional poetry, rhapsody, music, art, religious life, and paideia more vigorously than before, and his critique is not unexpected, for as he challenges traditional notions of the polis and its leadership, he must criticize as well those institutions that give shape to them.

In addition, Plato comes to realize that even in an ideal polis, most citizens will not be philosophers. Most will be farmers, artisans, and so on, accustomed to a religious regimen of festivals, sacrifices, divination, and personal worship which satisfies important needs and moreover which may be harmless and even beneficial to the polis at large. In other words, Plato admits that the special ecstatic character of philosophical inquiry as a type of religious rite may be unsuited to most citizens, and so he permits the establishment of a regimen for "common" religiosity that is akin to but not identical with traditional Homeric and Delphic piety.[16]

Ultimately, Plato's treatment of religion in the *Republic* has several dimensions. The first is his use of religious language to characterize philosophy and philosophical education. The second is his treatment of immortality and his use of myth to describe posthumous reward. The third is Plato's critique of traditional religion, poetry, and paideia. The last is his willingness to permit a revised style of traditional Greek piety in the ideal polis. In the following sections I shall deal with them all, although in slightly different order.

IN earlier chapters I have tried to show how Plato's deepest religious commitments were critical of Homeric religion, the Athenian system of sacrifice and divination, and what I have called the Delphic theology. In the *Republic*, however, we find a surprising complication. On the one hand, both early and late in the *Republic*, Plato engages in lengthy critique and revision of religious myth and its

poetic vehicle. Broadly speaking, this critique seems to meet our
expectations. On the other hand, Plato explains how the temples
and the sacrificial calendar of the ideal polis will be established
according to the will of Delphi, and he implies, through Adeimantus' objection, that Orphic and Bacchic initiation and purification rites are to be disdained and rejected. The result is an apparently deep ambivalence, if not an outright paradox, for the *Republic* appears to contradict itself and our expectations about whether
to advocate traditional piety and whether to impugn ecstatic ritual.[17]

Such conclusions, however, are not inevitable. It can be shown
that in the *Republic* Plato deals with Greek religion in a manner
coherent and consistent with what we have already seen. The solution to the apparent confusions follows the recognition of the
Republic's special contribution, the focusing of attention on the
philosophical life in its worldly, political setting and the implications of that situation for the philosopher's education, his role, and
his polis.

Early in *Republic* IV, Plato turns from an account of the guardians' supervision of education and upbringing to a discussion of the
areas in which they ought to legislate. The final area he discusses
concerns religious rites and worship, the establishment of which is
left not to the guardians but to the Delphic Apollo. They are the

> greatest, most beautiful, and first enactments . . . the establish-
> ing of temples, sacrifices, and other forms of service to the gods,
> spirits, and heroes; then again the burials of the dead and the
> services which ensure their favor. We have no knowledge of
> these things and in establishing our city we shall not, if we are
> wise, accept any other advice or use any other than our ances-
> tral guide. This god is the ancestral interpreter of these things
> for all men as he sits upon the rock which is the center of the
> earth. (427b6–c4)

The first thing to be said about this charge to the Delphic oracle
and Apollo is that it is completely normal. Fontenrose has shown
that "the largest part of the [Delphic] responses either command or
sanction cult acts and cult laws."[18] Apollo is to be the religious
exegete or interpreter for the ideal polis, just as—according to an

inscription dated to the Peloponnesian War—he is the "*exegete* for the Athenians."[19] Plato's charge to Apollo to establish the temples, sacrifices, and festivals of the ideal polis is wholly characteristic, and it extends to fixing burial practices for the guardians and regulating the taking of spoils and their dedication during wartime.[20] But precisely because the role of Delphi in the fixing of religious practices is traditional, we are led to wonder how Plato could so easily endorse it; this is part of our problem.

The answer is not far off. The Delphic establishment of religious practice and the traditional character of sacrifice, cult, temple, and festival—all this must be understood within the limitations of the polis. The ideal polis is largely made up of nonruler guardians whose education is limited to artistic and physical training—farmers, merchants, craftsmen, and artisans. These are the people who, in the end, Plato says will be "enslaved" to the rulers but in a positive way, such that the rational and divine order directly guiding the philosopher's life and endeavors will govern their lives indirectly.[21] Just as not all people are born with a philosophical nature and not all potential philosophers remain uncorrupted, so not all are capable of or inclined to ecstatic piety, to Bacchic-Orphic-Eleusinian rites of initiation and purification. Traditional polis religiosity— with its temples, its cultic acts, its system of sacrifices and festivals, its burial rites—is appropriate and suitable for the vast majority of its members. Plato is not being inconsistent, but rather realistic, in recognizing the limitations of normal polis life.[22]

In addition, if the ideal polis is to maintain internal unity and reduce external strife, it must love all Greece, and to do so, Plato suggests, it must "share the religion of the other Greeks."[23] This must mean that the ideal polis should remain faithful to the dominant pitch of Greek piety, to its festivals, its sacrificial-oracular character, and much else. Once Plato realizes the importance of treating philosophy in its social, political, and historical context, he comes to recognize how diverse are people's religious and philosophical commitments and capabilities. The installation of traditional Greek religion through the medium of Delphi and Apollo is as necessary for most forms of polis life as the philosophical paideia is for the life of the philosopher-ruler.

But Plato is not uncritical of traditional Greek religion, education, and poetry. He does not simply endorse its establishment. Earlier in the *Republic* he uses two opportunities to register his concern and recommend revisions.

Plato's elaboration of the guardians' upbringing and paideia includes a critique of poetry, traditional myths, and traditional Greek education. This critique is already announced earlier, in Glaucon's and Adeimantus' twin challenges that begin *Republic* II. Glaucon begins the assault by telling the tale of Gyges, the Lydian, and his discovery of the magic ring that enabled him to assassinate the king of Lydia and replace him. According to Glaucon, if the just man were provided such a ring, he would appropriate property with impunity, have sexual relations with anyone he wanted, kill and "do the other things which would make him like a god among men" (360c2–3). The just and the unjust would behave the same way, and both would be models of divinity among men. In the end, the unjust man is completely successful and prosperous; because he is not afraid to be unjust, he is always the winner, accumulating wealth and benefiting his friends while harming his enemies. "To the gods he offers grand sacrifices and gifts which will satisfy them; he can serve the gods much better than the just man . . . with the result that he is likely to be dearer to the gods" (362c2–6).[24] As Glaucon portrays him, then, the unjust man imitates the Homeric gods—willful, grasping, prosperous—and hence he is best able to sacrifice to them and ingratiate himself with them. Sacrifices and liturgies were sufficiently expensive that only the extremely wealthy were able to subsidize them.[25] In the traditional scheme, wealth, power, and piety were mutually supporting features of an increasingly smaller group of people's lives, the ideal embodiment of which was a tyrant such as Dionysius or Jason.

What Glaucon initiates as an objection, Adeimantus continues. Glaucon emphasized the prosperity of the unjust; Adeimantus begins by describing the way that fathers recommend justice to their sons, praising not the quality itself but rather its reputation and the results of its reputation, especially the "abundant blessings (*agatha*) which, they say, the gods grant to the pious" (363a6–7). This, Adeimantus shows, is the teaching of Hesiod and Homer, a doctrine of divine retribution. It is also taught by Musaeus and his son,[26] Adeimantus says: in Hades, the just banquet with the pious, are crowned with wreaths, and spend all their time drinking "as if they

thought that the finest reward of virtue was perpetual drunkenness"
(363d1–2).[27] The impious and unjust, on the other hand, are buried
in mud in Hades, forced to carry water in a sieve, and more. One
is hardly surprised to find Plato disdainful of Homeric retribution,
but it is a bit startling to find him berating what seems to be an
Orphic eschatology.

Adeimantus' attack is filled with passages both difficult and important for the study of Orphic texts, rites, and teachings. He claims
to be complementing Glaucon's challenge, but on this point he is
not sufficiently precise to be helpful. If we are to assess Plato's attitude toward Homeric religion and the phenomenon of Orphism,
we must understand the overall structure of what Adeimantus adds.

Adeimantus claims that his objections will supplement Glaucon's
by examining the praise of justice and the reproach of injustice,
presumably to show that even here justice is not commended for
itself and for its consequences for the soul.[28] The objections are
these:

1. When fathers speak to their sons, they praise justice for the
   reputation it brings, its rewards, both in this world and after
   death.
2. Justice is difficult, while injustice is easy though more profit-
   able; in fact, people honor the unjust, whom they think are
   happy because of their wealth and power.
3. Indeed, the gods inflict misery on the good and bring good
   fortune to the wicked. There are priests and diviners who offer to use sacrifices and incantations to rectify the ill effects
   of crime, and for little cost one can induce the gods to harass
   the good and the just.
4. Hence, the real issue is not between genuine justice and injustice but rather it concerns the appearance of justice.[29]
5. Praise of justice never explains what justice does for the soul;
   it always harps on the "reputations, honors, and rewards
   which follow justice" (366e4–5) and not the fact that the one
   is the greatest good for the soul, the other the greatest evil.

The gist of Adeimantus' remarks is that the account of justice that
he and his brother desire will not concern itself with reputation or
rewards; rather it will concern the way in which being just benefits
the soul of the just man—regardless of the ways in which gods and

men react to his justice or injustice. The portions of Adeimantus' remarks that especially interest us concern points (1) and (3) and the account of appearing just while being unjust (365d–66b).

In these passages, Plato has Adeimantus make two points about the gods, poets, religious practitioners, and justice. First, he claims that the posthumous rewards of justice are of dubious repute, while the punishments are given both to the unjust and to the just who have a reputation for injustice—in such a way that the distinction is confused. Second, he adds that the gods can be "bribed" to forgive the wicked and harm the just; prayers and offerings can be used to manipulate the gods to obliterate the distinction between the results of justice and injustice. If the distinction between justice and injustice is to mean anything, it cannot depend upon their respective results.

Plato's criticism of religious teaching and practice is global, hurled at any element of polis piety that manifests a view of providence and retribution that suits his critical purpose.[30] We should notice how imprecise his attributions are, or better, how they mix precision and imprecision to give the impression that he has a total tradition in mind and that it is, as a whole, guilty of supporting injustice. This strategy seems intentional; it enables Plato to indict together the poets, diviners, and priests of the classical tradition and the more recent practitioners of heterodox piety by distinguishing his own views from both. He quotes Homer and Hesiod twice, mentions Musaeus and his son—unidentified "begging priests and prophets," who use spells, incantations, and ad hoc sacrifices, practitioners too of absolutions, purifications, and teletai, "geneologizing poets," and prophets. "Conspiratorial societies," "political clubs," and "teachers of persuasion" also come in for criticism. Surely Plato is not singling out particular figures and groups as much as criticizing a widespread tendency among many who shaped the religious character of Athens and other actual poleis in the 370s.

The criticism of the sacrificial tradition and of the poets is akin to criticism we have noticed elsewhere. The system separates radically the human and the divine only to make men servants of the gods. Here Plato emphasizes another feature of the separation, that the gods can be manipulated to inflict misfortune and distribute well-being where they are not deserved. Plato characterizes the human situation and divine dominion this way: if the gods do not exist, then one need not be concerned with how they might respond to justice or injustice. If they do exist, then either they are concerned with men or not. If not, once again their response is irrelevant. If they are concerned, then we learn that they "can be persuaded and influenced by gentle prayers and by offerings"; indeed we can even avoid posthumous penalties through teletai and rites of absolution.[31] In a sense, the gods play no role in human growth and excellence; they are *there* to be influenced, manipulated, and bribed, but they are indifferent to real justice and hence to real excellence or arete. And this is as true for the gods of the teletai and rites of purification as it is for the gods to whom sacrificial offerings are made and in whose names spells and incantations are uttered. If there is novelty in Plato's criticism, it lies in his fairly explicit indictment of corrupt Bacchic-Orphic rites of initiation, alongside that of traditional Homeric piety.

But exactly what sorts of rites, practices, teachings, and works is Plato attacking? These passages (363c–e, 364b–c, 364e–65a, and 366a–b) have been subject to extensive analysis, especially with an eye to determining what they reveal about Orphism in the early fourth century. Fortunately, it is not necessary for us to examine each text in detail. What we need is a reasonably acceptable overall portrait of the types of teachings and practices that Plato is criticizing.

First, the passages are especially interesting because they refer quite clearly both to teachings and books, on the one hand, and to teletai, rites of purification, on the other. The two are not unconnected, of course, but the emphasis on teletai shows that Orphism was not exclusively a tradition of books and teachings. It involved or was associated with rituals of purification and absolution as well. We have seen this association already, and the *Republic* merely confirms the conclusion.[32] But this text need not mean that the rites or practices were Orphic in some restricted sense, only that Orphic teachings were associated with these rites—including Bacchic rituals and perhaps the Eleusinian mysteries.

Furthermore, since the Orphic texts, teachings, and rites are incorporated into Adeimantus' general critique, it seems clear that Plato is identifying what he takes to be corrupt versions of rites and practices, and such a selection suggests that there are other, noncorrupt cases, which Plato does not choose to attack. We might notice, for example, that Plato identifies certain political clubs, "teachers of persuasion,"[33] as targets for criticism—as he does eristics and misologists elsewhere—without implying that all sophists or politicians are of this sort or that all deserve criticism. We can infer more correctly that there are probably other Orphic teachings and rites that Plato admires, or at least that they have aspects or dimensions which Plato views more positively, and it is these which form the background for his own understanding of philosophy in the *Meno*, *Phaedo*, and *Symposium*.

With these caveats, then, what do the texts tell us about the rites, teachings, and books under attack? There are two issues involved here, the nature of the rites and teachings and their association with Orpheus. The first of the four texts (363c–e) cites a doctrine about posthumous reward and punishment: the just are treated to perpetual feasting and drinking, the unjust to burial in the mud and carrying water in a sieve.[34] The teaching is ascribed to "Musaeus and his son" (363c3), a reference which some commentators interpret as broadly Orphic,[35] others as "Eleusinian eschatology . . . attributed at this period [the 370s?] to Musaeus and Eumolpus, not Orpheus."[36] To a certain degree, the attribution seems to depend upon how seriously one takes the exclusion of Orpheus' name, given the apparent connection between the eschatological passage and the later reference to a "hubbub of books by Orpheus and Musaeus" (364e). In truth, however, Plato often associates Musaeus and Orpheus, and this might be sufficient to see in the doctrine an Orphic style. Moreover, the texts (363c3 and 364e) probably are connected; the latter (364e–65a) refers explicitly to a "dreadful fate" awaiting those who are unjust and fail to receive absolution.[37]

If the first text (363c3) introduces an Orphic eschatology, the second (364b–c) describes ritual acts that can be used to deter the stern decree. The third (364e–65a) can be read as a kind of summary, recalling the purifications and their role vis-à-vis the "dreadful fate [that] awaits the uninitiated." If the writings of Musaeus and Orpheus confirm the eschatology and the efficacy of these rites, then the latter are, broadly speaking, *Orpheotelestai*. Burkert reports the details this way:

> [The Orpheotelests] are wandering people making money (*agyrtai*), wherefore they go to the "doors of the rich": they perform

"purifications" (*katharmoi*) and "initiations" (*teletai*); they claim these are effective for the living as well as for the dead, and refer to terrible sufferings awaiting the uninitiated after death; they can make amends for an evil deed committed by a person or his ancestors; they can as well bring evil upon an enemy by "binding" him or raising a demon against him; they use sacrifice and magical formulas (*epoidai*).[38]

There is one ingredient in Plato's description that Burkert omits, and it is somewhat surprising that he does so. These mendicant Orpheotelests "persuade not only individuals but whole cities" of the efficacy of purification, sacrifice, and charms. West wonders whether the Eleusinian mysteries are not in Plato's mind; perhaps they are, but I am more inclined to think that what Plato is alluding to are waves of Bacchic or Corybantic enchantment, prominent at times of stress and uncertainty. One can easily imagine that the wave that overcame Athens during the Peloponnesian War did not abate in the fourth century but rather became thoroughly vulgarized, and that it is just such vulgarized ritual—therapeutic, Bacchic, Orphic—that Plato is attacking in the *Republic*. Rites that were once serious and modest have become mechanical, mercenary, and malignant, cheapened by phoney practitioners who prey on the insecurities of the wealthy and the vacuity of the wicked.[39] Plato is not mocking institutionalized magic and religious mercenaries; he is mocking their informal dominance in the way that one might have attacked witchcraft and astrology in early modern Europe or the way one might be inclined to ridicule popular cults and television evangelism today.[40]

It is not the elevating, genuine type of teletai that Plato is attacking, but rather the vulgar kind, which accepts the radical separation of the divine and the human and exploits the use of sacrifice, incantation, and purification to manipulate divine providence. In Plato's mind, the vulgarized form of Orphic practice and teaching is akin to traditional piety. Its practitioners are as keen to quote Homer and Hesiod as they are to refer to Musaeus and Orpheus. The key to their religiosity lies not in its association with Orpheus and a tradition of Orpheotelestai but rather in its continuity with Delphic, Homeric texts and teachings and with the sacrificial, oracular tradition. As we shall see shortly, Plato's critique of that tradition is as strong as ever; what these passages add is a new twist to that critique—and a touch of guilt by association. It extends the attack to the vulgarized aspects of Dionysiac, Orphic piety, as they have been co-opted by the Athenian population during the decades following the end of the Peloponnesian War.

These passages signal Plato's continued dissatisfaction with traditional piety and the Delphic theology that grounds it, but they do so in a novel way, by exposing Plato's antipathy to an amalgam of Orphic and Homeric vulgarized magic, sacrifice, and divination. Such piety is condemned as bribery, the work of swindlers and charlatans. If the spirit of these texts is largely negative, then that of the later treatment of traditional piety is largely positive because revisionary. In the lengthy elaboration of the guardians' artistic and gymnastic education, Plato does not dispense with that piety, its texts and teachings, as much as he tailors them to his new purpose. In the end, of course, this education will be only preliminary; the rulers will require something more and indeed something different in order to become philosophers. But at this stage and in this context, what Homeric, Delphic piety needs is adjustment, not abandonment or supersession.

THE guardians' early education has two familiar components, *mousike* and *gymnastike*. Plato's basic innovation is that while he appropriates the traditional division, he does so with a new intent. As he mentions, traditional paideia was well established in the fifth century and was conceived as training for the body and the soul.[41] For Plato, however, *both* gymnastic and artistic training have as their object the soul—the one its spirited part, the other its wisdom-loving part—and in general the harmony between the two.[42] Mousike, then, is concerned to cultivate the potential guardian's love of learning, wisdom, and knowledge; gymnastike is devoted to his swiftness, strength, and high-spiritedness (see 376c). The revision of polis piety and the Homeric tradition occurs in the account of mousike, its content and its form (376e–403c).

For the moment we can defer discussion of tragedy and comedy, of imitation and the forms of artistic education, and can focus on the discussion of content (376e–92c). One aspect of Plato's criticism is well known and does not originate with him—the attack on Homer and Hesiod, among others, for portraying gods and heroes in undesirable ways.[43] Socrates charged that such portrayals are poor models, encouraging crime and impropriety and disposing young minds to impiety rather than virtue.

As Socrates reminds Glaucon at the conclusion of *Republic* II, the education of the young, potential guardians is aimed at preparing them "to become god-fearing and divine, as far as it is possible for man" (383c4–5). Teaching the stories of Homer and other poets will not serve this purpose. But poetry about the gods is desirable. If the ultimate goal of philosophical paideia is quasi-divine status, then its early stages must be guided by appropriate portraits of the divine. Plato has Socrates formulate and defend two rules or guidelines (*nomoi te kai tupoi*, 380c7) for poetry about the gods, and in these two rules we can hear echoes of Plato's predecessors and the origins of what might be called "natural theology." The two rules outline a conception of the divine as good, as the cause of worldly goodness as perfect, unchanging, and wholly true. They are: (1) "The divine is not the cause of all things but only of the good" (380c8–9); (2) The gods "are not sorcerers who change themselves, nor do they mislead us with lies in word or in deed" (383a3–5). To be sure, the arguments for these rules are not without their difficulties.[44] Nonetheless, the point of (1) is clear; Plato wants to avoid implicating the divine in the responsibility for evil. The sources of evil must lie elsewhere.[45]

The second rule is about deception and change.[46] Genuine divinity engages in neither, for it is perfect and true as it is. If the first rule recalls Xenophanes, this one recalls Parmenides as well, along with the notion of changelessness.[47] Once again, Socrates' argument is not without problems, but again, its point is clear: The deep error of the traditional poets—epic, lyric, tragic—is that they falsely portray the nature of divinity. Particularly if education is to result in emulation and to proceed according to it, then an accurate theological picture must be employed. The two rules are hints in the direction of such a theology, in which the divine is somewhat depersonalized and yet maintains its goodness and perfection. This passage identifies a stage on a line that stretches from Xenophanes and Parmenides to the *Timaeus* and the *Laws*, and from there to *Physics* VIII, *De Caelo*, *Metaphysics* XII, and beyond. At the same time that Plato has appropriated the Socratic interest in transcendence through cognitive inquiry, he has adopted other interests in the divine. Here in the *Republic* the two stand side by side and do not significantly mingle. One wonders when, if ever, Plato will ask whether natural theology, any more than Delphic theology, is compatible with ecstatic rites of initiation and philosophical transcendence.[48]

In *Republic* II and III Plato examines and revises poetry as a vehicle for the guardian's education, exploring both its content and its form. In *Republic* X, once the Forms and the philosophical education have been introduced, Plato returns to his critique of poetry, specifically of poetry about human beings.

What is Plato's judgment in *Republic* III about the forms of poetry—about tragedy, comedy, imitation, and so forth? The problem he poses at 394d is whether the guardians' education should include the work of imitative poets, for example, tragic and comic playwrights. Should the guardians be imitative (394e)? Or does imitation fly in the face of the one-man–one-occupation rule? Socrates argues that imitation occurs in diverse modes demanding special talents and expertise; the guardians are to be devoted only to the polis' freedom and hence should imitate only those excellences, including bravery and self-control, that will best enable them to achieve that single goal. They should not, then, be permitted to imitate women, slaves, evil men, cowards, or other inappropriate types (395d–96e). The prospective guardian should imitate only the good man, engaging in the pure style of narration and not the mixed style that ultimately appeals to children, slaves, and the mob (397c–98b).[49] In sum, Plato does not in *Republic* III condemn imitation in and of itself; what he criticizes and indeed rejects is imitation of inappropriate models. In fact, imitation as a form of training is a valuable component of the young guardians' education. Poetry with revised content and recited in an appropriately pure way would be a worthy vehicle of paideia.

In *Republic* X Plato returns to poetry but in a spirit of intense and vigorous opposition.[50] At 608b, with the lengthy critique completed, he classifies poetry with wealth and honors as alien to and destructive of justice and the other aretai. To the degree that epic, lyric, and tragic poetry are associated with Olympian religion, Delphic theology, and the polis tradition, they are appropriate objects of Platonic criticism.

Plato's argument against imitative poetry (595a–608b) has several parts, but I think that it is helpful to view it as having two main stages. In the course of the first and lengthier stage, which ends at 605c, Plato tries to show that the imitative poet, like the painter, "is a maker of images which are very far removed from the truth" (605c3–4) and is one who strengthens an inferior part of the soul, thereby destroying the reasonable part.[51] The complex argument that leads to these twin conclusions utilizes the theory of Forms, the conception of the soul as tripartite, and the distinction between knowledge and true belief, among other views not yet introduced or developed in *Republic* III. It incorporates a metaphysical, epistemological, and psychological analysis of imitation, including a comparison between scene painting, for example, and imitative poetry, and an inquiry into the nature of mimesis.[52] The final indictment is twofold: epistemic deficiency and educational-psychological corruption.

The second stage begins with Socrates' words: "we have not yet, however, brought the most serious charge against imitation, namely that it is able to corrupt even good men, with very few exceptions, and that is a terribly dangerous thing" (605c6–8). This stage involves a relatively brief argument (605c–7a) that the bad kind of imitative poetry can have a powerful effect even on the good man, pandering to and enhancing his evil or destructive desires, pleasures, and pains, to the point where he comes to be ruled by them rather than by "*nomos* and the *logos* that is always and by all thought to be best" (607a6–8).

Thus the core of Plato's attack concerns the effects of imitation on its audience and not merely the defects in its nature. In other words, imitative poetry qua imitative may be deficient intrinsically. It may be a faulty expression of knowledge and an erroneous mode of depicting the truth. But these twin facts may be, by themselves, insufficient to exclude imitative poetry from the ideal polis. For that exclusion another aspect of imitative poetry may be required, an aspect that is related to but not identical with its character as imitative art. If this is so, then imitative poetry of a sort may be banished from the ideal polis but not simply and exclusively because it is imitative.

At 598d7–601b8, Socrates wants to say that tragic poetry is, like painting, a form of imitative art. The issue is whether tragic poets are at a third remove from reality and depict their subjects without knowledge of the truth (598e–99a). If they had the relevant knowledge, then they would surely employ it to advantage. But they have failed to do so. Hence, it is clear that "all poetic imitators, beginning with Homer, imitate images of virtue and of everything else they write about and have no contact with the truth" (600e4–6). The tragic poet knows not excellence and the human good; what he knows is how to imitate.

Socrates' argument turns on the analogy of poetry with painting and the accuracy of his criticism of the latter. The painter is a maker who makes an image (*eidolon*) of a physical thing, in a way similar to the way one makes an image by holding up a mirror to something. Often the painter depicts people, and Plato is especially interested in such cases (598b–d, 600e–601a), for they are the best analogy for tragic poetry and its depiction of people. The painter uses color and shape and perspective (601a, 602c–d). The one type of painting that Plato explicitly refers to is shaded painting; he calls it a form of magic, a charge that recalls the similar charge against painting and all the imitative artists, that they are deceivers and magicians (598d).[53]

There are, of course, a variety of reasons that painting might have appealed to Plato as the fulcrum of his charges. Two seem especially important. The first is that imitative painting, more vividly than any other form of imitation, shows that an imitation depicts the image of a reality as that image appears, that is, via its perspectival adumbration, rather than as it is, as a totality.[54] The second concerns Socrates' reference to shaded painting. This type of painting is referred to five times in the *Republic*, although at 602d it might be taken to refer to scene painting and the use of perspective as well as shading.[55] Both techniques were discovered in the late fifth century, shading by Apollodorus and scene painting by Agatharcus.[56] Plato's examples at 602c–d—the stick that appears both crooked and straight and the use of color to make something look concave or convex—can be taken to refer to both innovations.[57] But the point is nonetheless the same: that distance, context, color, and so on can result in a confused perception in which the same thing is two sizes or appears both crooked and straight or concave and convex. What we have here of course is a reminiscence of the classic text at 523a–24d and the contradictory perceptions that conduct the intellect to the "contemplation of reality." Imitative poetry—shaded painting and scene painting—appeals to and capitalizes on a non-intellectual part of the soul.[58] The two basic features of painting, then, indicate that painting appeals to sensory perception and non-rational impulses. Once these facts are developed, it will be clear that any form of poetry that does the same will be poorly equipped to aid the guardians' and philosophers' development and thereby the polis' goals.

At 602c4–5 Socrates turns to the core of his attack; he moves from an account of mimesis to an account of its effects on something in man, that is, on its audience. Although the introductory passage once again uses painting as a model, Socrates quickly sets painting aside in favor of a direct assault on poetry.[59] The differences between representational, realistic painting and tragic poetry are significant and obvious enough to warn us against forcing the analogy. Plato's target is poetry, for unlike visual art it has a religious, political, moral, and educational role that is a threat to the ideal polis.[60] Plato uses painting as a case study to develop general criticisms of mimesis, which he then applies to tragic poetry.

As Plato begins to consider the effects of imitation on its human audience, he introduces the final ingredient in his critique, a division within the soul between the intellect and nonintellectual components. That part of the soul which engages in calculation and measurement—the best part—forms beliefs based on these results.[61] Imitative painting, on the other hand, appeals to one of the soul's inferior parts, which forms beliefs contrary to those of the rational or intellectual part. "Imitation . . . being an inferior thing and consorting with an inferior part, produces inferior offspring" (603b4). Painting and other imitative arts, that is, are the objects of one of the soul's nonrational parts, and the results of their relation are beliefs contrary to those generated by reason and calculation. This part of the soul is later called "unreasonable, idle, and friendly to cowardice" (604d9–10), "peevish" (604e2), "mindless" (605b), and "lachrymose" (606a8–b1). But the most helpful comment comes at 606d1–7, where Socrates says this about the impact of poetic imitation on its audience: "So too with sex, anger, and all the desires, pleasures, and pains which we say follow us in every activity. Poetic imitation fosters these in us. It nurtures and waters them when they ought to wither; it places them in command in our soul when they ought to obey in order that we might become better and happier

men instead of worse and more miserable." Clearly, the part of the
soul to which imitation appeals is the seat of pleasure, pain, and
nonrational desire. At the descriptive level, imitation results in false
beliefs, for the nonrational part of man's nature readily accepts the
confused perceptions of imitative arts as accurate and generates
beliefs contrary to the truth. Not recognizing an appearance or illusion for what it is, the soul believes a straight stick to be crooked,
a proximate scene to be distant, a flat object to be concave, and so
on.[62] As a result, if the goal of education is knowledge, then imitative art is a bad vehicle for it, since it appeals to and exercises
precisely the wrong psychic capacities.[63]

The gist of Plato's criticism, then, is that imitative poetry—not
all poetry perhaps—appeals to the nonrational soul to generate erroneous beliefs rather than inspiring the rational soul to generate
truth and knowledge about the subjects that the poetry depicts.
Education in particular and the polis in general benefit from the
cultivation of reason and inquiry. Imitative poetry would make a
bad educational tool and an equally poor cultural institution. It
would encourage the flourishing of error and illusion, the peevish
and mindless rather than the wise and patient, in the polis' citizens.

In the end, then, the presence or absence of imitative poetry in
the ideal polis is a matter of benefit and utility (607e). Imitative
poetry harms the soul and the polis; it encourages indulgence in
pleasure, joy, and satisfaction and impedes the governing of rational
desire. Ultimately it encourages the young and indeed all citizens
to accept appearance and the contrarieties of false belief rather than
to desire knowledge and aspire to it. In short, imitative poetry sab-
otages philosophy and therefore the philosophical polis in two ways,
epistemically by generating false beliefs and *affectively* by destroying the desire for knowledge.

Near the end of this critique, Socrates warns that imitative poetry
will make pleasure and pain rulers in the polis, and hence "hymns
to the gods and eulogies of good men are the only poetry which we
can admit into our city" (607a3–5). Such hymns and encomia are
among the proper objects of the pure diction described in *Republic*
III.[64] Imitative, tragic poetry tends to depict emotion, pleasure and
pain, grief, joy, and sorrow. When it does so, it is a threat to the
polis and to philosophy. Hence the "ancient quarrel between philosophy and poetry" (607b5–6). But not all poetry is imitative—

though Plato is hardly interested in nonrepresentational poetry—
and not all imitative poetry is drawn to the depiction of the passionate and the sordid. In principle, poetry is not the appropriate
vehicle for philosophical inquiry and research; it is too far from
truth and does not even aspire to know it. But poetry of a specific
sort can be an appropriate vehicle for the education of rational
desire and for enhancing public fidelity to the role of logos and
nomos. In the end Plato's indictment of imitation, imitative painting, and tragic poetry in *Republic* X is very selective, and by being
selective it does not bar the doors that were opened in *Republic* III.[65]
What the critique does instead is ground the right of passage through
those doors by clarifying the precise ways in which indulgent, sen-
suous, hedonistic imitative art, especially poetry, threatens to sub-
vert the cognitive and noncognitive dimensions of philosophical
growth and inquiry. The paradoxical conclusion of Plato's critique
is that Homeric poetry and tragic drama are antireligious forms of
art.

In the course of his argument that tragic poets do not have knowledge of war, governance, and education—all the things which their
writings depict—Plato contrasts Homer unfavorably with Pythagoras. One who genuinely knows about education and public life
would surely teach others and promote among friends and disciples
a "way of life" (600a–b). It is not hard to believe that Plato is doing
more here than registering a casual challenge to the poetic progen-
itor of the polis tradition and Greek piety. More than any earlier
dialogue, the *Republic* articulates the shape of a "way of life," a
form of social and political life, an account of human nature and
its best state, and an elaborate account of paideia, the elementary
and advanced forms of training and inquiry that enable philosophical aspiration. All along we have called this enterprise as much
religious as moral, political, and "scientific." It is now time to show
that Plato conceived of it this way, for if he did, he would surely
have framed his vision in a religious vocabulary, as I have argued
he did in the *Phaedo* and the *Symposium*.[66]
    To identify ways that Plato employs religious vocabulary to char-
acterize and conceive philosophical education and its results, we
might best turn our attention to two features of the *Republic* and
restrict ourselves to them: (1) the way Plato describes the ultimate

achievement of the philosopher and his or her rewards, and (2) the terminology Plato uses for describing knowing access to the Forms, the nondiscursive aspect of dialectical knowledge.

In describing the state of philosophical achievement, Plato uses religious terminology, but it is general and modest, in sharp contrast with the more precise allusions of the *Phaedo*. At 521c, for example, having completed the image of the cave, Socrates fixes on two questions, how the philosopher will come to rule in the polis and "how one will lead them into light, as some are said to have gone up from Hades to the gods" (521c2–3). Against the background of this comparison of philosophical illumination with divine status,[67] Socrates proceeds to set out the curriculum of mathematical and dialectical study appropriate for the philosopher. Near the conclusion of this discussion, Socrates summarizes the effects of dialectic, aided by *dianoia*: "It gently draws the eye of the soul, which is really buried in a kind of barbaric mire, and leads it upwards" (533d1–3). In a famous paper Hermann Fraenkel has argued in behalf of the Heraclitean heritage of the evocative phrase "*borboro barbariko*" (d1), "in a kind of barbaric mire."[68] Even if his interpretation is correct, however, the phrase surely has Orphic overtones as well and may very well allude to the *Phaedo*.[69]

The contrasts between lower and upper, dark and light, dirty and clean, tainted and pure are not new in Plato, and they recur throughout the *Republic*. A notable case occurs in *Republic* X, where Socrates compares the incarnate and discarnate soul to the sea god Glaucus, whose original nature is damaged and hidden as long as he remains beneath the sea.[70] So it is with the incarnate soul, "beset by countless evils" (611d7). To understand what the soul is genuinely and purely, we must consider

> the soul's love of wisdom, and realize what things it apprehends, what company it longs for as it is akin to the divine, the immortal, and the everexisting, what it would become if it followed this with the whole of its being and if that impulse lifted it out of the sea in which it now dwells, if the many stones and shells, the many stony and wild things which have been encrusted all over it by those so-called happy beasts as it feeds on earth, were scraped off. (611e1–12a3)

Once again, philosophy is thought to lead to purity, to divinity, and

to immortality.[71] And at the same time that the philosopher ultimately achieves everlasting bliss,[72] the polis that he has served is
expected to honor him—indeed, as a divine spirit (*hos daimosin*) if
the Pythia agrees, but if not, then as happy and divine (*hos eudai-
mosi te kai theiois*, 540b7–c2).

Throughout the *Republic*, then, Plato refers to the philosopher
and his achievement as divine,[73] and he contrasts the nonphilosophical life, the incarnate life, with the philosophical in terms of
purity, light, and so on. The imagery occurs in Parmenides and
Heraclitus but is also prominent in texts that reflect Orphic teaching
and practice.[74] Plato is a great synthesizer, and there is no reason
to think that he intended his readers to keep the strands separate
as much as to appreciate the whole cloth that he wove from them.[75]
It is easy for Plato to draw on Orphic teachings and other traditions
in order to characterize the incarnate life and nonphilosophy as
dirty, impure, and tainted, and the life of the philosopher as pure,
illuminated, and divine. But there is more than tradition operating
here, I think, and the new ingredient concerns Plato's discovery of
the Forms as the appropriate objects of the highest kind of knowledge.

Plato does not call the philosopher "divine" in a wholly honorary
way. Poets, mantics, and oracles are inspired and hence "divine"
as a matter of usage or custom. But the philosopher is divine in a
deeper sense, and Plato tells us why at 500b–d:

> As [the man whose thought (*dianoia*) is truly directed to real
> existence] looks upon and contemplates things that are ordered
> and ever the same, that neither do wrong nor are wronged, one
> to another, all being in order according to reason (*logos*), he
> imitates them and tries to be as like them as he can. . . . So the
> philosopher, who is with the divine and the orderly, becomes
> as ordered and divine as it is possible for man. (500b8–d1)

Here we have a type of imitation that is not only acceptable in the
polis but even desirable.[76] As Plato goes on to explain, the philosophers qua rulers are like painters who use a divine model for their
work. Their goal is to shape existing social and political life into
the best life it can be, based on that element in man that even
Homer called "divine and godlike" (501b7). Their goal is to make

human character as much like the divine (*theophile*) as they can (501b–c).

In this passage, Socrates uses terms such as "divine," "divine-loving," and "divine-like" of the philosopher, of reason, of the human character patterned after the ideal. But the central, determinative objects which are called "divine" are the Forms themselves, the ordered realities that the philosopher seeks to "look upon and contemplate." Indeed, in the text at 500b–d Socrates says that the philosopher becomes well ordered and divine because and insofar as he imitates the Forms.[77] At one level, this must mean that the philosopher seeks rational order in his own life and in the life of the polis; at another, however, it must mean that he seeks for himself the everlastingness and unchangeability that come with perfect knowledge. Just as justice in the *Republic* is systematically equivocal, with the Form of the Just and then the just soul as the central and then derivative types of justice, so divinity in the *Republic* is equivocal. The Forms and the god of natural theology are primarily or focally divine; then follow the philosopher, philosophical reason, the ideal polis, and its members. Tradition may refer to many things and many persons as "divine" in some vague, honorific manner. Plato, however, uses the term more precisely and systematically. In the *Republic* and doubtless earlier, in the *Phaedo*, the philosopher is called "divine" because he is like the objects which he knows and tries to exemplify.

It is no surprise, then, that throughout the *Republic* when Plato refers to the philosopher's knowledge of the Forms, he uses a terminology that emphasizes the nondiscursive, referential aspect of knowing.[78] There is hardly any need to pay special attention to the visual terminology Plato uses. Terms for seeing, looking at, gazing at, and contemplating occur everywhere.[79] Nor is it necessary to do more than notice that there are at least two likely settings from which such visual vocabulary is derived: the dramatic contests at Dionysiac festivals and the Eleusinian mysteries.[80] Without quite the same degree of intensity or of explicitness as the *Phaedo*, the *Republic* does employ a religious vocabulary—often associated with ecstatic rites, initiations, and so on—to describe philosophy, its objects, its goal, and its importance. Together with the critique of traditional piety, the use of this vocabulary is a powerful expression of the religious character of rational, philosophical inquiry and education.

HAVING disposed of the type of poetry that leads one to neglect justice and excellence, Socrates returns to a theme already introduced by Glaucon and Adeimantus in Book II. In order to respond adequately to Adeimantus' challenge, Plato had to show why justice is good for its own sake, that is, what it does for the incarnate soul. But a problem still remains: what are its rewards?[81] What benefit is justice to the discarnate soul? As the time from childhood to old age is slight compared with all of time, so is the earthly to the posthumous reward for justice, excellence, the good life.[82] In the waning pages of the *Republic*, Plato turns to this subject, prefacing it with a brief but telling discussion of the nature of the soul.[83]

As Annas points out, the argument for immortality is embarrassingly flawed.[84] It is hardly necessary to review its obvious shortcomings.[85] Socrates himself seems to use it as a device for drawing some further conclusions—beyond the facts that soul always exists and is immortal (611a1–2). He believes that souls are always the same in number and that they are each, in their truest nature, either simple or well organized, rather than complex and factitious, as *Republic* IV–IX imply. The real purpose of this argument for immortality is that it points to the *Republic*'s central theme and a difficulty that the theme seems to generate. For the soul's immortality seems to entail a structure that is different from the diversity and complexity of the incarnate soul.

Like the *Symposium*, the *Republic* dwells on the soul's earthly career only to point ahead, at a crucial juncture, to something beyond, to a state in which the best or philosophical soul exists in an untainted, pure way. The analogy with the sea god Glaucus is surely intended to highlight the contrast between the soul as it appears at present, in its incarnate state, and the soul in its pure state, contemplated by reason.[86] As incarnate, the soul appears "full of great variety and unlikeness and difference" (611b2–3), "not put together in the finest way" (b6), and "maimed by its association with the body and other evils" (b10–c2). Basically, the incarnate soul is burdened with competing desires, pleasures, and pains, continually subject to struggles for dominance by the desires for wealth, honor, and physical satisfaction. Once the connections with the body and worldly pleasure and pain are severed, however, the soul appears in a different light, in "its truest nature" (611b1, 612a3–4). But Socrates admits that he and Glaucon have no direct access to such a state; they cannot see what the soul is like in its true nature. What they can do is contemplate the soul by reason (*logismo*, c3–4). That is, they can examine the one aspect of the soul that points to its truest, most perfect nature. In other words, if the soul's real nature is what it has lost and what it strives for, then even if we cannot examine it in that state, we can learn of its true nature by learning from its aspiration. And because the highest form of aspiration of the incarnate soul is the love of wisdom, we should examine the soul's *philosophia* in order to see its true nature (611e1–12a5).

But why should the study of the soul's highest or best form of love or desire, its striving for knowledge, communicate anything about its highest state? Plato's answer, in the vein of 500b–d, is that the nature of the objects of wisdom reveals the state that the soul itself seeks, for the soul seeks to become like what it aspires to know.[87] The way to understand the soul's truest nature, its *telos*, is to come to know "what things it apprehends and what company it longs for, being akin to the divine and immortal and always existing, what it would become if it followed this with all its being and if that impulse lifted it out of the sea in which it now dwells" (611e1–5). Ultimately, one learns what the soul aspires to be by examining what it aspires to know—what it itself would be if its love for wisdom were wholly successful. In the end, we can be sure that the soul is immortal because rational argument shows it to be so,[88] and hence it is divine,[89] but whether in the end it is or strives to be multiform or uniform is not known. One is inclined to believe that just as the domain of Forms is plural but rationally ordered, so the ideal soul-state is one of plural but harmonious desires and capacities.[90]

It is against the background of this projection about the soul's truest nature that Socrates returns to the second aspect of Glaucon's and Adeimantus' twofold challenge, that he show the rewards of justice and virtue, both in life and after death (612b–c). The culmination of this stretch of dialogue is the account of soul's posthumous reward as it is revealed in the myth of Er (614b–21b).

The real purpose of the *Republic* is not to give an account of dikaiosune that suits only the soul's worldly career; it is instead to give an account of the philosophical life and the religious character of rational inquiry and cognitive ascent, an account that is true both to its otherworldly goal and to its this-worldly context. The *Republic* is about eternity and history, about transcendence and everyday life, and the account of justice, virtue, and philosophy that it produces must ignore neither of these twin dimensions of Platonic piety.

THE most dramatic novelty in the *Republic* is Plato's recognition that, against the background of the contemplative, ecstatic ideal, historical-political factors must play a central role in his defense of the philosophical life as the best human life. In order to see how this novelty is expressed in the *Republic*, we must address three problems. First, given the separation of the ultimate objects of philosophical aspiration and dialectical knowledge, how is education or inquiry possible?[91] Second, what does the *Republic* say about the desire for knowledge, about the noncognitive or affective dimensions of learning? Finally, what role should philosophers play in the just polis? Once we have answered these questions, we can return to the myth of Er and Plato's weaving together of the this-worldly and otherworldly rewards of the philosophical life.

RECENT commentators have been reluctant to take the "contemplative ideal" of the philosopher very seriously.[92] Some, for example, argue that its role in the *Republic* is a mistake on Plato's part, and that his conception of justice and the good already contain an altruistic component that is incompatible with the ideal of study, inquiry, and wisdom portrayed most vividly in the Cave. The error in such interpretations, however, runs deep. The aspirations of the philosopher can be reconciled with a demand for political and moral activity, and the "contemplative ideal" of rational, ecstatic aspiration is central to Plato's thought. The author of the *Republic* is the author of the *Phaedo*, and the historical and political character of his interests in the *Republic* do not alter but only deepen his reverence for philosophy as an ecstatic rite whose ultimate goal is divine bliss.

Philosophy is paideia, inquiry, learning. If the ultimate goal of this philosophical paideia is knowledge of the Forms, which it surely is, then we have seen how the separation of the Forms presents a potential threat to its success. The *Republic* confirms the gap that separates Forms and the physical world; it also confirms the difference between belief, even true belief, and knowledge.[93] Not only is knowledge firmer and more reliable and capable of giving an account of its objects, but it also has a different object altogether— whereas belief is in some sense about the physical world, knowledge is of the Forms. Hence, education is possible only if the believer can be made first to recognize his limitations and then to turn his attention to what he has yet to apprehend. The central epistemological task of the *Republic* is to show how this process is achieved and thereby to show what genuine learning is and how it occurs.

Plato's account begins at *Republic* V and continues through the images of the Sun, Line, and Cave, concluding with the mathematical curriculum of *Republic* VII. First, the knowledge obtained as a result of dialectical study involves both contemplating the Forms and giving accounts of what they are. Commentators either struggle to make sense of these twin dimensions of knowledge or choose to dispense with the contemplative dimension, as a Platonic excess— antiquated, romantic, unnecessary, and mystical. But the evidence that Plato endorsed both dimensions is overwhelming,[94] and once one sees Plato's philosophical development within the context of Greek religious thinking, it is simply impossible to jettison the contemplative aspect. Belief and knowledge involve both the apprehension of an object and the affirmation of some logos as being true of that object. Plato has no conception of a believing or knowing that would not involve apprehension of its object, that would lack "referential access," as we might call it.[95]

Second, in the *Republic* Plato accepts as part of his Socratic heritage the caveat that real or preeminent knowledge is always knowledge of what *x* is; let us call this "essential knowledge." Hence, the goal of philosophical education is not just any kind of knowledge— such as historical or everyday knowledge. Rather it is precisely essential knowledge, and to have it is both to have the Form in one's ken and to know a certain logos to be true of that Form, a logos that spells out what the Form really is, its nature or essence. In short, Platonic knowledge is about the essence of Forms, for strictly speaking only essential knowledge is real knowledge and only Forms have (or are) essences.⁹⁶

If this account is correct, then inquiry or learning, which involves the transition from belief to knowledge, incorporates two steps. One step is the identification and confirmation of logoi that give true accounts of what the Forms are. The second is recognition that these logoi are true of separately existing entities, the Forms, and apprehension of them.⁹⁷ Although Plato pays some attention to how the first step is achieved, especially in his discussion of method concerning both mathematical thinking and dialectical investigation,⁹⁸ in the *Republic* his primary attention is on the second step. In *Republic* V he frames an argument to persuade the nonphilosophical believer that he has beliefs but not knowledge precisely because the proper objects of essential knowledge are not within his ken; they are other than the objects with which he is preoccupied. In the images of the Line and Cave, Plato shows how, via the mechanism of mathematical thinking, the inquirer's or learner's attention is turned from physical objects to the Forms.⁹⁹ In this way Plato shows what role mathematical thinking plays in attaining referential access to the Forms. In the end, that access is the standard for assessing the truth of any proposed logos and at the same time gives the soul the subject of that logos. The logos guides the awareness to its clearest and most vivid apprehension of the object and then confirms the accuracy of the awareness. Essential knowledge or philosophical wisdom, for Plato, is impossible without both dimensions of knowing, and genuine inquiry requires their joint progress.

Plato's treatment of the philosopher's education and inquiry begins in *Republic* V. He is fond of the contrast between dreaming and waking.¹⁰⁰ Once it is introduced, at V, 476c2–d4, as a metaphor for the knowledge (*gnome*, d5) of the philosopher and the belief (*doxa*, d6) of the nonphilosophical lover of sights and sounds, the contrast provides one of the operative motifs that run through the later analogies. Dreaming and waking represent states of confusion and clarity, of error and accuracy, and their objects represent what is unreal and dark as opposed to what is real, clear, and brightly illuminated.¹⁰¹

There are three points to notice about how the pair function in *Republic* V. First, the dreaming-waking analogy is part of Socrates' answer to Glaucon's question about who the genuine philosophers are (V, 475e3–4). That answer takes shape as a contrast between the philosopher, who loves the sight of truth (the Forms), and the nonphilosophical believer, who loves the sights and sounds of worldly experience. The difference in type of thinking (dianoia, 476b7; 477d5)[102] is the difference between knowledge and belief, but these can be understood only once a distinction is made between two orders of objects—between the one and the many, for example, or between the Beautiful itself and all those shapes, colors, and tones that share in it (476a4–b12). The dreaming-waking analogy, therefore, depends for its application upon this ontological distinction between two orders of objects. It is meant to clarify in some manner two ways of apprehending these objects.

Second, these ways of apprehending the two orders of objects need not and in fact do not occur as an isomorphic pairing, one way of thinking for each type of object and only for that object. To be sure, those with sense-bound beliefs cannot apprehend the Forms, nor can they follow someone who tries to get them to apprehend the Forms (476c2–4).[103] But the philosopher, in contrast, is able to apprehend each Form and "those things that share in it" (476d1–2). What Plato tries to show by means of the dreaming-waking analogy is not that the types of thinking have exclusive objects but rather how they differ in the ways they apprehend all the objects they are capable of apprehending. This realization brings us to the third and crucial point: the nonphilosopher is a dreamer; he thinks "that a likeness is not a likeness but rather that which it resembles" (476c6–7). The dreamer, that is, fails to realize that what he sees is only a dream image; he takes it to be real, substantial, "the genuine article," when it is in fact only a copy. The philosopher, on the other hand, is awake; he "thinks neither that the things that share in [a Form] are [that Form] nor that it is the things that share in [it]" (476d2–3).

In sum, the philosopher does not confuse Forms with observable properties and objects; he does not mistake one for the other and most notably does not think that observable properties and objects are what is real. Only the Forms are real (compare *Phaedo* 83a–b). Such a person is like one who is awake and does not mistake his wakeful experiences for dreams, and, more important, he is like a person who is awake much of the time and who realizes that the objects experienced in his dreams are only dream images. The wakeful person knows that his dream images are not sensible objects; similarly, the philosopher knows that observable properties and objects are not what is real.

The nonphilosopher, in contrast, thinks or believes that observable properties and objects are real; he has no inkling of the existence of Forms and mistakes the ontological status of observables. What precisely is his mistake? It is a special case of mistaken identity. Both the dreamer and the man awake have views about what is real and genuine. The former thinks that beautiful colors, shapes, and tones are what real beauty is; the latter realizes that this is an error. The colors, shapes, and tones are like the Beautiful but are not identical to it. Both address the question, "What is it that makes beautiful things beautiful? What is really beautiful?" and both search for what beautiful is. But the philosopher's cognitive scope provides him with more possible solutions, and his perceptiveness and accuracy allow him both to identify the right one and to recognize the ontological relationship between the right one and all the wrong ones.

What then is belief? Belief occurs when a nonphilosopher senses an object or property that has a certain characteristic, being beautiful for example, and believes that object or property is what real beauty is. And what is knowledge? Knowledge occurs when a philosopher knows a Form, say the Beautiful itself, and knows of the Beautiful that it is what real Beauty is; he knows too that the beautiful shapes, tones, and colors are beautiful because they are copies of the Beautiful itself. In both cases, the central question concerns thinking about what real being beautiful is, or what real being F is. "Belief" and "knowledge" are technical expressions for two ways of thinking about a thing described in that way, two ways of apprehending the solution to an inquiry framed in these terms. This fact is a restriction that together with the dreaming-waking metaphor is retained and developed in *Republic* VI–VII.[104]

As we turn now to the Sun, the Line, and the Cave themselves, I want to begin in an unorthodox manner. Some commentators argue for a strict correspondence between the Line and the Cave.[105] Others notice the significant differences between the two.[106] The differences must be taken very seriously. The Cave in a sense unifies the Sun and the Line, but it follows them and transcends them as well. The

Cave ignores and supplements as well as includes features of the earlier analogies.

The nonphilosophical believers of *Republic* V are voluptuaries in a world of observable properties and objects.[107] Those who are chained from childhood in the deep cavern of *Republic* VII are prisoners in a world of shadows (VII, 514a2–c3). The former believe what is real and true to be the objects of their sensory experience—observed colors, shapes, and tones, felt pleasures, pains, and desires. So do the prisoners, for "they think that what is real is nothing else but the shadows of the artifacts" (515c1–2). The prisoners are, Plato tells us, "like us" (515a5). The nonphilosophical believers, we are told, are dreamers, unable to apprehend what is real, confusing image with reality. So also are the prisoners dreamers; the re-entrance of the philosopher into their midst is like the entrance of a waking person into a world of dreamers who "fight one another for shadows and wrangle for office as if that were a great good" (520c1–d1). In short, the prisoners at the base of the cave are nonphilosophical dreamers constrained by sense-bound beliefs about what is real. They "contend about the shadows of justice or the images that cast the shadows," having never seen Justice itself (517d8–e2) or Beauty or the Good (520c5–6). And the prisoner's world is our own world, the world of physical, observable objects and properties.[108]

Plato asks us to consider how bewildering it would be to wrench someone from that cavernous world. Just as the eye is blinded temporarily by unaccustomed light, so the soul is temporarily dismayed and perplexed by the change in illumination. Plato describes the disturbance that accompanies such a change (518a–b) as well as the bedazzlement; such a person does not come willingly but must be dragged. Plato's language is severe, so severe that it might be thought to reflect a profound worry that education faces such great opposing forces that it may never be capable of succeeding against them. So it might be thought—if the Cave were read alone, isolated from its surroundings. But the truth is that in the Cave Plato expresses this worry and the inertia of the prisoner's life, already having identified the key transitional stage that makes learning and hence education possible. For this reason, the worry of the Cave is a tempered distress, for the Cave follows and does not precede the Line.

The Line is about mathematical thinking,[109] and the account of learning as conversion, which the analogies jointly produce, has as its core mathematical thinking.[110] Neither the images nor their role can be properly understood unless we get the Line straight.

Thus far I have tried to show that the original position of the prisoners, like "our" situation, is identical with the dream state of the nonphilosopher. Now I want to suggest that this situation is elaborated in the Line, for both of the Line's lower sections, *eikasia* and *pistis*, are encompassed within the prisoner's original position.[111] The Line's lower sections represent the realm of the sun; it is the visible realm, populated by shadows, reflections, and the animals, plants, and artifacts that cast them (509d6–10a6; compare 476b4–8). The Line is first introduced as a development of the image of the Sun (509c5–d8), and hence its two main divisions are initially called "the intelligible" and "the visible" (*to horaton*, 509d2–3; see also d8). It only takes a short time, however, for Plato to revise his terminology and to reveal that the visible realm is in fact none other than the realm of belief, recovered from *Republic* V and newly developed (510a9, *to doxaston*).[112]

Within the dream-like world of sense-bound beliefs, the believer not only believes that observable properties and objects are what is real. He also believes that certain observable objects are not real. These include images, shadows, and reflections (509e1–10a3), which he recognizes as genuine objects of sensation and yet not *really* the things that they depict, copy, or represent. If the believer has such objects and his awareness of them pointed out to him, he can come to appreciate that within his own experiential range there are important differences of clarity and obscurity (509d8–e1). Furthermore, he may come to realize that also within his experiential range there is a difference between what is an image or a resemblance and what is an original, independent entity of which there are images. These distinctions are real for the believer even within the confines of his "dream" world. He can be made aware of them, and they can be intelligible to him—and even more so to Glaucon, who in *Republic* VI is someone who acknowledges the existence of a realm beyond that of observables. What the lower sections of the Line show, then, is that just as shadows and reflections are only copies of natural and artificial objects, so the objects themselves may be copies of something else—something beyond them and existing independently of them.

Moreover, just as eikasia is an awareness of shadows and reflections *qua* images, that is, seeing them with a full realization that they are only copies, so there is a mode of awareness or thinking by which natural and artificial objects can be experienced qua images, that is, with a full realization that they, too, are only copies. And just as eikasia is an enlightened awareness of images without yet involving awareness of their originals, so this other mode of thinking can be an enlightened awareness of observables without yet involving an awareness of their originals.[113] The purpose of eikasia is to point beyond itself and beyond belief to a kind of awareness or thinking that is intermediate between doxa as pistis, which is an experience of natural and artificial objects *qua* realities, and *noesis*, the full-blown knowledge of Forms qua realities. This kind of thinking, Plato says, is called—largely from custom or habit—"thinking" (dianoia), though we really need a more accurate name that indicates vividly that such thinking is clearer than belief and yet more obscure than knowledge (533d4–6).

Pistis and eikasia mark a real distinction within sense-bound belief, even though Plato's purpose in distinguishing them is primarily illustrative and heuristic.[114] But what kind of thinking is eikasia? If the prisoner's original situation, judged by Plato as one of error, were identical with eikasia, then the latter too would have to be a matter of error. That is, eikasia would be mistaking shadows, reflections, and images in general for natural and artificial objects. Not only is this completely unsupported by what Plato says about eikasia, but also, if eikasia is to be an analogue of dianoia, then such reasoning would indict the latter, too, as a type of thinking that mistakes some objects for realities, that is, for Forms. Such reasoning, however, would ruin the role of mathematics in education, leaving Plato without any special reason to emphasize the role of mathematical studies in *Republic* VII. This is sufficient to recommend against identifying eikasia with the prisoner's position and with erroneous belief.

Eikasia is illustrative not of error but of modest success, for it represents or exemplifies any kind of thinking that involves both an awareness of an image as an image and an anticipation, recommended by this awareness, of some direct way of apprehending the originals of which the images are only copies. Eikasia is honest and humble; it does only what it can do and does it well. But at the same time, it recognizes that more can be done, even though it is itself incapable of doing it. In this sense, and only in this sense, is eikasia an apprehension of natural and artificial objects *through their images*. Similarly, mathematical thinking will be an indirect apprehension of the Forms, in a severely restricted sense.[115]

Loosely speaking, both of the two upper divisions of the Line correlate kinds of knowing with the objects of knowing, or the Forms. In a stricter sense, the analogy of the Line and its symmetry breaks down here, for mathematics is an intermediate way of thinking,[116] and hence it is only a qualified kind of knowing.

Thus far I have tried to show that the realm of dream-like belief, the lower two sections of the Line, and the prisoner's original position are all in some sense coextensive. Furthermore, while eikasia is a genuine type of thinking for a "dreamer," it is introduced by Plato for heuristic and illustrative purposes to point beyond belief to a kind of thinking, namely, mathematics, that is soberly realistic and yet optimistic. If this is correct, however, mathematics must fit its billing, both in the Line and, more importantly, in the Cave. But to see whether mathematics succeeds, we have to look first at dialectic, for mathematics will define itself in terms of what it aspires to as well as what it transcends.

Dialectic in *Republic* VI–VII is a process, a way of studying and coming to understand a certain subject matter, namely the Forms. The knowing philosopher of *Republic* V was like a person awake, capable of apprehending both Forms and their copies and wise to the differences between them. The dialectician of *Republic* VI–VII is also awake (see VII, 533c1–3, 534c6–d1), for he is a relentless inquirer into the nature of the Forms who proceeds by abjuring the use of observable properties and objects and confining his attention to Forms. He conjectures, refutes, and ultimately certifies accounts of them until he grasps systematically the defining interrelationships that draw the totality of Forms under the umbrella of the Form of the Good. In part, the perfection and goodness of that totality lie in its unity and harmony. The pinnacle of dialectical study is an unsurpassable grasp of that unity.[117]

What in the Cave captures the spirit of dialectic thus described?[118] What stages of the prisoner's ascent correspond to this pilgrimage of study aimed at higher and higher degrees of knowledge? In the analogy of the Sun, Plato explains what factors must be present in order for vision to occur, and the Cave uses the Sun's visible world

as an analogue for the world of the Forms. Actual vision requires
(1) the eye with its *capacity for* seeing (*he tou horan aisthesis*,
507e6; see 507c, where Plato calls this a *dunamis* and identifies it
with *opsis*; compare VI, 508a11–b1); (2) the visual object[119] with its
capacity to be seen (*he tou horasthai dunamis*, 507e6–508a1; see
also 507c6–8, 509b2–3); (3) light (*phos*, 507e4–508a2); and (4) the
sun, different from (1) and (2) (*helios*, 508a4–b13).[120]

Where in the Cave are all four of these conditions satisfied?
Clearly they are present only when the eyes of the prisoner have
their capacity for vision, when there are objects before them to see,
and when the sun is present, shedding its light on the visible objects.
Such a situation occurs only once the prisoner is habituated to the
bright sunlight outside the cavern, when he views the "animals and
plants" (532b8–9), then the heavenly bodies, first at night, subsequently in daylight, and finally the sun itself (516b1–7; see 532b9,
509b2–3).[121] These are the final stages of visual acclimation, and
they represent degrees of knowledge, knowledge that becomes perfect and complete only when the sun—the Good itself—is known
through an ultimately confirmed and certified definition (534b–c).
These details show Glaucon that what had seemed simple and uniform in the dreaming-waking analogy is in reality complex and
ramified. Knowledge is both an achievement and a process, though
in its ideal and highest form it casts a ladder of dialectic aside in
favor of an enduring synoptic vision of reality (537c1–7).

We have identified those stages of ascent in the Cave that capture
the character of dialectical study. What remains, however, presents
us with a difficulty. For in the Cave, between the original position
of the prisoners and the final perusing of natural objects, heavenly
bodies, and so forth, lie a series of steps, most notably the prisoner's
being shown the puppets, the firelight, and his seeing reflections
and shadows outside the cavern. Aside from the problem of distinguishing discrete steps in the series, how can these several steps
correspond to the one remaining section of the Line, that is, mathematical thinking? How can one cognitive capacity correspond to
many? How can one object correspond to several?[122]

There are those who search for one kind of object of dianoia distinct from the observable objects and the Forms.[123] Such a search is
unnecessary, and its results are false. Plato explicitly says that
mathematicians use and talk about models and diagrams but think

about the Forms (510d5–11a1). Sense-bound believers take observable objects and properties to be realities; mathematicians—themselves not yet directly aware of the Forms—realize that observable
diagrams are but images of something else; what they do and the
theorems they prove are "for the sake of" those other things and
not "for the sake of the image[s] of [them] which they draw" (510d8–
e1).[124] Let us say, therefore, that in a sense mathematical thinking
has two objects; it involves a direct, "clear" apprehension of physical objects and an indirect, "obscure" apprehension of the Forms.
Such thinking is, we might put it, bipolar.[125]

This bipolarity of mathematical thinking is the crucial feature
which makes it so thoroughly suitable for the sort of education Plato
has in mind. Mathematics involves a certain kind of perceptual
awareness and produces, as a result of this awareness, bipolar beliefs. Plato calls this kind of perception "contradictory" (VII, 523b9–
c1), for it presents to the perceiver an observed object or property
under contrary descriptions: a painting as beautiful and as ugly, a
particular weight, for example, 100 pounds, as being heavy and as
being light. The result of such perceptions is a bipolar belief. The
perceiver believes, for example, that having internal angles equal
to two right angles is true of this drawn triangle only insofar as this
triangle is a copy or an image of some other entity, the Triangle
itself. The mathematical believer, that is, realizes that what he sees
is an image of something else, though he as yet has no direct referential access to the original itself.[126]

The Cave forces Plato to distinguish in imago what in reality is
a unity. Because of its rigid dichotomous structure, the image of the
Cave makes it impossible to picture a stage intermediate between
belief and knowledge. There simply is no domain between the cavern and outside. Hence, what represents mathematics in the Cave
are at least two stages, one inside and one outside the cavern, and
these two stages reflect the bipolarity of mathematical beliefs.[127] In
the first stage, the prisoner sees the shadows as shadows of the puppets; in the second, when he emerges from the cave and is forced to
look at shadows and reflections, he experiences these images as images of things he has not yet seen. In a sense, the puppets in the
cavern are the surrogates of the shadows and reflections outside the
cave, and the original shadows turn out to be shadows of "shadows," twice removed from the Forms themselves.[128] What appears

as a sequence of steps in the Cave is in reality a unity, two acts of apprehension with two objects occurring simultaneously as components of one state of thinking.

Mathematical thinking, Plato says, is darker than dialectical knowledge but clearer than belief. It is darker because while it grasps concrete objects as images, it has not yet grasped the Forms by themselves. And it is clearer because while it grasps concrete objects, it strives beyond them by recognizing their derivative status. Mathematics has no unique, single object—with the caveat that its twin objects be considered unique to it; its objects are those of the sense-bound dreamer and the wakeful knower. And in the confines of its single act of awareness[129] it encompasses "a craft of turning" the soul from one domain of objects to another (518d3–4). Mathematical thinking, that is, is the key to the nature of education as "conversion" (*periagoge*, 518d4; see also 521c6) and hence the solution to the inquiry into what genuine learning is.[130]

The account of education or paideia as periagoge (518d4) is just what Plato needs to solve the problems about education engendered by his own theory of Forms. Education, he says, is not like putting vision into blind eyes but rather like turning one's eyes from darkness to light (518b6–d1).[131] Vision is a *dunamis* of the visual organ, the eye, and it is that characteristic arete without which eyes cannot see well. Education is not a matter of putting such a dunamis into an organ that lacks it, for such an education would require conjuring or magic.[132] Rather education is a matter of putting the object or paradigm into the student's ken in order to enable the capacity to become an actuality, and this may involve a change of venue of the student or at least a redirection of attention.

There is a prominent example of Greek educational ritual that incorporated just such an alteration in the student's attention, and Plato may very well have had it in mind.[133] It involved an elaborate relocation of the initiate so that the object of his or her education could appear in a vivid and powerful way. I refer of course to the rites of the greater mysteries, conducted in the month of Boedromion for vast numbers of Athenian initiates (*mystai*) and others,[134] during which the initiates traversed by stages the distance from Athens to Eleusis and culminated their journey with the secret ceremonies in the sanctuary of Demeter and Persephone.[135] These rites were both serious and popular.[136] Complete descriptions of the nine-day ritual are available.[137] They elaborate, in great detail, the various activities of each day and the stages along the route from the Stoa Poikile to the sanctuary in Eleusis and back.[138]

For our purposes, two features of the mysteries are noteworthy. First, the ritual was a full-scale displacement of the *mystes* (initiate) from the scene of his everyday affairs, Athens and its agora, to another location, first to Eleusis, some fourteen miles away, and finally to the temple known as the Telesterion.[139] It was important to the ritual's impact that the locations and the officials of the stages of the ritual—chief among them the Hierophant and the priestess of Demeter—transport the initiate to a different location with a keen sense for the diplacement that was occurring.

Second, the culminating rites are shrouded in secrecy, yet some dim outlines show through the veil. The rites included three elements: "the *dromena* (that which was enacted), the *deiknymena* (the sacred objects that were shown), and the *legomena* (the words that were spoken)."[140] What is important here is that at the climax of their journey, the initiates see and hear things that are extraordinary, separated from all else by secrecy and unconditional privacy. There is extensive debate about these elements—whether they include a sacred pageant of the story of Demeter and Persephone,[141] a "simulated trip of the initiates through the lower world,"[142] a sacred marriage,[143] and sacred objects—perhaps an ear of corn or a phallus.[144] "We cannot be sure of the appearance and nature of the Hiera [namely, the deiknymena], but we can be certain that their revelation . . . formed the climax of the rites."[145]

The Cave illustrates what education is by portraying a reorientation from darkness to light, a light in which the objects of knowledge are first present within the philosopher's ken. This metaphor is unlike the procession of the mystai in many ways, but the two have this much in common. The central feature of education, which the Cave exhibits, is the fact of redirecting attention; in the greater mysteries this fact is exploited, and the end of the process is a sensory confrontation with something utterly remarkable and extraordinary. Platonic philosophical education appreciates the fact that attention to the objects of aspiration and knowledge requires a redirection of one's mental gaze—a redirection as radical and dramatic as the relocation of the initiates culminating with their remarkable vision in the sanctuary of Demeter and Persephone.

DIANOIA makes philosophical education possible but only in part. For philosophy is also a form of eros that requires more than an epistemological bridge; it requires special motivation as well.

At 376a–c, having described the origins of the polis, Socrates and Glaucon agree that in addition to being gentle and high-spirited, the guardian must be a lover of learning (*philomathes*) and a lover of wisdom (*philosophos*), which are of course the same (376b8–9, 376c1–2).[146] Plato seems to treat this desire for learning and wisdom as natural, in the sense that those who have it do not acquire it from others but possess it as part of their basic, natural repertoire of traits and desires. Physical training, for example, must be culti-vated in order to nurture the guardian's sense of spirit and verve, but one must be cautious and see to it that physical training does not so wholly dominate his upbringing that he loses his taste for learning and investigation so that the "love of learning in his soul" becomes "enfeebled, deaf, and blind." "Such a person comes to hate reasoned discussion and the arts" (*misologos kai amousos*, 411d7).[147] Some people come to education without a love of learning and an appetite for knowledge; others without a sense of spirit or without either. Artistic and physical education have these two traits as their concern, and in the end their goal is to cultivate and harmonize both.[148] Education does not, then, create or generate the love of wisdom; rather it stimulates, encourages, and directs an already existing desire.

In the *Meno*, a mere slave boy could arrive at knowledge and presumably desired to learn what he did not know. In the *Phaedo* Plato tells a more exclusive tale, and only the philosopher is said to desire knowledge as an end. Others are bound to physical desires, to the love of prestige, honor, wealth. In *Republic* V, having intro-duced the third wave of paradox, Plato gives an account of who the philosopher is (474b–480) and in Book VI a description of the philo-sophical nature (485a–487a), which he calls several times "the best nature."[149] He says explicitly that one of the purposes of these dis-cussions is to show that whereas some people by nature love wis-dom, others do not, and that this love of wisdom is coincident with the capacity to rule (474b–c).

At 485a–d Plato says that

    1. philosophers are always enamored (*erosin*) of studies

    (*mathematos*) that will reveal to them each being that is
    eternal and that does not wander from generation to
    corruption;

2. they desire not one or more parts of wisdom but rather all of
   it (compare 474c–d); and

3. they love the truth, for truth is most akin to wisdom (see
   489e–90b, 501d).

These three natural desires are the desire for knowledge of all the
Forms and the love of those studies that will facilitate or result in
such knowledge.[150] Clearly, the love of truth is the love of true being,
the Forms (501d, 475e). Moreover, the philosopher by nature desires
to know all of the Forms, for, as Socrates shows Glaucon (474c–
75b), the genuine love of knowledge is not selective and narrow; it
ranges over all the objects of study and knowledge. To be sure, the
argument in behalf of the comprehensiveness of this desire is not
persuasive; neither the principle on which it is based nor the examples invited to support it seem compelling.[151] But Glaucon does
accept the conclusion, as long as Socrates can show how the genuine
philosopher is distinguished from the *philotheamones* who are like
him (475d–e).

    In his treatment of the philosopher in *Republic* V–VII, Plato states
but neither explains nor defends the claim that some but not all
people have this natural desire to know the Forms (474b–c, 491a–b;
compare 493e–94a); indeed he remarks that such a desire is rather
rare. Second, he says that most of those who have such a natural
gift are corrupted by bad education and environment (490e–96a);[152]
this leaves a small remainder who are dedicated to their love for
knowledge (496a–97a; compare 494a, 499b, 503b) and available to
serve as rulers of the ideal polis (499b–c). Third, the desire for
knowledge is a passion of this uncorrupted remainder, a longing that
in turn becomes a desire to imitate the eternal, unchanging order
that they gaze upon and admire. "The lover of wisdom, associating
with the divine order, will himself become orderly and divine in the
measure permitted to man" (500b–d). Fourth, the philosopher must
subsequently be compelled to serve the polis, to become a craftsman
of public virtue and not merely a person concerned with himself
(500d; compare 517c–d, 519c–21b). For this purpose, compulsion is
necessary, for such people are by nature lovers of wisdom and not
lovers of rule (521b).

This brief sketch permits us to see first that the desire for knowledge is not common to everyone, although it is a matter of nature. Only a small group is naturally inclined to seek comprehensive knowledge. Second, not all members of even this group will succeed. They require both the proper education and a favorable social environment in order to work at satisfying their natural desire to learn. Third, they also have a natural desire to know about the Forms, although even they will not realize this of course until they are suitably educated.[153]

In the *Republic* Plato says these things, but he does not satisfactorily explain them. Many questions remain unanswered. For example, not all souls are equally capable of recollection, because not all have a natural desire for essential knowledge. But Plato never explains in the *Republic* why this is so. Indeed, if all souls always have knowledge of the Forms, in some sense, then learning as recollection would seem to be equally possible for all.

Furthermore, we have thus far seen that a nonphilosopher with a philosophical nature will desire knowledge only if he does not think that he already has it, and he will desire knowledge of the Forms only if he is systematically confused by sense experience in such a way that his desire is directed away from sense objects altogether.[154] But one might demur. This confusion may lead to a redirection of attention, of one's mental gaze and one's epistemic search, but why think of it as redirecting also the nonphilosopher's desire? All along he may want knowledge, and knowledge may be restricted to Forms, but certainly the philosopher need not want the Forms.

Moreover, even within the philosopher's own affective life, one of the goals of genuine education is harmony among his competing desires and traits. The vehicle Plato uses to convey this goal of harmony or coordination is an image (eikon) of the human soul as a congeries of a many-headed, multiform beast,[155] a lion, and a man, hidden in the form of a man. It is an image, of course, of the threefold soul, introduced and elaborated in *Republic* IV. The soul or person is best and most beautiful when most just, when the beastlike parts—the multiform beast and the lion—are ruled by the human or divine part, so that the person values studies that lead to moderation and order, cultivates "harmony in his body" (591d), and acquires wealth and accepts honors with a sense of inner harmony.

The soul has three types of desire and three types of pleasure, and the best soul coordinates these for the purpose of inner peace and harmony. One part is dedicated to the acquisition of money, profit, and the satisfaction of diverse physical desires; the second is devoted to victory and honor, while the third loves study and learning.[156] In the best soul, the philosophical soul, the other desires—for wealth and honor—do exist, but their influence is directed by and subordinated to the love of learning. When the desires for wealth and honor are directed by knowledge and reason, they will maximize their satisfaction and the attendant pleasures, for each will reap its own reward without dissension and strife.[157] The reason for this result is that only the soul governed by rational desire knows what is just, moderate, and so on; it desires learning, but at the same time desires most of all to exemplify what is just and good. Hence, only if rational desires govern the soul are the other desires granted their own satisfactions, as long as they do not impede or overwhelm one another. Inner harmony, order, balance, satisfaction—these are possible only if rational desire is dominant, and then they are guaranteed. In this sense, the soul of the best man, of the philosopher, is the freest and the least servile.[158]

When reason and the love of wisdom direct one's conduct and shape one's character, the result is harmony, peace, and pleasure—in a word, eudaimonia. Plato's account of competing desires and psychic harmony shows how much he respects the complexity of incarnate existence. Moreover, Plato appreciates a further type of desire, one that seems less malleable and more uncontrollable, and this shows just how deep that respect is. Plato distinguishes desires such as that for bread, which are necessary, from other desires, such as the desire for strange foods and sex, which are unnecessary.[159] The distinguishing characteristics, presumably, are that the necessary desires contribute importantly to one's life, health, and well-being, while the unnecessary ones are harmful to body and soul. Among these latter desires, moreover, are some that Plato calls "lawless" (*paranomoi*, 571b5), and it is just these lawless desires that dominate in the tyrant and drive him mad. If we are to appreciate the deepest forces that genuine education and psychological nurturing must overcome, we must understand the nature and influence of these antinomian desires,[160] which are as natural and common as the desire for learning and wisdom with which they compete. Indeed, Plato shows that when praising the tyrant, who is ruled by these passions, one is praising them. It is hardly surprising that the love of wisdom is so easily overwhelmed or corrupted in existing poleis—given the character and frequency of these drives.

What are these antinomian desires? Socrates refers to them as a "dangerous, wild, and lawless kind of desires in each of us . . . [which] becomes most manifest in our sleep" (572b4–7). Earlier he had described these same desires as the result of an absolutely uncontrolled situation when the reasonable, ruling set of desires are inoperative and the wellspring of base desires leads to attempted sexual relations with one's mother, a man, a god, or a beast, or to murder, or to any kind of shameless deed.[161] Driven by such desires, one becomes frenzied and mad, the slave of Eros.[162] Such a man is the tyrant. He is uninhibited and insatiable, driven to new desires and further ones, far beyond his means, sacrificing anyone and anything to increase his satisfaction. No terrible murder, no theft, no shameful act is beyond him. He is without friends and wholly enslaved, the unfree man, for he is under the control of desires that are utterly antinomian and antisocial and perhaps antihuman—the desire to do what is disgusting and shameful—to commit sodomy, to spill blood, to eat impure foods, and so on.[163]

Plato is pointing to a dark and foreboding feature of human nature, a wellspring of what is terrifying and awful in the extreme,[164] a reservoir of desires and pleasures "probably present in everyone . . . [which] are held in check by the nomoi and by the better desires with the help of reason. In a few men they have been eliminated or a small number are left in a weakened state, while in others they are stronger and more numerous."[165] Surely it is those dominated by such desires whom Plato calls, in the myth of Er, the "incurably wicked" (615e) and whose permanent posthumous reward is to be dropped into Tartarus.[166]

For Plato the philosophical life, facilitated by rational inquiry and education, must cope with the complexity of human desire and in the end with the threatening power of these antinomian desires. By noticing these features of Plato's account, we add to our appreciation of his recognition that the philosopher must live in the world, in history, in society and in the polis.

AT 473e Socrates introduces the greatest of the three waves of par-

adox, the "smallest change which would enable a city" to become
a just polis: "Neither cities nor the human race will have respite
from evil unless philosophers are kings in the cities or those whom
we now call kings and rulers genuinely and adequately become philosophers, until, that is, political power and philosophy come together" (473c11–d3). Socrates says that this desideratum is "highly
paradoxical" (*polu para doxan*, 473e4). For this reason, he does take
time, via Adeimantus' objection and the image of the ship's pilot,[167]
to explain why Athenians would believe Socrates' claim to be so
surprising but why they ought not to do so. On the one hand, there
is a straightforward sense in which philosophers might be thought
to be so vicious, wicked, useless, and odd that they would be the
least, not the most, desirable rulers. But, on the other hand, although philosophers might be widely demeaned in the public eye,
it is not at all surprising that Plato would think of them as the ideal
rulers.

I have called attention to a thread of paradox that runs through
the *Republic*, and one way of unraveling it begins here, with the
proposal that political power and philosophy be united in the same
individuals. The paradox concerns the way in which Plato wants
to hold together an ecstatic ideal of the life of study and knowledge
with an ideal of political rule, an ideal of eternity with one of
history, of otherworldly bliss with this-worldly activity. The paradoxical effort to hold these poles together can be seen in the present
proposal.

Here—as often in the *Republic*[168]—Plato uses the term *basileus*
for the *archon*, or ruler; his proposal, then, is that philosophers
become *basileis* (kings). In Athens the title "basileus," of ancient
origin, still remained in force in the fifth and fourth centuries. By
then, however, his duties were largely religious, the basileus being
but one of nine archons. In the *Athenaion Politeia* (57.2) we are told
that the basileus' legal functions included introducing into court
cases concerned with impiety and disputes about the duty to perform a sacrifice or the right to claim a priesthood.[169] Both Andokides
and Socrates, for example, are brought to court by the basileus.[170]
In addition, the basileus first heard, usually from the relatives of a
person who had been killed, the charge of homicide and then pre-
sided over the case at the Prytaneion, together with the heads of
the four ancient tribes of Athens, the *phylobasileis*.[171] The basileus'

legal functions, then, were no less religious than were his strictly
"priestly" functions, such as being responsible for organizing almost
all state sacrifices, including the mysteries, the Lenaia, and the Anthesteria.[172] In Sparta, too, the kings had priestly as well as political,
legal, and military functions. In a sense, as Burkert nicely puts it,
the Greek polis was a "sacrificial community" with a basileus or
archon as the chief priest or religious official.[173]

When Plato comes to think that the position of archon or basileus
ought to be occupied only by a philosopher, he does so within this
context. Whereas others may find the identification beyond credi-
bility because philosophers are often popularly viewed as wicked,
useless, and odd, Plato may find the proposal remarkable because
of his—and Socrates'—unusual conception of philosophical piety.
That is, the traditional basileus was the central figure in a sacrificial
system, organized around festivals and an elaborate sacrificial calendar, supplemented by personal acts of devotion and petition. The
novelty in Plato's proposal is *not* that the political leader should be
a religious official, for that identification was common. It is rather
that the precise type of religious figure be a mystes, a devotee of
ecstatic rites, a philosopher.[174] In the earlier dialogues, from the
Euthyphro and *Protagoras* and beyond, Plato had come to be opposed to the polis tradition with its oracles, sacrifices, and so on.
How paradoxical that tradition and Athenian practice must have
seemed to Plato, then, when he came to realize the necessity of
combining his beloved philosophy with political rule. There would
have to be weighty reasons, one would think, that the ancient office
of archon basileus should be filled not by lot but rather by expertise,
the expertise of the least likely person, the ecstatic philosopher.

In the *Republic* Plato says a great deal about who such a philosopher is. To be a good ruler and guardian, a philosopher must be
both gentle and high-spirited;[175] such individuals must love wisdom,
of course,[176] specifically knowledge of the Forms.[177] Hence, they must
love the truth, learning, and the pleasures of the soul; they must be
moderate and not love money or physical pleasures.[178] The philosopher is courageous and quick, a person with a good memory and
a capacity to learn without difficulty.[179] Philosophers are, Plato says,
"divine and like daimones," people whom after death shall be worshiped and cared for like daimones.[180]

Given such a character, however, and especially his over-riding love of knowledge, why should a philosopher engage in political activity? Why in particular should a philosopher be willing, if not eager, to rule the polis? Clearly this question is ever-present in Plato's mind, for he returns to it directly and indirectly several times in the course of the *Republic*. Let us begin with a passage near the close of *Republic* VII. Having concluded the account of mathematical studies and dialectic, Plato, in an epilogue, produces a timetable. The philosopher must return to the cave twice, once between the ages of thirty-five and fifty and again periodically after the age of fifty. During the former period, the philosophers are "compelled to rule on matters of war and the government of youth, so that they shall not be inferior to others in experience" (539e3–5). After fifty, they return to their studies in order finally to look upon the Good itself "using it as a model to order the city, individuals, and themselves for the rest of their lives each in turn. They will spend much of their time with philosophy, but, when their turn comes, they must each labor and rule in public affairs, and they will do this not as something splendid but as a duty" (540a9–b5). In both cases, then, the philosopher engages in political affairs, but he does not willingly or eagerly return to the cave; he is forced or required to return and to engage in activity for the sake of the polis. There is no question that Plato's language reflects this sense of compulsion, duty, or necessity (*anankasteioi*, 539e3; *anankaion*, 540b4).

In the description of the cave and the philosopher's attitude when once free of it, Socrates says that he would "go through any suffering rather than share [the prisoner's] opinions and live as they do" (516d6–7). Already at this stage, then, we might have wondered what could force the genuine philosopher to return to the cave to be ridiculed and perhaps even killed. Socrates tells us that "he who is to act intelligently in public or in private must see [the Good],"[181] but we might still not understand why, having seen the Good, one is compelled to act in the cave at all. Indeed, as Socrates points out, it is quite natural for philosophers to be "unwilling to occupy themselves with human affairs." The implication of the image of the cave is that philosophers will be better able to satisfy their love for knowledge in study and hence will be happier in cognitive ascent and ecstatic contemplation outside the cave than in any political activity within it. To return to the cave, therefore, the real philosopher must be compelled or forced or bound.

How Plato accounts for this necessity is a complex matter. On the one hand, the philosopher should fear lest the polis be ruled by inferior people so that he would be required to live in a society that would inhibit his philosophical enterprise. The portrait of genuine philosophers surviving in unjust societies is not a pretty one:

> like a man who has fallen among wild beasts, being unwilling to join in wrongdoing and not being strong enough to oppose the general savagery alone, for he would perish, useless both to himself and to others, before he could benefit either his country or his friends, of no use to himself or anyone else; taking all this into account he keeps quiet and minds his own business. Like a man who takes refuge under a small wall from a storm of dust or hail driven by a wind, and seeing other men filled with lawlessness, the philosopher is satisfied if he can somehow live his present life free from injustice and impious deeds, and depart from it with a beautiful hope, blameless and content. (496d–e)

As long as the philosopher is alive, he can exist only poorly and in an unfulfilled way outside the perfect polis—like a man living among savage beasts or someone seeking refuge from a driving storm. What is needed is to save potential philosophers from corruption and the "education of the mob," and at the same time to recognize the philosopher's expertise as a ruler. Philosophical growth and development require a perfect polis in which to flourish, a polis with the best nomoi and the best forms of training and paideia.[182] Such a city will save potential philosophers from corruption, while arguments such as Socrates' will persuade people that genuine philosophers—not the poor, sophistical imitations—ought to rule. For philosophical rule is the solution to both problems, that of the city's well-being and that of the philosopher's salvation.

On the other hand, in the ideal polis the philosopher must return to the cave and rule because the nomoi require it, and they do so because their goal is the best polis, one in which eudaimonia is maximized for all, where happiness is spread throughout the community. The nomoi require philosophers to rule, that is, because by so doing they advantage both the philosophers and the rest of the polis.[183] It is better for the others because in virtue of philosophical rule the polis will be more stable and their lives will be more orderly

and rational than under any other regime. Plato puts this beauti-
fully, at the end of *Republic* IX, when he says that more passionate
citizens, driven by physical and monetary desires, can

> be ruled by a principle similar to that which rules the best man
> [by being] enslaved to the best man, who has a divine ruler
> within himself. It is not to harm the slave that we believe he
> must be ruled . . . but because it is better for everyone to be
> ruled by divine intelligence.[184] It is best that he should have this
> within himself, but if he has not, then it must be imposed from
> outside, so that, as far as possible, we should all be alike and
> *philoi* and directed by the same thing. (590c–d)[185]

Nonphilosophers benefit from philosophical rule by living more orderly, rational lives even if the ordering comes to them indirectly
and mediated through the philosophical rulers. It is surprising but
nonetheless true that the slave to reason is a genuinely free man.[186]

In the just polis the nomoi are already given, as it were, but in a
sense the philosopher's mandate to rule is nonetheless subject to his
acceptance.[187] He could, after all, choose to refuse rule. Why ought
he not do so? Why ought he to accept the nomoi of the best polis—
as Socrates, Glaucon, and Adeimantus, its "legislators," have fixed
them? Why should he not simply reject the decisions of these meta-
legislators? The answer is hardly surprising. Once he has contemplated the Good, the philosopher is most capable of distinguishing
the good from its contrary. He is aware of what is good for the polis
and for all others in it. To refuse to rule is to diminish their well-
being, to sever their tie with rational order, political stability, and
unity. But to be as perfect as possible requires of him that he strive
for wisdom while not doing injustice to others.[188] To diminish their
good even if to enhance his own is to commit injustice. It is also to
oppose the natural desire within him to produce exemplifications
of what is good and beautiful insofar as he is capable of so doing.[189]
In the end, then, the philosopher will destroy the best polis if he
refuses to rule it, and to do so would be to participate in his own
ruin.

In the course of the *Republic*, Plato thinks often and hard about
the place of the philosopher in the polis and in different sorts of
poleis. For although his final philosophical-religious goal transcends
history and politics, the philosopher lives in history and in the world

of the polis. Philosophical knowledge may be knowledge of the Forms, but its object is also a model of rational order for worldly existence.

AGAINST this account of the *Republic*, the myth of Er is no weak or messy ending but rather the dialogue's natural outcome. If we recall Adeimantus' attack on the eschatological rewards and punishments ascribed to Musaeus and his son (363c–e), the myth of Er is no surprise. For it does not reiterate posthumous reward and punishment, even though it could do so—in the mode of the *Phaedo*— by focusing on the splendors of eternal wisdom. Instead Er's tale concerns not everlasting bliss as much as intercarnate passage. The story of the soul's passage from one life to another, of the moral and cognitive dimension of reincarnation, is a story about initiation. Reading the *Republic*'s conclusion, the typical Athenian of 370 could hardly have failed to see the allusion to Eleusis. Adeimantus lampoons the bogus initiations and purifications that absolve with gimmicks and shams. Er tells the tale of genuine initiation that succeeds or fails depending upon the soul's worldly achievements. Reincarnation is a successful initiation to a new life when it capitalizes on the soul's prior cognitive or philosophical initiation. In response to Adeimantus, Er eschews alternate eschatologies in favor of a new conception of initiation, a transcendent initiation that builds on the achievement of genuine worldly initiation.[190] For the heroes of Er's tale are none other than the philosopher-rulers, the heroes of the remainder of the *Republic*, and the source of their heroism is none other than paideia itself.

Before we look at Er's tale, let us consider its form. In the *Gorgias* and *Phaedo*, the mythoi are primarily eschatological, and the dominant style of Platonic investigation is dialogical argumentation or inquiry. There, it seems likely, Plato reverts naturally to the traditional genre of religious representation, mythos, in order to portray posthumous reward and punishment. Philosophy as ecstatic rite may take the shape of rational inquiry, but its results are beyond its grasp. The philosopher aspires to wisdom; the poet portrays its fruits. In the *Symposium* Plato's centerpiece is a tale of the priestess Diotima, but its form is that of a typical elenchos. Against this background, the *Republic* presents a problematic profile, for on the

role and character of mythoi or stories, the *Republic* is more complex and variegated than its predecessors.

First, if *Republic* II–III is to be our guide, then Plato calls for a
revision of the content of stories but not their total rejection (compare 377a4–5).[191] And this recommendation, featured in the paideia
for the young guardians, seems to apply as well to the *Republic*
itself. For throughout the text Plato uses eikones or images that are
sometimes stories, sometimes metaphors, sometimes analogies, and
sometimes—at least once—myths.[192] At 614b2 the tale of Er is introduced by the Homeric term *apologos* and is called a mythos at
621b8. Introducing the Line, Socrates calls it and the Sun similes
(*homoioteta*, 509c6; compare *hosper*, d6).[193] He also identifies the
objects of the Line's lowest section as eikones (509e1), which he
then explains: "By images I mean shadows in the first instance, then
the reflections in water and all those on close-packed, smooth, and
bright materials, and all that sort of thing" (509e1–10a3).

I do not think we can confidently press this variety into a simple,
clear scheme. Literary eikones seem to be derivative from physical
ones—shadows and reflections; they are narrative descriptions or
depictions of some set of events—the story of the ship's pilot and
the cave's prisoners. Plato uses them as metaphors, and in the case
of the Cave they are intended to clarify relationships, practices, and
so on and also to constitute the teaching of what those relationships
are. In both cases, if the later discussion in the *Sophist* is reliable,
the eikones must be accurate representations of their model;[194] they
are other than but like what they imitate (*Sophist* 235d).

Mythoi differ from eikones. They are literary tales, but they do
not describe a mundane event and are not intended to complement
argument or analysis. Instead mythoi are the efforts of poets to
convey what can be conveyed in no other way, for educational and
other purposes. Er's tale is not only a good example of a mythos,
but it even incorporates a device that highlights its exclusive role.
It records the fact that Er alone was "forbidden to drink of the
water" that leads all reincarnated souls to Forgetfulness. In general,
Plato uses myth as a literary strategy for communicating the otherwise impenetrable; here he uses it for that purpose and as a vehicle
for salvation. If one believes that the soul is immortal and that it
undergoes reincarnation according to the way Er portrays it, then

the story "could save us if we believe it" (621c1). Like other myths, Er's tale is a device for revelation and salvation.

This distinguishes the *Republic* from the *Gorgias* and the *Phaedo*. If anything, their eschatological myths function in the way Adeimantus criticizes. Furthermore, they eulogize the otherworldly goal of philosophical aspiration, to become divine to the degree humanly possible. In the *Republic*, as we have emphasized, that otherworldliness is mitigated by a serious confrontation with historical context and the philosopher's worldly career. Hence, at the dialogue's conclusion, Plato employs no ordinary eschatological myth to picture everlasting bliss. Rather he invents or designs a tale of interim passage that neatly emphasizes the this-worldly rewards of virtue and wisdom but does so within the context of a belief in the soul's immortality.[195]

The precise sources of the myth are beyond our grasp. There are doubtless Orphic, Pythagorean, and traditional elements.[196] Like the *Phaedo* myth, it has a cosmological component that we can ignore.[197] The real point of the myth and our special concern is the role that the discarnate soul plays in the determination of its future and the influence of its past life on the choice it makes. Plato has made it clear, at least since the *Phaedo*, that a genuine philosophical life will yield an ultimate reward, the attainment of divine status. What he shows in the myth of Er is that such a life also has interim rewards; wisdom and the desire for it put the postcarnate soul in a position to choose best its next incarnation and also provide that soul with the finest interim existence.

According to the myth, the soul's postcarnate journey takes more than a thousand years, the bulk of that time spent in heaven or Hades, depending upon the judgment of the soul's most recent life. Plato tells us little of what takes place in heaven, the locale of the just souls, who return from their period above clean (*katharas*, 614e1), having benefited from the "incredibly beautiful sights they had seen" (615a4) and having been rewarded tenfold for their justice and piety in the most recent life.[198] The rewards for piety toward the gods and parents were even greater (615c2–4). Plato does take time to display the suffering of the tyrant in an effort to underline the *Republic*'s attack on injustice, but he only hints at the posthumous bliss of the philosopher.

Thirteen days after death, following a lengthy journey, the souls arrive at the spindle of Necessity, where—under the guidance of a messenger of Lachesis[199]—they are set to choosing their next incarnation, "another mortal round that will bring death" (617d7). By lot they are assigned a place in the order of choosing; all daimones and forms of life are available to all the souls; the responsibility is the chooser's, not god's (e4–5). Before them are placed samples of lives—animal and human, tyrannies, athletes, and so on—and they are instructed not to be careless or incautious, for the early choosers can err and the late ones can still make wise choices. Er relates that the choices are quite a spectacle, "pitiful, ridiculous, and surprising" (620a1–2). Generally, the choice depends upon the character of their previous life, some seeking to avoid calamities or anxiety, some seeking to find the peace they never had. After the choice is made, each soul is provided with the appropriate daimon, and its choice is confirmed. And prior to being carried upward to birth, they must drink from the river of Lethe, forgetting all that has taken place.

In the course of this account, Plato emphasizes that one's life, in any given incarnation, depends upon the choice made between lives, and that choice is not a matter of divine compulsion. It is up to the soul in question, constituted by its past experiences, attitudes, desires, and so on, to choose the life it wants. Plato is not claiming that such a choice is spontaneous; he is recognizing the role of character in shaping the decision of what type of person one will be. And the choice, while it is the soul's, is not made during the life in question. The reason for this, I imagine, is that Plato takes much of one's life—what species one is, one's city, one's family, status, and so on—as being *given* and not the result of choice. What the myth says is that if a soul's existence is considered as disjointed periods, the overall character of that existence, through these periods, is unified. The given features of any period are not determined by an external factor, for example the divine, but rather by the soul itself, by its character and the choice that character makes.

In the course of this general account, Plato always has his attention on the just man, the philosopher, and at one point he interrupts the tale to remind Glaucon of the special rewards of philosophy: "Therefore if someone, whenever he comes to live here on earth, pursues philosophy soundly, and the lot of the choice does not place him among the last, according to the message received from the other world not only is he likely to be happy [*eudaimon*] here but also his journey from here to there and back again will not be along the rough path below the earth, but rather along the smooth and heavenly [route]" (619d7–e5). Since Plato makes so much of the fact that those with late and early choices have the same opportunities and responsibilities, one wonders why he enters the caveat about the lot. Nonetheless, the gist of his observation is clear, that philosophy makes one eudaimon in the soul's next life and also guarantees a long period of heavenly bliss between lives. The reason for this confidence is that the philosopher is devoted to learning and to the knowledge that will enable him to distinguish the good from the bad life because he will know what justice is, what contributes to it, and why it is good for the soul to be just. Hence, such knowledge enables the soul to make a rational choice which is the best choice possible for itself and its well-being (618b6–19b1). In the end, the external rewards of philosophy and virtue are not disassociated from their internal rewards. Because the philosophical soul knows what is best, it thrives, and it continues to thrive because it knows what is best.[200]

As the *Republic* ends, then, it affirms its central theme, that philosophy is doubly beneficial, for it is aimed at transcendence at the same time that it is historically situated. Justice and wisdom (621c5) make the philosopher's life richer and fuller; they allow his fellow citizens to flourish as well. But beyond that, such a life is part of a process of ongoing flourishing for the immortal soul, whose aim is blissful detachment and divinity. The *Republic* seeks to return to the worldly involvement of Greek piety without abandoning the ecstatic character of rational inquiry. The myth of Er portrays the interweaving of these efforts.

ADVOCATING immortality and reincarnation, Plato engages in a critique of the Delphic theology and the polis tradition. In the *Republic*, that critique has become diversified, including a revision of traditional mythology, the ancient conception of the gods, the character of paideia, the character and role of tragic poetry, and more. The key word here is "revision." Plato retains as much as he rejects, but he does so in a new form. Within the context of the political and historical developments of the 370s, Plato must not be seen simply as an eccentric or as an unqualified opponent of Athens. He is instead a revisionary, an advocate of change who will not pander to Athenian self-esteem and who seeks a new political vision for his novel conception of piety.

That new political vision involves a critique of Athenian democracy and the affirmation of a more suitable political setting for rational piety. The critique of democracy is famous, and we need not review its details. But clearly Plato does think Athenian democracy a poor political setting for the flourishing of philosophical transcendence. One might have thought otherwise, for at least the democracy permitted philosophical discussion and debate.[201] Arguably the intellectual was freer in Athens than he was in any other Greek polis.[202] Why, then, is democracy so unappealing to Plato in the *Republic*?

According to Plato, the centerpieces of democracy are its freedom, diversity, and equality. The citizens of a democracy are free; "the *polis* becomes full of liberty and freedom of speech, and in it one can do anything one pleases" (557b4–6). The democratic polis is full of many kinds of people, with various skills, interests, desires, and goals. It is tolerant, open, full of praise for those who pander to desire. "It distributes a kind of equality to the equal and unequal alike" (558c5–6). That is, it gives a uniform distribution of public responsibility, decision making, and praise to everyone, whether skilled or not, well-intentioned or not.

The same features are present, too, in the paradigmatic democratic man. He is a mass of indulgent, unnecessary desires and pleasures, each dominant momentarily so that one day he drinks heavily, another he diets, another he engages in vigorous physical exercise, another he "pretends to spend his time on philosophy" (561d2). As Socrates puts it, "there is no plan or discipline in his life" (d5–6). Such a man calls himself free, joyful, and happy. Socrates describes the soul of democratic man as a citadel under attack by profligate desires that are victorious because the soul is unprotected by learning, fine pursuits, and true reasoning (560b8–9). In place of order and the primacy of at least some necessary desire, say for food or wealth, these profligate, indulgent desires introduce "insolence [*hubris*] and anarchy and extravagance and shamelessness" (560e2–3). These they camouflage, calling insolence "good training" (*eupaideusia*), anarchy "freedom," extravagance "generosity," and shamelessness (*anaideia*) "courage" (*andreia*). Socrates describes this process as one of purification: these rampant desires "purify by splendid rites the soul of the one who is victimized by them and initiated" (560d8–e2). If lucky and not utterly lost to this "Bacchic" frenzy,[203] an older democrat might readmit some of his more sober desires but still only structure his life according to one at a time, never forging an overall plan for his life.

Both individually and jointly, then, democracy encourages an anarchic display of desire and interest, a display without order or organization. There is no overarching goal, no recognition of what is best for human life in general. Just as in the democratic polis there is no appreciation of rational expertise concerning the good for man, just as all are given equal opportunity to rule and equal responsibility, and just as all forms of speech are tolerated, so in the democratic man, rational desire gives way to a crowd of conflicting desires, each gaining temporary ascendancy, with no rule, no order, no restraint, and no sense of limit or direction. The true democrat is purified—of order and reason; he is *initiated*—into a state of unrestrained indulgence; he is a *Bacchic*—devoted to a loss of self in a sea of disintegrated desire. Ironically, Plato uses his favored religious vocabulary to indict the Athenian ideal. In short, the democrat is free of his own self; in a democracy, equality is earned at the cost of coherence, order, and integrity.

It is no surprise that Plato finds his own form of Socratic piety, rational inquiry as a rite of philosophical transcendence, out of place in a democracy and hence out of place in fourth-century Athens. There it must struggle against tremendous odds; it can succeed only in dark corners—like a victim trying to avoid the winds and rain of a raging storm.[204] Genuine learning and a love for wisdom are threatened and assaulted in a democracy. Philosophy's ecstatic content, its capacity to purify its initiates and to transport them to a type of Bacchic displacement that is pure and clean—all this is corrupted in a democracy. The crowd of profligate desires that overwhelm everything make purification and initiation ugly and distorted. This is Plato's point when he uses the language of Bacchic rites and purifications to describe the effects of the lower desires as they overcome the soul. The result is not real initiation or real purification; it is corrupt initiation and contaminated purification.

At best, as he puts it, the democrat gives us the pretense of philosophy and not the genuine article.

As the 370s come to a close, the Platonic critique reaches a new stage. It has become deeper and bolder than before, and justifiably so. In earlier dialogues Plato had opposed his own ideal to that of Athens and defended the ideal of philosophical ecstasy vigorously. In the *Republic*, the battle is taken into the streets. For Plato can no longer afford the luxury of debating the virtues of otherworldly transcendence, while allowing the devotees of honor, wealth, and power to rule the polis. The philosopher may ultimately abandon the polis for a finer world, but in this life and in many others before and after, he must live in the polis, and the necessity of historical existence forces the issue. The confrontation between philosophy and democracy, Delphic theology, and the polis tradition makes the *Republic* a work of great dramatic intensity as well as one of subtle, moving philosophical depth. Some commentators are willing to acknowledge Platonic realism as emerging only much later, in the *Laws*, but they are wrong. The power and poignancy of realism are already present in the *Republic*.

CHAPTER SIX

PHILOSOPHICAL MADNESS
AND POLITICAL RHETORIC
IN THE *PHAEDRUS*

The Platonic dialogues are sufficient testimony by themselves that in the fourth century the terminology for verbal crafts (*technai*) was not yet firmly fixed. Not only confusion but also appropriation was possible. Sophists, rhapsodes, orators, poets, rhetoricians, philosophers—all these and more claimed territorial rights, but the boundaries shift and slide. Individuals moved from one domain to another, clinging to or changing titles as they or others saw fit. Similar developments occurred in the area of religious practice and ritual character; language was malleable, easy to adopt, to adapt, to challenge and to defend. The Platonic dialogues written during the 380s and 370s plot some of these movements and expose some of these conflicts, always reflecting on Plato's developing conception of philosophical inquiry and his need to carve out a special domain, strategy, and enterprise for that title to denominate.

These tasks have already burdened Plato—in the *Gorgias, Phaedo, Symposium*, and especially in the *Republic*. And even earlier we noticed how Plato, in his portrayals of Socrates—say, in the *Ion* and *Euthydemus*—makes an effort to compare and contrast Socrates against others with whom he might easily be confused. This matter of identification becomes a Platonic obsession, a fear of having one's identity stolen before it is firmly or clearly constructed, a phobia about preemptive impersonation and de-personation. The *Phaedrus* marks an important stage in this process of characterizing philosophy, defining its religious aspects, and distinguishing it from other cognitive crafts and noncognitive endeavors—from rhetoric and poetry to prophecy and mundane madness.[1]

The *Phaedrus* was probably written shortly after the *Republic* but before Plato's second Sicilian visit. Hackforth suggests 370, and that seems right.[2] If the *Republic* reflects the flux of the 370s that led to the Battle of Leuctra and the Theban victory, the *Phaedrus* may be Plato's first real response to that event and, in a way, to the new prominence of Isocrates and his school.[3] Plato already—in the *Meno*, *Protagoras*, and *Gorgias*—shows his opposition to Isocrates, among others. But commentators are wise to notice in the *Phaedrus* a renewal of that confrontation and this time at a moment of even more serious defeat for Athens and for Isocrates' Panhellenic dreams.[4] For many Athenians 370 was probably a year of shame and disgrace, when the old defeats coalesced with the new, generating a sense of monumental despair. But it was otherwise for Plato, and the *Phaedrus* is one record of his mood and of his response to the recent turmoil.

Many of the *Phaedrus*' themes converge on the historical situation of Athens and Sparta, and the emergence of Thebes. One of those themes is rhetoric and its relation to philosophy; another is the nature of philosophy with its cognitive and noncognitive components; a third is the nature of eros, and a fourth is the types and roles of *mania*, of madness. From madness we can start to trace the special configuration of the Platonic posture toward Athens and Thebes at that moment when the tide of fourth-century Greek history was decisively turning.

Plato's primary political and religious criticism focuses on Athens, but in 370 the historical spotlight has turned to Thebes and Epaminondas, "the dominating figure of his age in the judgment both of contemporaries and of posterity."[5] Xenophon, for example, knew and loathed Epaminondas and Thebes; his *Hellenica* bears his testimony, largely by omission,[6] occasionally explicitly. For his own exile to Corinth can be traced to Leuctra and the Spartan defeat.[7] And Xenophon's hatred is doubtless not misplaced. If the inscription on the statue of Epaminondas on the Theban acropolis is any clue, the liberation of Missenia and the foundation of Megalopolis in Arkadia were widely revered as his greatest achievements, at the cost to Sparta most of all.[8]

The details of Athenian attitudes to Leuctra and its aftermath are easy to surmise but hard to document. Forced into alliance with Sparta and nearly all other Peloponnesian cities, Athens spent much of its military time for a decade defending its Peloponnesian allies against Thebes and seeking to reestablish itself in the Aegean. As Davies puts it, nearly two decades were to pass before one could observe "a major though subtle shift in public opinion away from the heroics of power."[9] Appearances suggested that Athens acted out of a fragile posture of fear, imperialist ambition, and faded hopes of yesteryear. Thebes and Epaminondas were the enemy, the threat, and the objects of fear, but it was the hunger for power that had really sent Athens scurrying to its traditional enemies for aid and alliance.[10] Clearly, after Leuctra, the crucial Athenian decision concerned its alliances and with whom it should side,[11] and it was no small victory for Callistratus, together with Chabrias and Iphicrates, to have lobbied effectively for the Spartan alliance.[12] Perhaps their victory is sufficient for us to infer the existence of another outburst of Athenian hubris and nostalgia, but it is not remarkable that Pausanias records greater honor bestowed upon Timotheus, their exiled opponent, than upon them.[13] Xenophon as usual is not helpful about the Athenian situation; we are left with little on which to base an account.

Among the characteristics appropriate to a description of Athens in the 370s and to Athenian leadership, self-indulgence and over-grasping desire for power are surely two. The portrait of the tyrant as the man gone mad is a sketch of Athenian and Greek mental illness. And even if Athenians happened to be blind to their own situation, they should have learned from what had happened to Thebes. Against this background of political excess, the *Phaedrus* is Plato's testimony to the possibility of recovery by transformation. Its lesson is that salvation means not becoming less mad but rather becoming *more* mad, only differently so.

Two millennia later a great satirist will portray English society as exalting the virtues of madness and as seeking its leadership in Bedlam.[14] Swift's barbs are aimed at Catholicism, at reason and natural philosophy, and at contemporary modes of literary discourse. His famous "Digression on Madness" in *A Tale of a Tub* is really neither a digression nor about madness. Rather, Swift uses madness as a vehicle for his satirical dismembering of English religion, politics, and culture. Plato's treatment of madness in the *Phaedrus* differs in fundamental ways. Plato is serious, not satirical, and although he is critical, he does not use the concept of madness as an indirect device for his criticism. Plato is intensely interested in *mania*; he endorses philosophy as the highest form of madness, the most genuine form of rhetoric, the truest expression of *eros*. Having defended philosophy as the best vehicle for political rule and as the highest form of piety, Plato finds himself in the midst of a heroic, yet seemingly paradoxical enterprise—to place madness at the heart of Greek life and indeed at the heart of human living. Plato can be playful and ironic, and satire is not beyond him. But the light touch of Plato's pen in the *Phaedrus* does not really hide the seriousness of his task, to show that the philosopher is as mad as the tyrant—indeed, a great deal more so.

The *Phaedrus* builds on old foundations—the treatments of eros and *philia* in the *Lysis*, *Symposium*, and *Republic*, the encounter between dialectic and oratory in the *Gorgias*, and the encomium to philosophy in the *Phaedo*. But the most important background for us here is the account of the tyrant in *Republic* IX, an account of a person in the throes of a madness baser than any described in the *Phaedrus*. In a sense, the *Republic*'s descent from the rational control of the philosopher to the rule of passion in the tyrant is, in the *Phaedrus*, reversed into an ascent from the most corrupt to the noblest form of mania. For while the *Phaedrus* deals with four kinds of divine madness, it is a fourfold classification that implicitly is built on the fifth sort of madness described in *Republic* IX. This further kind is the human madness of political rule run wild. If the philosophical ruler's real nemesis is the tyrant, then the genuine antipode of philosophical mania is not the divine madness of oracles or prophets; it is the madness of self-indulgent and unbridled lust for political power.

FOR Plato the issue in the *Republic* is not one of classifying a variety of phenomena under rubrics of mania. It is instead the task of describing the emergence of a particular political-social-psychological type, that of the tyrant. And what is striking about how Plato performs this task is that in his view this development, which occurs as an alteration in the arrangement of a person's desires, is described as the rise of a kind of madness. This may not be the only type of madness that for Plato occurs naturally and has no divine aition, nor might it necessarily be the best example of nondivine madness.[15] But in the *Republic* and in the *Phaedrus*, this tyrannical madness is one of the most important kinds of mania.

Plato begins his discussion of the tyrant by identifying a "dangerous, wild, and lawless type of desire that exists in each of us" (572b4–5). He describes this kind of desire as normally controlled or inhibited by rational guidance and yet as aroused during sleep in the form of wild, antinomian dreams. In these dreams, Socrates says, we are free of shame and prudence, willing to commit foul murders, to eat anything, or even to have sexual intercourse with one's mother or indeed with any man, god, or beast.[16] Yet all these base desires that are hidden in our dreams become determinative for the tyrant: he will sacrifice his mother and father to his own desires, steal from others, rob temples, lie and accept bribes, and in the end, if necessary, subjugate his own polis.[17] Such a man is "intoxicated, lustful, and melancholy" (c9), the slave of eros. He will want anything and will do whatever must be done to get what he wants. He is mad (573a8, b4), a man who "expects to be able to rule not only over men but over the gods, and attempts to do so" (573c3–5).

In the 370s the examples of such madness would not have been hidden from view—Epaminondas preeminent among them, along with Callistratus, Timotheus, and many others, from Dionysius of Syracuse to the Great Kings. If this form of madness, moreover, is the soul's greatest sickness, then the remedy must be equally powerful. In the *Republic* Plato calls it philosophia, in the *Symposium* eros; in the *Phaedrus*, it is eros too but now eros as mania. In short, the antidote to madness is nothing but madness itself.

Unlike the *Republic*, the *Phaedrus* uses an explicitly religious vocabulary to portray, in a brilliantly phenomenological way, the nature of philosophical inquiry. Much of that vocabulary is set in contrast to the terminology of the other three forms of madness. Plato wants to make precise what kind of religious enterprise philosophy is and what kinds it is not.

The project begins with Socrates' speech concerning love as a madness "that comes into being by means of human ailments" (265a9–11), an evil thing.[18] It is a tale or mythos initiated by Socrates' solicitation to the Muses (237a7–b1) and punctuated by Phaedrus' agreement that Socrates is the bearer of a "divine pathos" (238c6), which is wholly appropriate in a place that really seems to be divine (c9–d1).[19] In other words, Socrates' first speech is a sketch of human and not divine eros as a kind of madness, but he presents it as a poetic tale, which is the product of divine possession. The left hand of madness already points ahead to the right.

The first speech not long concluded, Socrates introduces his second in no less a religious fashion. His daimonion comes to him, forbidding him to leave the spot until he has atoned for some offense (*hamartema*) against the divine. As a *mantis*, Socrates understands what that offense is, for he says the soul has a certain mantic capacity. The offense was that he accepted the charge to deliver a speech on eros as an evil thing, when Eros is a god or divine being and hence cannot be evil.[20] There is a reminiscence here of the natural theology of *Republic* II and a revision of the *Symposium*'s claim that eros is a daimon.[21] Socrates' mantic powers, somehow associated with his daimonion, register in a syllogism: if no god produces evil, and if Eros is a god, then Eros produces no evil. The offense is an offense against truth, and it is discovered by divinatory logic.

As a result Socrates feels the need for katharmos, purification, and chooses an ancient method, the delivery of a palinode (243a2–b6). He anticipates a noble form of love, a divine madness, that will outweigh its sinister counterpart. Mantic prophecy recognizes a poetic flaw and recommends a poetic purification, all in response to an original error—that of Lysias' speech—and against a background of bogus purification. For Corybantic and Bacchic rites can be cleansing, and Socrates showed explicitly that he had expected Lysias' speech to purify him of ignorance.[22] Indeed, he described Phaedrus as just such an initiate. But, as the sequel has shown, Socrates comes to recognize both Lysias' rite and his own poetry as offenses, sins against the divine, against Eros, and he once again calls on poetic inspiration to enable him to purify himself.

On one hand, then, the palinode will compensate for Socrates' error, his gullibility about eros and sinister madness; on the other, of course, it will not compensate at all. The *Phaedo* has already made it clear that the real offense is far deeper and concerns physical desires, a slavish attention to pleasure and the avoidance of pain, and a thoroughgoing ignorance. For *this* flaw no mere poetic recantation will suffice; for this only philosophy can serve as purificatory rite. In the end, the *Phaedrus*, with greater descriptive brilliance than any earlier dialogue, sees this role for philosophy too and appreciates the way it achieves its goals, through poetry and myth—a remarkable innovation.[23]

The early speeches warned against the lover on the grounds that he is mad and on the assumption that whoever is mad is always evil. But the truth is that the greatest goods come from that madness which is a divine gift.[24] Socrates' impressive second speech is an attempt to explore this truth and to expose its core, that the highest form of divine madness, which yields the very greatest goods for man, is philosophy. It is, at the same time, the most perfect and beneficial form of religious rite.[25]

At 249d4–e4 Socrates indicates that he has arrived at the fourth kind of divine madness and that "it is the best of all forms of divine possession, both in itself and in its sources, both for him that has it and for him that shares therein" (249e1–3). The account of the first three kinds is a preface to this description; the purpose of the account is to introduce the notion that some madness is both divine in origin and beneficial in result. Socrates treats this statement as a proposal needing confirmation, and the account of the fourth kind of madness is offered as a proof or demonstration of the proposal.[26] Early on there is no suggestion that the four are intended as a classification, that they all carry the same weight, or that they are arranged in some kind of order or hierarchy.[27]

The lack of hierarchy in the account of the types of madness is especially important.[28] Plato may employ poetic and mythic tactics in the *Phaedrus*, but he does not explicitly rank the poet higher than the telestic or mantic or tell us what would determine such an order or ranking.[29] He does, however, describe each type of madness in such a way that both aspects of his proposal are clear, that *some* madness is divine and beneficial, and that not *all* madness is human-natural and evil. Given this understanding of their purpose, then, what do these descriptions tell us?

The first type of madness is mantic; it is best exemplified by the oracle at Delphi and the Sybil.[30] When mad or inspired, such oracles performed acts both individually and publicly beneficial; when self-controlled, they did little or nothing (244a8–b3). The dignity of such madness is ancient, according to Socrates, as long as it was thought to be the result of divine dispensation (*theia moira*, c3). Socrates contrasts mantic prophecy[31] with the practice of those "controlled" prophets who read entrails or other omens in order to see into the future.[32] Madness that comes from god is superior to sophrosyne that comes from men, and in this case, as Socrates later points out, the god in question is Apollo.[33]

From this account few details can be culled. The contrast with magician-diviners simply distinguishes good religious functionaries from bad social servants but tells us nothing about the details of their respective practices. The one feature that Socrates underlines is the fact that mantike has its source in the divine (244a7–8, b4, c3, d4). Indeed, this point is so often repeated that we can confidently take it to be Plato's central claim about what occurs in a mantic consultation. The Pythia is a case of mediumistic possession in which the oracular utterance itself is taken to be the speech of the god.[34] This state of divine possession was precipitated by ritual acts; there were no gases or aromas, no inarticulate babbling or frenzied ecstatic ravings. The oracle sat on a tripod, attended by priests and assistants, heard the request, and uttered the god's response. This rather lean view of the nature of the mantic consultation, which rejects most of the later, Hellenistic accounts and opposes earlier descriptions, such as Farnell's, is now a virtual orthodoxy.[35] Indeed, Fontenrose points out that the later Hellenistic and Roman views of the Pythia's madness—including her ecstatic, frenzied state—in fact originate with the *Phaedrus*, its etymology associating mantic and mania, and what is understood as a parallel with telestic, poetic, and erotic madness.[36] In the end, we are not at all sure what took place in a mantic consultation, at Delphi or elsewhere, and Plato is little help in this regard. What he emphasizes is just what we were led to expect, that such occasions were frequently beneficial and that the oracle was thought to utter the god's speech.[37]

For a host of reasons, such mantic practices are inferior to philosophy, not the least of which are the facts that the oracle is a mere vehicle or instrument and that the end has no effect on the oracle's soul and its well-being. In both regards—and they are not of course unrelated—the practice of telestic rites, the second kind of mania, is an advance.

Linforth's two articles, together with the comments of Dodds, Burkert, and Parker, put us in an excellent position to understand the single difficult sentence in which Plato describes telestic puri-

fications.[38] For our purposes, the following are the crucial details:
(1) the rites are katharmoi; (2) they cure or purify homeopathi-
cally; (3) they cure misery with madness; (4) they are Bacchic and
Corybantic.[39] The cathartic madness took the form of "prayer and
submission to the gods," ritualistic frenzy that helped purge the
celebrants' misery and distress. If Linforth is right, the noble lineage
of these rites is part of Plato's strategy to give dignity to the practices. "Socrates is concerned to show that madness, which was, after
all, as distressing an affliction in the Greek world as it is anywhere,
could at times be an experience productive of blessings to mankind."[40] What doubtless seemed repugnant to many had been co-
opted by old aristocratic families for public benefit. The god of the
ritual was Dionysos, the god of liberation and joy. If in the *Republic*
Plato makes much of the corrupt versions of such practices, coupled
with magic and wizardry, here he does not. Indeed, unlike mantic
art and poetry, telestic purifications are not presented in contrast
to a corrupt form; they are treated as ecstatic rites, sponsored by
Dionysos, that seek to purify by dislocation. Here there is no contrast with evil or corrupt forms. As we have argued, however, this
model for Socratic and Platonic philosophy is not yet identical to
it, for obvious reasons.[41]

The description of poetry, the third kind of divine madness, is like
that of mantic prophecy. It is brief and sketchy, incorporating a
contrast between good and bad poetry that is parallel to a contrast
between divine and humanly based art.[42] Commending a poet for
being a vehicle for divine expression is not novel in Plato; Democritus clearly states that "all that a poet writes when possessed and
divinely inspired is truly excellent" (B18). We have already seen
similar commendation, although qualified, in the treatment of poetry in the *Ion*, and there as here Plato's point is that the poet is a
vehicle, caught up in divine rapture, expressing great deeds in behalf of paideia. But as in the case of mantic possession, the divinely
inspired poet is the god's instrument. What benefit there is comes
to all those who learn from inspired poetry, but the poet's soul
remains unchanged.[43]

By returning to this earlier strategy, of distinguishing divine-
passive from human-active poetry, Plato leaves open another possibility. It is the possibility of a kind of *poesis* that is cathartic, like
telestic rites, but that is also a poetic craft that is divine in one

sense and human in another. And in the end it transcends the mantic in every important way, for its agent is not a passive instrument but an active inquirer, and its fundamental commitment, unlike that of the Pythia, is that the human soul, via its divine route, can ascend toward the divine, becoming as much like the divine as it is possible for man to be. Thus, there is no explicit hierarchy in the three types of mania that prepare the way for philosophy, but implicitly they do form an ordered progression. In so doing, the three indicate the religious shape that philosophical inquiry must take.

OSTENSIBLY Socrates' second speech is about Eros as divine and about the philosopher as lover.[44] The bridges between these twin claims are the relationship between mania and Eros and the account of philosophy as the highest form of madness. If these bridges are constructed on religious foundations and with religious materials, as I have tried to show they are, then ultimately philosophy will be characterized as a religious ritual. Moreover, such a characterization will develop on the basis of a fundamental commitment to the continuity between the divine and the human, and we have seen that such a continuity turns on the question of the soul's immortality. It is not surprising, then, that Socrates announces as his first step an account "of the nature of the soul, both divine and human, its experiences and tasks" (245c2–4), nor is it surprising that he commences by setting out a proof of soul's immortality.

Hackforth—following Frutiger, Skemp, and Bury—points out the "close connection" between the current argument and the final argument for immortality in the *Phaedo*.[45] The latter ties together soul and life, the former soul and *kinesis*, so that, in Hackforth's words, "What the *Phaedrus* does is to remold an argument about the relations of words and concepts into one based on observed physical fact, the fact namely of *kinesis*."[46] In addition, commentators have generally noticed the pre-Socratic origins of Plato's proof—or at least antecedents, especially the role of Alcmaeon of Croton, a younger contemporary of Pythagoras, who took the soul to resemble the heavenly beings in its immortality since all are always in motion.[47] This claim, drawn from Aristotle's report,[48] is confirmed and supplemented by Aetius' version, that "Alcmaeon supposes the soul to be a substance self-moved in eternal motion, and for that reason immortal and similar to the divine."[49]

Pythagorean or quasi-Pythagorean elements are not as prominent in the *Phaedrus* as they are elsewhere in the dialogues, but it surely seems right that Plato has taken his basic idea from Alcmaeon—or someone like him. Furthermore, the *Phaedrus'* argument does mark a departure or at least a development in Plato's thinking about the soul's immortality. If the argument has a teleological character,[50] there is some reason to think it constitutes a stage between the *Phaedo*, on the one hand, and the *Timaeus* and *Laws*, on the other. At the same time, however, there is another connection worth noticing, and that is to the critique of Homeric theology in *Republic* II.[51] Viewed against the background of that critique, the *Phaedrus'* conception of the soul as self-moved and immortal occurs at the point where a refined Platonic conception of divinity as natural theology intersects with his treatment of philosophical inquiry as ecstatic ritual. That point is a new conception of soul in its cosmic role, coupled with and as support for its status as immortal and divine. Plato is on his way to the notion that the end of philosophical aspiration is assimilation to divine cosmic agency, or to the world soul.

Until the *Timaeus*, *Laws*, and other later dialogues, and unlike the Aristotelian analysis of kinesis, arguments like that in the *Phaedrus* must remain sketchy and programmatic. Such reasoning indicates more about Plato's reach than it does about his grasp.[52] What seems like a gratuitous discussion of *arche*, for example, does not bother him, nor does the formal and impressionistic character of the argument or the ad hoc way soul is introduced at its end. The basic structure of the argument, however, seems easy to grasp:

1. What is always-changing is immortal.   *Why?*
2. What changes itself is always changing.
3. Therefore, what changes itself is immortal.
4. Soul is something that changes itself.
5. Therefore, all soul is immortal.[53]

Unfortunately, Socrates' arguments for each of these steps are not without difficulties. There are unexpressed assumptions, conceptual imprecision, and apparent disorder in development, and the central notions—kinesis and arche—are not fully clarified, nor do they seem to play a significant role later in the dialogue. It appears that Plato, needing to demonstrate the soul's immortality for later purposes in the dialogue, employs a new argument whose important ties extend outside the *Phaedrus*. The precise structure and validity of the proof are less important than its intent, which is a definition of soul as *arche* of *kinesis* as the foundation of its immortality. The gap between immortality and imperishability or everlastingness is closed by taking soul to be not life or kinesis but what is *responsible* for all kinesis.

This proof of the soul's immortality—or of all soul's immortality—serves as a reminder, if not more, that for Plato the soul is capable of attaining fully divine status.[54] The central role of philosophy in the *Phaedrus* shows how that divine status must be sought. But, as in the *Symposium* and *Republic*, Plato does not merely identify philosophy's preeminent task; he also wrestles with difficulties in his conception of it. In the *Republic* he was concerned with the nondiscursive dimension of inquiry, belief, and knowledge and, to a certain degree, in the affective, noncognitive conditions relevant to learning. In the *Phaedrus* Plato seems to appreciate and address further noncognitive difficulties. At the same time, he begins to turn to the discursive and propositional aspect of cognition and inquiry. These twin tasks—to explore further the noncognitive dimension of philosophical inquiry and to develop a technique for discovering the discursive aspect of philosophical knowledge—are among the *Phaedrus*' achievements. But both are presented in a novel way that underscores the intensely religious character of Plato's endeavor.

The account of philosophy in Socrates' second speech is aimed at showing why and how the philosopher is the genuine lover and hence why he is divinely mad. But this goal can be achieved only if Plato can describe the philosopher's experience, what he does, and this requires a description of philosophical inquiry and its presuppositions. But all of this description and analysis is based on what the philosophical soul, in comparison with other souls, is and does. It is no surprise, then, that with the soul's immortality demonstrated, Plato turns to the soul's nature, its "experiences and activities."[55] His vehicle of presentation is myth or likeness.

We have seen how Plato has appropriated and adapted Greek myth, both its form and content, to express what seemed beyond human experience.[56] We have also seen him use myth or likenesses for other purposes, as an illustrative device for advancing an argument, as a vehicle for teaching an interlocutor what he is really unprepared to learn in a nonfigurative way, and as a helpful gloss on difficult argumentation.[57] Plato seems to realize that myth differs from argument or logos, but where the dividing line is to be drawn is not easy to say. Although Plato does not, for example, ever appear to call a definition, argument, or theory a myth, what is called a mythos or story at one point might well be called a logos or eikon elsewhere.

Even if no precision emerges from what precedes the *Phaedrus*, the results in this dialogue do have a certain distinctiveness. Part of what makes this use of myth unusual may derive from intuitions similar to those that led to the myth of the Cave, for example, but another part may have to do with the *Phaedrus'* effort to carve out a precise territory for philosophy, a territory that leads Plato to call it a higher form of madness than others, a more genuine kind of rhetoric, and a purer form of poetry. To cast the deepest lessons in the form of poetry, myth, and religious activity is to emphasize the continuity between philosophy as Plato conceives it and Greek life. At times an innovator wants to emphasize novelty not by being blatant and radical but rather by a subtler strategy of starting with similarity and showing how difference and preeminence emerge from it. Plato's use of myth here, together with his use of religious vocabulary and rhetorical style, is an expression of this tactic, part of Plato's ambitious design for locating the place of philosophical inquiry both within and in opposition to Hellenic culture.[58]

Myth is a construction of language; it is story, told and retold, appropriated, revised, passed down, reappropriated. The *Phaedrus* myth of the soul, with its biography of the philosophical lover, possesses some features of mythic storytelling but not others. It is certainly not a paradigmatic Greek myth, for although it borrows from the tradition, it does so under the severe guidance of a master poet and a profound philosopher. Plato—like Aeschylus, Sophocles, Herodotus, and others—is no mere transmitter of tales. Furthermore, the *Phaedrus* myth is largely a creative tale; its most important features are Plato's special contribution, concocted in an attempt to show what philosophy is and how it is related to oracular prophecy, telestic purifications, sexual love, and political rhetoric. Hence, the question of its history, as a traditionally transmitted and applied tale, is less relevant for us than is the question of its importance for Plato's enterprise at the time of its telling.[59] The implication of this realization is somewhat surprising: that we should decline in this special case Burkert's valuable reminder that myths have a "historical dimension," that they involve "consecutive changes of crystallization and application."[60] Insofar as we are interested in the myth of Socrates' second speech vis-à-vis the current stage of Plato's religious epistemology and psychology, we should read the myth with an eye to its context and the way in which it represents and justifies related elements of that context. The historical element vanishes; the real issue is what role the myth plays with regard to philosophical experience and practice. In a sense, we can borrow leaves from the books of two schools of myth interpretation. From the structuralist, we borrow the notion that the *Phaedrus* myth is part of a larger whole which it mirrors in terms of its overall structure and order. From the older ritualist school, we borrow the idea that for the interpretation of myth the primary component of the myth's social context is ritual, in this case that of philosophical inquiry.[61] The *Phaedrus* myth, then, should be read as Plato's attempt to articulate the nature of and provide a justification for the philosophical rite of ecstatic aspiration to divine status. It is the story that grounds rational inquiry and hence, even independent of its rich epistemological gains, marks a momentous stage in Plato's development.

My reading has three main goals. First, I will point out some ways in which the myth employs religious vocabulary in its portrayal of philosophy. Second, I will explore what Plato tells us about the noncognitive aspects of learning and knowledge, and third, I will examine the technique he proposes for fulfilling the discursive requirements of knowledge.

As we might expect, in his speech Socrates uses Orphic, Bacchic, and other telestic terminology and motifs to describe the soul and its experiences.[62] At 249c6–d3 the philosopher is said to be a man who uses correctly reminders of the Forms and thereby comes to be really perfect (*teleos*) "by always being initiated into perfect rites" (*teleous aei teletas teloumenos*). In this way, "standing aside from busy human affairs and turning to the divine, he is rebuked by the multitude as being crazy and is possessed by the divine (*enthou-*

siadzon, d2), which they do not realize." Hence, the philosopher is mad in a fourth, preeminent way, for this is the best form of divine possession (249e1–3; *enthousiaseon*, e2).[63]

Moreover, "when the lover of beautiful things partakes of this madness, he is called a 'lover'" (249e3–4). Recalling, a few lines later, the original, precarnate vision of the Beautiful, Plato says that "we were initiated (*eidon te kai etelounto ton teleton*) into that mystery which it is right to call most blessed" (250b8–c1).[64] The celebration is referred to as frenzied (*urgiadzomen*, c1) and the initiates as "whole, unblemished, free from alloy, steadfast and blissful" (c1–3), terms also used for the sights that we saw and the light that shone on us (c2–5). The celebrants are also called mystes and their vision an epopteia (*myoumenoi te kai epopteuontes*, c4), terms that are especially reminiscent of Eleusis, while the subsequent reference to the prison of the body that surrounds and taints us now is certainly Orphic.[65]

Later, in his account of the types of lover, Plato says that each lover wants his own beloved to be like the god he worships (253b4) and like himself (b7–c2). Responding to both his god and his lover, he is like a Bacchant, pouring out what he takes from the divine onto his beloved (253a6–b1).[66] At 253c3, these acts of love are once again called initiations or teletai, rites of possession and perfection.

These are good examples, I think, of the way that Plato, in the myth of the second speech, uses the language of Orphic and Bacchic rites to describe philosophy, both the end of rational inquiry and the precarnate vision that is its presupposition and origin. Into these religious forms, Plato pours the wine of philosophy, but it is a conception of philosophy that is more nuanced and developed than that presented in earlier dialogues.

At first reading, this may be a difficult claim to accept. The *Republic*, with its discussion of mathematical thinking in *Republic* VI and VII, surely looks more detailed and sophisticated, and the portrayals of philosophical thinking look more tooled in the *Meno* and *Phaedo*. But one should not be misled. The mythic form should not be a veil hiding the philosophical developments that are portrayed in poetry, allegory, metaphor, and imagery. The myth, remember, is to be read as a description and justification of philosophical inquiry. In this role, it must say or show what philosophical inquiry is and how it is possible.

On the one hand, the *Phaedrus* myth recalls features of philosophy that have been elaborated in earlier dialogues, but on the other it extends beyond earlier accounts. In two areas, the *Phaedrus* myth offers novel answers to old problems. First, it introduces a new strategy for constituting the discursive aspect of knowledge—the method of collection and division—thereby indicating what structure that discursive aspect should have. Second, it identifies factors that show why not all people are potential philosophers and why the capacity for learning or inquiry differs, sometimes dramatically, from person to person. The *Phaedrus* myth, in other words, incorporates an epistemological psychology, couched in a rhetorical effort to associate love, philosophy, and divine madness. The *Phaedrus* myth complements the detached assessments of the philosophical quest and its obstacles that occur in the *Phaedo* and *Republic* with an almost phenomenological portrayal of "the difficulties, triumphs, and disasters that lie behind [the soul's] struggle to catch sight of the objects of knowledge, the Forms."[67] Within this portrayal Plato develops his understanding of the role of desire in learning.

THERE are, Plato says, divine and human souls (245c2–4; compare 246a6–b4, 247a8–48a1). He describes both the variety of human souls that exist prior to physical incarnation and their differing knowledge of the Forms by contrasting what such prenatal souls undergo with the "experience" of the divine souls. These divine souls see perfectly and completely that which is, or true being (247c7, d3–4), including the Forms of Temperance, Justice, and Knowledge. In the case of Knowledge, for example, the Form they see "is not close to becoming, nor is it different for different things we now call 'beings,' but [it is] the knowledge of what really is" (247d7–e2). Compared with these divine souls are nondivine souls, some of which are capable of human incarnation. Some succeed in a god-like vision of the Forms but only with difficulty; others are able to see only some of the Forms; a final group fails altogether.[68] Of these nondivine souls some are able to remain discarnate. These dwell permanently with the gods, periodically returning to a vision of the Forms.[69] The others enter into physical bodies and cycles of incarnations.[70] Among incarnate souls, some are at least capable of human lives, nine kinds of which Socrates identifies. The highest form of human

incarnation is the philosopher—also called the lover of beauty—
and a certain kind of musician, and the lover.[71]

Philosophical souls can reunite with the gods after three thousand
years. Others take ten thousand. In the course of a nonphilosophical
soul's cycle of incarnations, it can find itself in both human and
nonhuman bodies, but, as Plato is careful to emphasize, in order for
a soul ever to enter a human body it must have seen the truth or
the things that are, that is, the Forms (249b5–6, 249e4–50a1). The
reason Plato gives for this stipulation is that human beings must be
capable of recollection, "to go from many perceptions and collecting
them together into a unity of reasoning. This is recollection of those
things which the soul saw when it journeyed with a god, surveyed
what we now say 'is,' and gazed up at what really is" (249b6–c4).
If, in other words, learning what x is, for all relevant x's, involves
realizing that knowledge of x is knowledge of the Form of x, then
such learning is possible only if the Forms can be recalled, and
recollection requires prior acquaintance. All human beings must
have the capacity for such recollection; those thoroughly con-
founded souls that were never able to view the Forms cannot be
incarnate in human beings. Plato does not seem to say here, however, whether a human soul must have "once" seen *all* of the Forms
or whether it is sufficient to have seen some.

Two things remain unclear. Why does a human soul now desire
knowledge and especially knowledge of those Forms which it has
since forgotten? And second, given the overall uniformity of the
precarnate experience of human souls, what accounts for the fact
that all persons are not equally eager for and adept at recollection?

Nondivine souls, Socrates says, might be compared to a charioteer
and his team of horses.[72] In the case of human beings, there are two
horses, one fine and good (*kalos te kai agathos*), the other the opposite. The combination, as Plato later describes (253c7–54e5),
makes the charioteer's job of guiding and controlling them difficult,
to say the least.[73] It is fairly clear that the charioteer, in this image,
represents the intellect or reason and knowledge (*nous* and *episteme*; see also 247c7–d2), conceived as having a natural desire for
the Forms. This is proved in part because the soul is said to be perfect
when "winged," which means when it rises naturally to the domain
of the gods and when it is as fine, wise, and good as it can be (246b7–
c1; compare 246d6–e1). It is also shown by 247d1–5 and 248b5–c2,

where Plato tells us that intellect and knowledge are the proper food and nourishment for the soul and that the Forms are in fact the food for the noblest part of the soul and nourishment for its "wings." Indeed, at 248b5–c2 Plato uses this fact to explain why the souls, even in their precarnate state, are eager to behold the Forms. They are, in short, as attracted to it as any form of life is attracted to that which keeps it alive and perfects it. As a *philosophos* and *erotikos*, the philosopher is that kind of human being most perfectly given over to the guidance of his charioteer and that means to the dominant desire to see the Forms once again. The soul desires knowledge of the Forms now in part for the same reason it naturally aspires to contemplate the Forms, in order to sustain and perfect itself.

In the *Republic*, however, we are told that not all persons are equally capable of education; not all seek knowledge as their dominant goal with equal intensity. To be reminded of the Forms by things in this world is not easy for everyone (250a1–2). In order to explain why some people are poorer learners and why some lack any serious desire for knowledge and hence lack the desire to learn, the *Phaedrus* should show why for some people their natural desire for knowledge is not their overriding desire, and why in certain circumstances it does not manifest itself at all. In addition, it should show why even some of those with a zeal for knowledge of the Forms might be poor learners.

For a number of reasons, Plato takes as his example the recollection of the Form of the Beautiful.[74] It is, he says, doubly suited to be recalled, first because it was especially brilliant and vivid when originally contemplated, and second because its worldly exemplifications are accessible to vision, the keenest mode of bodily perception (250b5–e1). Beauty would have made the most permanent, deepest impression on the discarnate soul, and seeing beautiful things, including fine and handsome people, will have the most stimulating effect on incarnate souls. Why, given the advantages of recalling the Form of Beauty, do some find doing so difficult? Some, Plato says, originally saw the Forms too briefly (250a2), and of course others were unable to control their horses completely and so never did see *all* of the Forms (248a5–6). Some, having come to the performance of acts of injustice, forgot what they had seen (250a2–4; compare 248c7). Only a few remain whose memory is sufficiently vivid to facilitate the recollection of the Forms when a sensible likeness presents itself (250a5–b1). Later Plato summarizes the three factors that play important roles: (1) how recently the original contemplation had taken place, (2) its scope or comprehensiveness, and (3) the subsequent "purity" of the soul's desire (250e1–51a2).

It is no easy task to extract a precise doctrine from such an account. Yet a picture of the relevant factors does emerge. The natural desires of human souls form a complex mixture, a struggle between the desire for wisdom, which constitutes the charioteer's desire for survival and perfection, and the disparate noncognitive desires of the horses. Even in their original states, all souls did not contemplate the Forms in the same way, and this variety influences their capacities to learn or recollect when later incarnate. The scope and duration of the soul's original vision of the Forms, then, comprise the first relevant factor. Second, souls in later incarnations, when distant in time from the original one and without intermediate recollections in earlier incarnations, will find it increasingly difficult to gain knowledge of the Forms. This is what Plato means by his distinction between recent and distant vision of the Forms at 250e1–51a2. Finally, some souls, in the course of their incarnations, become impure. That is, their desire for knowledge of the Forms is no longer dominant. In the case of Beauty this is expressed as the surrender to pleasure that Plato speaks of at 250e3–51a1. What happens to one whose experience with the Form of Beauty is recent and vivid is brilliantly described by Socrates as the experience of a love that is love for the Beautiful and for the beloved beauty who exemplifies it. But if one's desire for knowledge is now dominated by a desire for physical pleasures, one "pursues a pleasure that is unnatural" (250e4–51a1). In short, the scale of priorities regarding one's desires will influence one's capacity to turn from sensible exemplifications to the Forms.

At the deepest level, therefore, each human soul has a desire to gain knowledge of the Forms and an ability to do so that are determined by two factors. The first is the soul's nature, the original character of its noncognitive desires and their relation to the initially dominant desire for knowledge. For it is the soul's nature that determined the manner in which the soul first contemplated the Forms and the mode of its first incarnation. The second factor is the soul's conduct once incarnate and whether the desire for knowl-

edge—the dominance of intellectual desire—persisted or was over-
ridden by nonintellectual, often physical desires. The result of these
two factors is the situation of each and every incarnate soul. Some
are philosophical by nature, which means that for them sense experience is a ladder to apprehension of the Forms and to that combination of anguish and joy that Plato brilliantly describes and so
dramatically calls "madness" of the fourth kind (249d4–e4). Others,
however, are not philosophical by nature, even though at their
deepest and most profound level they do have a natural desire for
knowledge of and kinship with the Forms.[75] But this desire is, as it
were, dormant within them or at best manifest only in a qualified
way. For some of them, the desire for physical pleasure alone motivates what they do; for others, the desire for knowledge must continually compete with desires for prestige, honor, and wealth. Some
of these souls are capable of limited education, some of very little
indeed. The philosopher alone responds eagerly and capably to education. The rapture that marks his success Plato calls "love," and
the look of otherworldly devotion in his eyes others call "madness."

A "demythologized" summary will indicate how the account of
recollection in the *Phaedrus* can best be viewed as a contribution
to the noncognitive dimension of Plato's theory. Let us call the
desire for knowledge of the Forms "intellectual desire." Consider a
person in an educational situation that Plato might have envisaged
in the *Phaedo*, *Republic*, and *Phaedrus*. For example, one is asked
whether a given person is beautiful or an action just or whether the
base angles of an isosceles triangle are congruent. A person with a
philosophical nature has, as a dominant interest, the satisfaction of
intellectual desire; such an individual desires to know the truth. At
first this interest involves testing personal beliefs about the problem.
Then desires urge further questioning about the nature of beauty,
justice, and triangularity. At some point, this process results in the
recognition that the knowledge sought is knowledge not about persons or actions or physical objects but rather about dimly recalled
objects of an earlier vision, objects separate from this world, the
Forms. For such a person, intellectual desire is constantly manifest
and dominant. It is expressed and effective as the primary reason
for what the student does.[76]

Others confronted with a similar situation, however, are not
philosophical by nature. They have intellectual desires, to be sure,

but these are at best latent, waiting to be called into play.[77] For others, their intellectual desires must always contend with other desires, so that even if their overall reason for acting as they do is determined by rational calculation, they tend to act for nonintellectual reasons. For others, their latent intellectual desires never even become occurrent; they are suppressed or sublimated to other desires.

Earlier we saw that in the *Phaedrus* both the original vision of the Forms and later incidents of recollective learning are in part explained by the soul's nature, in part by its experiences. Furthermore, every soul has intellectual desire as part of its nature, and the explanation for this phenomenon was that knowledge of the Forms is the natural sustenance and nourishment of the soul. I would like to emphasize this teleological function of the Forms once more. For Plato a person's intellectual desire is properly satisfied by contemplation of the Forms. What accounts for this nearly religious dimension of Plato's epistemology is a powerful attraction. As Plato showed in the *Phaedo*, the soul and the eternal, pure, simple Forms are similar in many ways. There is, as it were, a natural kinship between them (*Phaedo* 78b4–84b8). An Empedoclean principle of attraction is endorsed by Plato, and it becomes natural that the Forms, the objects of the soul's highest aspirations for knowledge, both attract and are the objects of its desire.[78] The more excellent was a soul's prenatal apprehension, the more constant and pure, the more compelling is the Forms' attraction of it. In the *Phaedo* we were puzzled that recollection might be thought to have a nonvoluntary, almost automatic character. We can now see that what might underlie this nonvoluntary turning, when it does occur, is the attractive force of the Forms themselves.[79]

THE *Phaedrus* myth, then, provides a psychological ground for the possibility of learning and hence a noncognitive foundation for philosophical inquiry. It does this within the framework of an account of love and divine madness, the centerpiece of which is a discussion of what philosophical inquiry achieves, that is, how it gains knowledge and what that knowledge involves.

We are moving into familiar, well-traversed territory. Beginning at least with Robinson's classic study, modern commentators have worked hard to spell out the nature of the Socratic what-is-x question, the character of definition (logos), and the dialectical method that is intended in part to discover such definitions.[80] Thus far, I have emphasized the referential, nondiscursive aspect of inquiry and knowledge. But commentators have spent more time on the discursive or propositional dimension, for obvious reasons.

When Plato inherits the Socratic definitional requirement and couples it with the commitment to transcendent Forms as the objects of inquiry and knowledge, he says little about what constitutes a good definition. But he certainly continues to believe that knowledge requires them. This is evident in both the *Phaedo* and the *Republic*. For Socrates, definitions were needed to provide a standard for distinguishing things that are virtuous; that is, having divine knowledge was associated with judgment and discrimination in the polis. For Plato, all sensible objects have both of a pair of opposite properties, including evaluative ones. So, as White has pointed out, the old use of definitions as standards of judgment can no longer apply. The Copy Theory, adumbrated in the *Phaedo*, is fully developed in the *Republic*, but there the primary use of knowledge is constructive and not judgmental.[81] In the *Phaedo*, knowledge includes logos as a lingering Socratic requirement. But in the *Republic*, with its new attentiveness to political participation and philosophical rule, the role of definitions becomes central, for if the ruler is to use the Form of the Just as a standard or blueprint, then his knowledge of it must involve more than recognition or referential access; it must have some content, so that institutions, practices, and policies can be modeled after it and evaluated in terms of their degree of resemblance to it. As an object of aspiration, divine knowledge has given way to divine providence and rule.

But there is another function that definitions serve for Plato after the *Phaedo*, and this concerns the very nature of knowledge. To know is to pick out, to see, to grasp, to point to; hence knowing involves, as part of its very nature, recognition or discrimination. Plato inherits this conception, I think, and appreciates all along that knowledge involves both referential access and a discursive element that functions to articulate this discriminatory aspect of knowing. Definitions of Forms, for Plato, are locative, for the possibility of confusing one Form with another is always there, unless a precise specification is had as part of the process of coming to know and then of knowing.[82]

In the *Phaedo* and *Republic*, implicitly if not explicitly, the method for gaining knowledge—the course of philosophical inquiry—was conceived as a process of recollection. But probably in the *Phaedo*, if not earlier, Plato came to realize that the quest for knowledge could not simply be a case of recollection. Its presuppositions and mechanism might account for the availability of the object of knowledge and referential access to it; what recollection could not do is account for the discovery of logoi. For that, even in the *Phaedo*, Plato sought another method—a method of hypothesis which, one might argue, is coupled with Socratic questioning in the *Republic* account of mathematics and dialectic to yield a method for developing a map of the world of Forms in terms of relations to the Good. In the *Phaedrus* the language of recollection, with its Orphic overtones, is still present, but it is yoked with a new method for arriving at logoi of identification and a new interest in language, both of which reflect a Platonic distrust with the current arts of language but also a new Platonic concern about the linguistic shape of logoi and their effectiveness as cognitive maps. Hypothesis fades as the partner of anamnesis, and division takes its place.

The real lover loves another in terms of his love of Beauty and seeks to shape the beloved in terms of what he knows.[83] As the *Phaedrus* shows, however, this love can be a love for many as much as for one, and the implement for shaping the beloved can be speech itself. In the political arena, the role of speech is most certainly felt; to shape the polis and its citizens according to the standard of the Good and the Beautiful, one needs to persuade, and for such a task speech and rhetoric are necessary.[84] The real lover in the *Phaedrus* turns out to be none other than the *Republic*'s philosophical ruler, now cast in the role of a philosophical orator whose dominant desire for knowledge issues in a desire to make his beloved, the polis and all of its citizens, "like himself and the god they worship" (253b8–c1). On this matter the *Republic* is programmatic; the *Phaedrus* is a study in implementation.

Between the philosopher-lover's nondiscursive access to the Forms and the philosopher-rhetorician's verbal dexterity, there is a gap to be filled. It is the gap between an immediate, nonconceptual event which is itself provisional, on the one hand, and a fully conceptual, linguistic discourse, on the other.[85] Plato fills that gap with logoi of the Forms and with the notion of knowledge that must be both discursive and nondiscursive at once.

The account of the role logoi play in genuine rhetoric and how one should arrive at them occurs later in the dialogue, when the dialectical method is shown to be central to the rhetorical task. In his speeches Socrates identifies the philosopher as the real lover and gives a stunning description of the process of learning and loving. In the later account of rhetoric, Plato projects this account of love onto a political screen and supplements his earlier account of philosophy with a picture of dialectic. When the mechanism for the lover's conduct is language, the dimension of knowledge to be explained is discursive. But the two aspects complement each other.

Dialectic involves a new method for Plato[86]—what he describes at 265d3–66c1 as a method of collection and division. Socrates has already gotten Phaedrus to agree that the best speaker will know the truth concerning all the things about which he speaks (259e–62c). Later Socrates will describe a genuine, philosophical rhetoric, at one point requiring that the real orator have dialectical knowledge (269c–74a; especially 273d8–e4).[87] The method of collection and division, then, is integral to the orator's knowing the truth and hence to the possibility of genuine, philosophical rhetoric. The method mediates the referential access to Forms and the linguistic expression of the philosopher's desire to create after the paradigms he knows, and it does so by yielding logoi of the Forms.[88]

WITH the return to genuine rhetoric as the philosophical ruler's instrument for shaping the polis and its citizens, we are thrust back into Plato's situation in 370. What is the relation between the *Phaedrus*' treatment of rhetoric and writing and the trauma of that moment in Athenian history? How does Plato's religious revisionism manifest itself in a critique of rhetoric and writing?

I begin with two observations. The first concerns the place of oratory in Athenian and Greek life in the fourth century and specifically in 370. On the one hand, as Field reminds us, "the fourth century is the age of political oratory . . . the age in which political oratory is becoming more and more divorced from executive, particularly military, responsibility."[89] Political oratory here must of course include forensic speeches as well as political set pieces.[90] But although this specialization is doubtless true to a degree, it is false to think that in practice rhetoric was restricted to professionals. In fact, like Isocrates and Lysias,[91] most professionals were ill-equipped to deliver speeches effectively and especially in political contexts, in the *boule* and *ecclesia*, where the situation required that the political leader himself do the speaking. In the 370s such leaders included Epaminondas, Callistratus, and Timotheus, and if Plato's interest in the *Phaedrus* is the realization of rhetorical skill in political action, it is they, rather than Lysias and Isocrates (who merely write) who must be uppermost in his mind. This fact, moreover, is perfectly compatible with Plato's criticism of rhetoric and writing. For it is reasonable to think that his criticism may be aimed at professional rhetoric for two reasons, both because of its own internal flaws and because of its failure of application.[92]

Second, we should notice something about the prominence given to Lysias in the *Phaedrus* and the attention paid to Isocrates at the dialogue's end. As Hackforth shows, the dramatic date is about 410, when Lysias had just returned from Thurii and Isocrates was twenty-six years old.[93] The dialogue's idyllic setting jars against the painful realities of those years, sandwiched as they are between the disastrous Sicilian expedition and Athens' ultimate capitulation to Sparta. But to the dialogue's readers Lysias and Isocrates would really appear not as they were in 410, but rather only as they had become by 370. The twenty-six-year-old Isocrates, presented by Plato as a man with the option of genuine philosophical rhetoric before him, had nonetheless become the Isocrates of the *Panegyricus*. Whatever optimism and openness there is in the *Phaedrus* must be tinged by the readers' knowledge that the road was not taken. Isocrates could have become a noble critic, a philosophical leader. Instead he had become a mute who writes but does not speak, who teaches but does not criticize. The enchanting scenery mirrors the dialogue's optimism, but both figures express a certain pathos, for both are, by 370, tarnished by history. By implication, real hope lies not with Lysias or Isocrates but rather with an alternative. I prefer not to see irony in Plato's attitude to Isocrates, for irony implies more vindictiveness than sober regret.[94] Plato's conception of philosophical rhetoric is the true descendant of the Isocratic promise, and in pointing this out Plato celebrates not ironic disdain nor self-congratulation but instead sober realism.

Phaedrus 259e–79b incorporates a two-pronged critique of rhetoric, one concerned with its epistemological deficiencies, the other with its written form.[95] With echoes of the *Gorgias*, the first question raised about rhetoric is whether it is a techne.[96] At 277b5–c6 Socrates gives us a precise summary of the results of this examination.[97] If rhetoric is to be a techne, two conditions must be satisfied: "First, you must know the truth about the subject that you speak or write about: that is to say, you must be able to isolate it in a definition, and having so defined it you must next understand how to divide it into kinds, until you reach the limit of division" (b5–8). This passage refers to the dialectical method of collection and division, with its goals of arriving at the best logoi and thereby of facilitating "implementation" of one's knowledge of and love for the Forms. In part, rhetoric, as a technique for such "implementation," is made a techne by having such knowledge as its foundation. And it needs such a foundation if it is to persuade the polis to do what is really good, for even if the citizens have only beliefs about what is good, the orator must know what is good in order to press for genuinely beneficial policies. To pander to the beliefs of the citizens is to be a sophist and not a genuine politician-statesman.[98] Furthermore, as Socrates shows, even if one thinks the object of rhetoric is not to persuade according to the truth, still the orator must know the truth.[99] That is, even if an orator—whether in law courts and the ecclesia or in private disputes—seeks to mislead others,[100] he must have knowledge so that he, but not they, can perceive fine distinctions and be able to tell similarity from dissimilarity (262a–c).[101] To be sure, dialectic is not by itself rhetoric; for that, more is required. But philosophy is at the heart of genuine rhetoric, and this is the first condition necessary for rhetoric to be a techne.

The second condition is this: "You must have a corresponding discernment of the nature of the soul, discover the type of speech appropriate to each nature, and order and arrange your discourse accordingly, addressing a variegated soul in a variegated style that ranges over the whole gamut of tones, and a simple soul in a simple style" (b8–c3). Speeches have components, and their authors employ a variety of literary techniques, styles, and tropes. The proper use of such strategies requires a knowledge of the soul of the listener. Socrates draws on a comparison of rhetoric with tragic poetry and medicine; in all three cases, it is one thing to have at one's disposal the raw materials of the techne in question, and another to know how to organize and employ them effectively.[102] Not Lysias and Thrasymachus but rather Pericles turns out to be the preeminent practitioner of real rhetoric—a good reminder that Plato's attention is on rhetoric as a vehicle for philosophical rule and political persuasion.[103] For Pericles associated himself with Anaxagoras and learned from him how to examine the nature of things, especially the nature of the soul.[104] This is what Socrates' summary requires as part of the second condition for rhetoric's being a techne, and it is what he elaborates when he explains how the soul should be examined in order to discover "precisely [its] real and true nature" (*ten ousian . . . tes physeos*, 270e3–4).[105] Here he applies a three-stage process of inquiry. First, one should describe the soul in order to see whether it is "single and alike" or pluriform, like the body. This amounts to exhibiting the soul's nature (*physis*, 271a5–8). Second, one should consider its capacities to act and be acted upon. Finally, one should classify the kinds of logos and of soul, and classify how souls are affected and why, considering what type of logos is appropriate to what type of speech, and so on (271b1–5).[106] Real rhetoric, then, involves a heavy dose of cognitive psychology.

The second aspect of Plato's critique of rhetoric concerns writing; when is writing proper and when not? Here Socrates begins with the tale of Theuth and its message, that writing encourages forgetfulness; it is a "medicine not for memory but for reminder" (275a5). Writing provides the semblance of wisdom but not its truth. It does nothing more than "remind one who knows that which the writing is concerned with" (275d1–2). At best, then, written logos can precipitate recollective knowledge; at worst, it can deceive and suffers from indiscriminate distribution and density.[107]

In fact, written logos is properly called an "image" (eidolon), of which the original is the "living, ensouled *logos* [that is] associated with knowledge and is written in the soul of the learner, that can defend itself and knows to whom it should speak and to whom it should say nothing" (276a5–9). Here Socrates uses the metaphor of the serious farmer and the gardener of the Adonia,[108] comparing the genuine orator—who has knowledge of just, beautiful, and good things[109]—with the serious farmer, who sows his seeds only in rich, fertile soil. Similarly, the real orator sows his seeds not on scrolls or stone but rather in the souls of his audience. He may write, to be sure, but he does so as a reminder for the time when age and forgetfulness overcome him (276d) and as a reminder for his students and disciples. But more important than this written vehicle for recollection is the living conversation itself, which proceeds by the "*techne* of dialectic" and "plants and sows *logoi* together with knowledge" (276e4–77a4). By this method the seed gains immortality and its possessor eudaimonia, to the greatest degree possible for a human being.

Socrates, then, does not denigrate written discourse totally. What is wrong or dishonorable is to claim more for writing than is appropriate. To think that written texts contain the most certain and clearest truth is to be deluded; to be ignorant of the differences between dreaming and being awake in things just, unjust, fine, and good is to be a subject of disrepute. Here, in terms as explicit as one would expect, Socrates calls on the dreaming-waking contrast of *Republic* V to distinguish the false from the true orator.[110] And just as there the genuine philosopher was properly cognizant of the deficiencies of sensory evidence in a way that distinguished him from the *philodoxos*, so here the real orator—the philosopher—appreciates the limitations of written discourse. It is "really a means of reminding those who know the best things" (277e9–78a1). "Lucidity, perfection, and serious significance belong only to those lessons on just, fine, and good things that are taught and spoken for the sake of learning and are really written in the soul" (278a2–5). Hence, while some small value is saved for written texts, preeminence resides with dialectical, conversational inquiry.[111] For the latter has a temporal, progressive dimension that employs interrogation to arrive at knowledge. The best writing can do is remind one of truths already grasped. Writing can, at its best, be a mute occasion for learning or inquiry to begin. It cannot clarify the nature of Forms and yield clear and precise knowledge.[112]

Hackforth, following Friedlander, advises that Plato's criticism of written speeches and rhetorical set pieces should be understood against the background of the emergence of writing in fourth-century rhetoric.[113] Isocrates, as Jebb puts it, responded to the political pamphleteering of the late fifth century by raising "the dignity and worth of this intermittent journalism."[114] He explicitly advocated the production of literary works that would endure and have lasting value.[115] In the 380s Isocrates became party to a dispute

over written and spoken discourse, or rather over written and prepared discourse in contrast to extemporaneous oratory.[116] His opponent was Alkidamas, a student of Gorgias, who extolled the
power of extemporary speech against Isocrates, whom he called the
"maker of words" (*poetes logon*).[117] Indeed, Alkidamas' own expressions, in his speech "Against the Authors of Written Speeches,"
closely match Plato's language in this last section of the *Phaedrus*,
for he refers to spontaneous speech as ensouled and alive (*empsy-
chos esti kai dze*, 28) and calls a written speech a copy (*eidola kai
schemata kai mimemata logon, eikon logou*). Both Friedlander and
Hackforth are surely right that Alkidamas' speech furnishes Plato
with some of his terminology, but they are wrong to think that
Isocrates alone serves as Plato's real opponent.

As I have suggested, Plato's real opponents are as much Epaminondas, Callistratus, and Timotheus as Isocrates, Lysias, and the
tradition of rhetoricians and sophists. And behind them all, of
course, lie the polis tradition, Athens' inflated sense of political
leadership, and the Delphic theology with its festivals, sacrifices,
oracles, and so on. The attack on the primacy of the written word
is an attack on this totality—on the courts, the boule, the ecclesia,
Athenian pride, the fragile uncertainty of political life in Athens,
the false confidence in temporary alliances, and the failure of individuals to commit themselves to the search for knowledge and the
implementation of the Beautiful, the Just, and the Good.

One might leave the *Phaedrus* thinking that Plato's criticism of
contemporary rhetoric is merely technical, that such rhetoric is not
founded on an adequate psychology, that it requires greater conceptual precision, and that it should rely, for effectiveness, more on
extemporaneity. One might think, that is, that a genuine orator
or a genuine craftsman of rhetoric could remedy these defects and
still deceive, manipulate, pander, and delude. But this narrow interpretation cannot be correct. The critique of rhetoric must run
deeper than this. It must be understood against the background of
Plato's larger interests and his overall response to Athens' historical
situation. The real orator's interest must be the good, the beautiful,
and the just and their application. Ultimately, the most promising
context for creating beautiful and good lives is the personal relationship that provides the setting for philosophical conversation and
the attainment of knowledge.[118] But every such relationship occurs

amid others, so that the polis becomes the proper social setting for a life of rational inquiry and, if not that, then at least for a life ordered by its devotees.

The real core of the critique of rhetoric is the claim that genuine rhetoricians must be philosophers, and, coupled with the substance of Socrates' second speech, this means that they must be genuine lovers as well, partisans of the highest form of divine madness. In the end, then, these rhetoricians become "politicians of reality,"[119] the true devotees of rational ecstasy. They become philosophers. The *Phaedrus* exemplifies the imagery of the Cave in a subtle way, for although the idyllic conversation between Socrates and Phaedrus takes place outside the city, its point is that the genuine rhetorician, who is a philosopher, must return to an active role within the polis. Philosophical inquiry and conversation may take place outside the city but the philosophical life cannot.

Now, with the *Phaedrus* behind us, we can see better what being a philosopher means for Plato and how philosophers are to be distinguished from so many others who populate fourth-century Athens. The philosopher is drawn to acquire as much knowledge of the Forms as man can acquire; his soul has those characteristics that make learning maximally desirable, accessible, and possible. And he has had that experience of the Beautiful and the Good that moves him to want to realize these paradigms in his own life by bringing others to share in the most fulfilling and blissful features of his experience. Ultimately, the philosopher desires to become divine or akin to divine, and he is hopeful that such transcendence is possible and not only temporarily so. But it must be *at least* temporarily so, for the philosophical life necessarily involves deep personal relationships and genuine political concern, the temporal and temporary content of philosophical aspiration. His life is a rite of passage, a constant process of initiation in which rational inquiry, *mathesis*, paideia enable him to "do what is pleasing to the gods" and to gain "the fullest measure of *eudaimonia* that man can attain unto" (277a3–4), both here and beyond.

CONCLUSION

The *Phaedrus* marks a natural break in the story I have been telling. With the dialogues written shortly after it, the *Theaetetus* and *Parmenides*, impressive changes occur in Plato's thinking and in the tone of his writing. One of these changes concerns the religious vocabulary and framework that has been the primary vehicle for our study of Plato's epistemological interests and their historical context. While religious issues do arise in the later dialogues, the enthusiastic, almost exuberant use of religious expressions and motifs, so prominent thus far, ceases. At the end of Plato's career, the *Laws* best expresses the continued importance of religious matters for Plato, but even it does so in quite a different way.[1]

Even though we shall conclude with the *Phaedrus*, it is tempting to consider what lies ahead historically for Plato—at least during the next decade, from 370 to 360. His literary output will be remarkable—the *Theaetetus*, *Parmenides*, *Sophist*, and *Politicus* (perhaps the *Cratylus* as well).[2] Many of the issues he confronts are ones that fit nicely the program already established, but he does so in a period of personal and social turmoil that influences, if not the content, then at least the form—the style and tone—of the results.

The years that separate the Battle of Leuctra in 371 from that of Mantinea in mid–362 were exciting but troubling ones for Plato. If the *Theaetetus* is an accurate witness, the Academy, by 369–367, had become a flourishing center for mathematical study.[3] By then Eudoxus had returned and, if the evidence is correct, had become interim head of the Academy during Plato's second visit to Sicily.[4] Indeed, it was at about this time (367–366) that Aristotle arrived in Athens at the age of seventeen, while Plato was absent and, as Field conjectures, Eudoxus was in charge.[5] The Academy's reputation was great enough to lure Aristotle from a significant distance, and he was not the only one.

Plato's return visit to Sicily was undertaken at Dion's request. With the death of Dionysius I in 368–367, the realm and rule passed to his son, Dionysius II. There is no need to retell the story of Plato's ambivalence about the journey, of the scheming that led to Dion's banishment, and of the discomfort that increasingly overcame Plato. With the outbreak of war in Sicily, Dionysius allowed Plato to return home in 367–366 but with the expectation that both he and Dion would return to Syracuse when peace had been arranged. Such plans were never realized, of course, nor were there realized any of those Platonic political and moral interests that were probably the basis for Plato's acceptance of Dion's invitation. Morrow's itemization of these reforms includes "the substitution of lawful government for the tyranny at Syracuse, the curbing of the luxury and license of Sicilian life, and the reestablishment of the Greek cities in Sicily."[6] These proposals are already practical declensions away from the *Republic*'s ideals, but even they are too demanding for Dionysius II and Sicilian affairs. It is small wonder that the *Politicus*, written between 365 and 362, already shows the effects of Platonic sobriety born of this experience and that the earlier exuberance and optimism of the *Republic* and its companion pieces are mitigated, if not altogether lost.

During these years Plato seems to play no significant role in Athenian politics, but this is not to say that he did not care about the well-being of his native polis.[7] And it is hard to imagine Plato either uninformed about or unmoved by Athenian affairs during this decade. From an independent perspective, the dominant role in Greek politics in the 360s is played by Thebes, and as usual in the fourth century Athenian affairs work themselves out in terms of relations with Sparta, Persia, and Thebes, and against the background of lingering hopes for renewal of her fifth-century preeminence. With regard to such hopes, there is little reason to think that the 360s brought greater Athenian success than had the previous decades.

Theban foreign policy, Hornblower reminds us, "develops in three theatres" in the decade prior to Mantinea.[8] In the Peloponnese she is called upon to defend the newly established federal state of Arkadia, helps to found the new league in Aetolia, and liberates Messenia from centuries of Spartan control.[9] In the north, Pelopidas complements Epaminondas' efforts in the south by "seeking to neutralize Athenian influence and ambitions," especially regarding Amphipolis.[10] And in the Aegean Epaminondas expresses an interest in upsetting Athenian naval supremacy. By the time the 360s end, however, Thebes' ambitions lie largely unfulfilled, while Pelopidas and Epaminondas themselves lie dead, emblems of the Theban failure.

One might think that with Sparta's loss of Messenia, with the establishment of federations and leagues on the Peloponnese, and with the ultimate failure of Thebes, Athens would have been the primary beneficiary of the 360s. In fact, however, this is not so. On all fronts Athens seems eager to reestablish its presence and influence, but events rarely go its way. When Athens refuses support for the Arkadians against Sparta, Thebes is invited to give aid, and the Theban invasion of the Peloponnese results in the liberation of Messenia and the eventual demise of Spartan hegemony.[11] When Callistratus sends Iphicrates with aid for Sparta, it is a modest act, too late to be useful. Subsequently, in the north, Iphicrates' efforts are thwarted by Pelopidas, whose capacity to gather support must be gauged in part as a response to Athenian designs on Amphipolis. Again, in 367, Pelopidas engineers a peace conference in Susa that generates, among its proposals, the directive that the Athenian navy be beached. Indeed, Timagoras, one of the two Athenian delegates to the conference, is executed on his return for agreeing to the pact.

Callistratus' policy of anti-Theban imperialism was not achieving secure results. In 366, when Thebes seized Oropus on the border between Attica and Boeotia, the policy's failure was glaring, and opposition turned into reconciliation. As Hornblower puts it, Athens chose to concede Theban rule over Boeotia and Oropus in trade for recognition by the great king of Athenian rights in the north, the Chersonese. Hence the King's Peace of 366–365.[12] Callistratus was tried, eventually to be exiled, and Timotheus was recalled. Almost immediately, feeling overly secure about Amphipolis, Athens turned eastward, sending Timotheus on a mission of aid to the satrap Ariobarzanes. Finding a Persian garrison on Samos, Timotheus expelled it and laid siege to the city, installing a cleruchy when it fell and evicting its citizens.[13] The result, however, was shock and animosity, renewed Athenian unpopularity among its allies. Together with its obviously imperialistic interest in Amphipolis, Athens' heady show of self-confidence struck fear in the hearts of its confederates and was in fact just the encouragement Epaminondas needed to initiate the Theban challenge to Athenian naval dominance.[14] As charitably as one looks, it is hard to find Athenian successes in the 360s.

Viewed against the unstable character of Greek affairs in the 360s, Plato's second visit to Sicily reveals itself to be a case of justified pessimism. And with the trip's failure, the scheming against Dion, and the realization of Dionysius' inadequacies, Plato's pessimism must surely have deepened. Perhaps Ostwald is right that the science of the statesman discussed in the *Politicus* is, even at this stage, not identical with philosophy.[15] But by the time the *Laws* is being composed, Plato's appreciation of the recalcitrant nature of man and society is so thoroughgoing that in his final work the rule of law has nearly replaced any notion of personal administration. In the *Republic*, Plato appreciated the demands nature places on philosophy, that ecstatic ritual as a rite of passage must occur in society, in a polis, and that the proper role for the philosopher is archon basileus, ruler. By the time the *Laws* are being composed, Plato still adheres to his conception of human eudaimonia as philosophical ascent, but his sensitivity to nature and history have led him to rethink the administration of the best polis. Law and not philosophical cultivation can best cope with such factors—with human desire and all that is associated with it. The commitment to philosophy's preeminence and its religious character remains; the opposition to the polis tradition and Delphic theology as the desired form of piety also remains. What has been jettisoned is the economical commitment to philosophical rule as the *Republic* envisages it.

The writings of the 360s testify to Plato's abiding commitment to the preeminence of philosophy and to the religious centrality of the soul's aspiration to divinity via philosophical inquiry. The religious terminology may not be as vivid or as strident; Plato's mood and style have changed but not his underlying conception of philosophy as a ritual of transcendence, a way to the human attainment, as much as is possible, of divine knowledge.

Nor did Plato forget his Socratic legacy. In the 360s he projected a trilogy, the *Statesman*, *Sophist*, and *Philosopher*, the final dialogue of which was never written. Cornford believed that had the dialogue on the philosopher been completed, its chief inquirer would have been Socrates.[16] In Plato's eyes, Socrates always remained the paradigmatic philosopher. There are doubtless many reasons for this veneration, but one must surely have been that Socrates best exemplified the novel type of rational piety that Plato had vigorously adopted, defended, and enriched. This piety was for Socrates and continued to be for Plato a revolutionary form of religious commitment and conduct.

Alongside a full regimen of civic festivals, sacrifices, and other rites, Plato developed the conception of a lifelong ritual of intellectual aspiration, a new paideia founded on the soul's immortality and aimed at attaining divinity—or something near it. I have tried to show the prominence of this theme in the dialogues of Plato's middle period. The dialogues of the 360s do not break with this conception of Platonic piety; they deepen it, revise it, and extend it, all within a period of personal and public turmoil. They are the product of a man of rare vision and literary skill, whose intellect yearned for hope in a historical period in which frustration and uncertainty were daily fare. Hope may have eluded him; his later writings exhibit little of it. But intensity did not. Nor did the conviction leave him that old separations and old animosities were never more than artificial boundaries to be transcended, bleak reminders of ancient prejudices that blocked the way to genuine piety, to human flourishing, and indeed to philosophy itself.

NOTES

INTRODUCTION

1 There have been a few studies of Plato and religion, but their orientation has been quite different from my own. See Solmsen, *Plato's Theology*; More, *Religion of Plato*; and Despland, *Education of Desire*.

2 I have in mind the Straussians, but one could include others as well. See Griswold, *Platonic Writings, Platonic Readings*.

3 For example, N. P. White, *Plato on Knowledge and Reality*; Irwin, *Plato's Moral Theory*; and Kraut, *Socrates and the State*.

4 See, e.g., Rorty, Schneewind, and Skinner, *Philosophy in History*.

5 Which, it can be argued, it surely is, insofar as all recovery of the past is constitutive of the self, the community's conception of itself, and so forth.

6 To avoid simple accommodation or construction. See Morgan, "Goals and Methods"; and "Authorship and the History of Philosophy."

7 Quentin Skinner, *The Foundations of Modern Political Thought* (Cambridge: Cambridge University Press, 1978); Richard Ashcraft, *Revolutionary Politics and Locke's Two Treatises of Government* (Princeton: Princeton University Press, 1986); James Tully, *A Discourse on Property* (Cambridge: Cambridge University Press, 1980); Richard Tuck, *Natural Rights Theories* (Cambridge: Cambridge University Press, 1979).

8 Bryan Wilson, ed., *Rationality* (Oxford: Oxford University Press, 1970); Martin Hollis and Steven Lukes, eds., *Rationality and Relativism* (Cambridge: MIT Press, 1982).

9 Richard Rorty, *Philosophy and the Mirror of Nature* (Princeton: Princeton University Press, 1980); Alasdair MacIntyre, *After Virtue* (South Bend, Ind.: University of Notre Dame Press, 1981); Stanley Cavell, *Claim of Reason*. One should not neglect the influence of Thomas Kuhn, *The Structure of Scientific Revolutions* (Chicago: University of Chicago Press, 1962; reissued 1970).

10 For a provocative attempt to argue for a similar approach to music theory—the wedding of historical research and formal analysis—see Joseph Kerman, *Contemplating Music* (Cambridge: Harvard University Press, 1985); Carl Schorske, *Fin-de-Siècle Vienna* (New York: Vintage, 1981). On Baron's seminal work see Gene Brucker, *Renaissance Florence* (Berkeley: University of California Press, 1983), 234–37.

CHAPTER ONE: SOCRATIC PIETY AS PLATO SAW IT

1 Cassirer, *Kant's Life and Thought*, 98–99.

2 Henceforth, my references to Socrates are based on the portrait of Socrates that Plato gives us in the early dialogues. I take this account to
reveal Socratic moral thinking, inquiry, and piety as Plato saw them
and hence as they came to influence him. In addition, this portrait may
be historically accurate in the sense that it provides us with knowledge
about Socrates that goes beyond Plato's perceptions of him. But I am
not concerned with this question of historical accuracy; I am concerned
rather with the question of historical influence, the impact of one powerful intellectual and religious personality on another.

3 See Ehnmark, "Socrates and the Immortality of the Soul." The notion
of the soul's immortality is present in the fifth century not only in
Orphic and Pythagorean traditions but also in Euripides (*Helena* 1014–
15), in Diogenes of Apollonia (B4, B5, B7, B8), in Empedocles (B112,
B115), and elsewhere. See Burkert, *Greek Religion*, 320.

4 Why do we begin with the *Apology* rather than the *Euthyphro*, which
after all deals explicitly with piety *(to hosion)*? The *Apology*, I believe,
is the primary evidence for Plato's interpretation of Socratic religious
thought and conduct. The *Euthyphro* may illuminate ordinary religious
thought and also fanatical excesses; the *Apology* portrays Socratic theology. Although tailored to the beliefs and attitudes of the jurymen,
the speech must be consonant enough with popular and intimate
knowledge of Socrates so as not to shock those familiar with him, and
in a jury of five hundred dicasts surely some were intimate with Socrates. And among the likely readers of Plato's dialogue, surely many
were Socratic confidants and disciples. See Brickhouse and Smith, *Socrates on Trial*, 2–10, and Allen, *Socrates and Legal Obligation*, 33–36,
on the reliability of the *Apology* and the nature of philosophical rhetoric. Also see Dover, *Greek Popular Morality*; and Mikalson, *Athenian
Popular Religion*, 7–8.

5 This is not to say that earlier, at least from the time of Peisistratos in
the sixth century, there had not been significant changes in religious
practice and thought in Athens. In private correspondence Robert Parker has reminded me that Greek polytheism was always open and in
flux. This does not however conflict with my suggestion that this
change was prominent in the late stages of the fifth century. See G. E.
Lloyd, *Magic, Reason, and Experience*, 10–14; and, for an influential
paper on the open character of traditional polytheisms, J. A. North,
"Conservatism and Change in Roman Religion," *Papers of the British
School at Rome* (1976), 1–12.

6 But see, e.g., Erwin Rohde, *Psyche*, 2:463.

7 Throughout this work I shall try to illuminate a Platonic association

between philosophical inquiry and ecstatic ritual. I shall introduce evidence that Plato came to understand particular occasions of philosophical inquiry as "akin to" particular ritual episodes, and the philosophical life as a life of ecstatic ritual, similar to a Pythagorean way of life or a life of Bacchic-Orphic religiosity. I use the expression "akin to" because I do not think that we can say with precision how Plato felt about this relationship; whether it was a loose association or an identity or something in between. Nor can we be sure how he felt at any given time. All that we can do is remember that for a fourth-century Greek thinker our own distinctions among religion, morality, politics, and so forth would have made little sense. When Plato carries over the vocabulary of ecstatic ritual into the epistemological domain, it is not likely that he meant it only figuratively. More than this we cannot say.

8 There is extensive discussion of the notion of *daimon*. See Gernet, *Anthropology of Ancient Greece*, 11; Vernant, *Myth and Society in Ancient Greece*, 107; and Burkert, *Greek Religion*, 180–81.

9 *Euthydemus* 302c4–3a3. See Mikalson, *Athenian Popular Religion*, 31–32, on the juror's oath, and 33–34, on the ephebic oath, contra Kraut; also see 70 and n. 32. On Zeus, Athena, and Apollo as the most prominent deities in the Athenian demes, see Whitehead, *Demes of Attica*, 206–07, n. 179; also Roberts, *City of Sokrates*, 118, 122.

10 Even though the Pythia is possessed, the message is one of separation; see I. M. Lewis, *Ecstatic Religion*, 56 and esp. 58; and Gernet, *Anthropology of Ancient Greece*, 55. But note the relationship between Delphi and Dionysos in Burkert, *Greek Religion*, 224–25.

11 Hugh Lloyd-Jones discusses this extensively in *The Justice of Zeus*. See also *Menexenus* 247e5–6, "Nothing too much"; Parker, *Miasma*, 65–66; and Burkert, *Greek Religion*, 148, 188–89, 201–02.

12 For a recent interpretation of Socrates that distinguishes between human knowledge and divine wisdom, see Vlastos, "Socrates' Disavowal of Knowledge," esp. 12–18 and 26–29. Vlastos argues that for Socrates human knowledge is elenctic and revisable, whereas divine wisdom is certain and infallible. I do not think that in the *Apology* Plato adopts this ambiguity or the notion of elenctic knowledge for Socrates. His terminology is not that precise. For a critique of Vlastos along different lines, see Reeve, *Socrates in the* Apology, 33–62.

13 This is the intellectual dimension of the issue; the popular dimension concerns divine foreknowledge. See Mikalson, *Athenian Popular Religion*, 20; and Xenophon.

14 *Pronoia* (providence) is a notion found in Herodotus (3.108) and one that Xenophon ascribes to Socrates (*Memorabilia* 1.4, 4.3). See Burkert, *Greek Religion*, 319.

15 Parke and Wormell, *Delphic Oracle*, 1:401–03.

16 See also the famous story of Xenophon, *Anabasis* 3.1.4–8. Socrates sends Xenophon to Delphi to seek personal guidance but Xenophon asks a presumptive question.

17 See Dodds, *Greeks and the Irrational*, chap. 1; and Allen, *Socrates and Legal Obligation*, for his commentary on the *Crito*. Dodds' understanding of Greek life, culture, and thought is indebted to anthropology. See Dodds, *Ancient Concept of Progress*, 29: "It would be possible to show how recent developments in social anthropology and social psychology open the way to a fuller understanding of Greek religion as an element in the complex pattern of Greek [life]." Dodds' own use of modern anthropology, most notably in *Greeks and the Irrational*, did not benefit from the Oxford school of Evans-Pritchard and others or from structuralism or recent comparative and cultural anthropology, such as the work of Geertz and Douglas. G. E. R. Lloyd's *Polarity and Analogy* and especially Parker's *Miasma* are indebted to these more recent developments. See too Lloyd's *Magic, Reason, and Experience*, 1–4.

18 This reading, which is looser than Vlastos would allow, runs against his conclusion in "Socrates' Disavowal of Knowledge," 12–18, and in "Paradox of Socrates," 10.

19 Kraut, in *Socrates and the State*, argues that Socrates believed knowledge to be possible and wisdom attainable.

20 See *Hippias Major* 289a8–b8 on Heraclitus and the comments on this fragment by Charles Kahn in *Art and Thought of Heraclitus*, 173–74.

21 See Ehnmark, "Socrates and the Immortality of the Soul," 116–17; compare with the *Phaedo* and its ending.

22 Athens is reputed to have more wisdom and power than any other polis.

23 The importance of immortality for distinguishing the divine from the mortal is widely acknowledged. See, e.g., Lloyd-Jones, *Justice of Zeus*; and Guthrie, *Greeks and Their Gods*. Also see Griffin, *Homer on Life and Death*, 82–83, 92–93, 167.

24 The kind of reason that Socrates points to is however a very special sort. It is a reason for believing that is not a reason for the truth of the belief.

25 Socrates' final remarks might be understood differently: that the jurors or citizens are worse off without him than he is going to be without them. Earlier in his speech Socrates did emphasize his value to the citizens of Athens, but it would be singularly unappealing for him to refer to this at the end of his speech. It is much more in character to have him comment on the citizens' lack of wisdom—about death and about the human good.

26 See 40e and 41c, "if the stories are true."

27 *Apology* 41b–c. Socrates shows a familiarity with Orpheus and Mu-

saeus, as well as with Hesiod and Homer, and imagines engaging in philosophical interrogations with Agamemnon, Odysseus, and Sisyphus.

28 Vlastos, in "Paradox of Socrates," 5, believes that *Crito* 54b–c is sufficient evidence, but I do not think it is decisive. The remark about an afterlife occurs in the Speech of the Laws and may very well be rhetorical.

29 In correspondence Robert Parker has expressed to me some dissatisfaction with this expression, and I thoroughly share his concern that the expression "smacks of the old and I think discredited way of viewing Delphi as a kind of Greek Vatican, the effective source of orthodoxy." Clearly, I do not intend that there was a single orthodoxy in Greek religion, nor that Delphi was an authoritative source of practice or belief for Greek religiosity. But I need an expression to capture the widespread belief in divine-human separation, and since that belief is so clearly associated with the teachings of Delphi, I use this expression, "Delphic theology," for such a purpose.

30 In his important studies of the Azande and Nuer, Evans-Pritchard emphasized the lack of an articulated native theology. He said it was largely the ethnographer's questions that precipitated religious reflection; resulting contradictions and confusions simply highlight the ad hoc nature of that reflection. See also G. E. R. Lloyd, *Magic, Reason, and Experience*.

31 Our best evidence for ritual conduct, festivals, and so on comes from Xenophon, the fourth-century orators, Diodorus Sicilus, Herodotus, Aristophanes, Pausanias, Plato's *Laws*, the *Athenaion Politeia*, and epigraphical material; our best sources for late fifth-century and fourth-century religious thought are the writings of the sophists, Sophocles, Euripides, Thucydides, Plato, and others.

32 In addition to Dodds, *Greeks and the Irrational*, and Lloyd-Jones, *Justice of Zeus*, see the many books and articles of Nilsson, Festugière, Burkert, Otto, and, on selected themes, Henrichs. For complete references see the bibliography and subsequent notes.

33 Older works, like Nilsson's *Greek Folk Religion*, are helpful but lack a historical dimension. Mikalson's recent book *Athenian Popular Religion* focuses on the fourth century, but is essentially a survey of material from the orators and other sources without any reflective depth. Dover's excellent work *Greek Popular Morality* is already a classic. One should also consult Parke on the festivals and MacDowell on the legal aspects of religious life and the context for the profanations around 415.

34 For a classic alternative see Taylor, *Socrates*.

35 B25; see also the famous first line of Protagoras' work *On Gods*, B4. Dover discusses the critique of traditional religion in the context of

trials for impiety and intellectual freedom in "Freedom of the Intellectual," esp. 44–46. See also Burkert, *Greek Religion*, 313–17; and Drachman, *Atheism in Pagan Antiquity*. For a sober comment on the
relatively conservative results of this critical attitude, see Burkert,
Greek Religion, 321. See also Kerferd, *Sophistic Movement*, 165–67; and
G. E. R. Lloyd, *Magic, Reason, and Experience*, 14–15.

36 On Protagoras see Dodds, *Ancient Concept of Progress*, 79, 96–97; Dodds
takes the influence of the rational critique and especially Protagoras to
be great, like that of Darwin in Victorian England. See Dodds, "Euripides the Irrationalist," in *Ancient Concept of Progress*, 84. See also
Guthrie, *History of Greek Philosophy*, 3:226–49; and Kerferd, *Sophistic
Movement*, chap. 13. In addition there are two excellent papers by
Henrichs, "Two Doxographical Notes," and "The Sophists and Hellenistic Religion."

37 G. E. R. Lloyd emphasizes this point; see esp. *Magic, Reason, and Experience*, 29–32.

38 See Parke, *Festivals of the Athenians*; Mikalson, *Sacred and Civil Calendar*; and Deubner, *Attische Feste*.

39 See Nilsson, *Greek Folk Religion*; and Scully, *The Earth, the Temple,
and the Gods*.

40 Perhaps the most visible expression of that kinship were the games at
Olympia; note also the role of Zeus. See Burkert, *Greek Religion*, 130–
31, on Zeus as a panhellenic god, and 170, on the hearth at Delphi as
a common hearth for all of Greece. See also Plutarch *Arist.* 20.4.

41 See Mikalson, *Athenian Popular Religion*, chap. 11; and Henrichs,
"Greek Maenadism," 154. See also Whitehead, *Demes of Attica*, 176–
222.

42 One should probably add divination to sacrifice as the most common
type of religious act. See Mikalson, *Athenian Popular Religion*, chap. 6;
and Powell, "Religion and the Sicilian Expedition," esp. 19.

43 Cf. Demosthenes 4.35–4.36, though an exaggeration. See also Mikalson,
Sacred and Civil Calendar; Whitehead, *Demes of Attica*, 44, 185–208;
and Dow, "Six Athenian Sacrificial Calendars."

44 See MacDowell, *Andokides*; Powell, "Religion and the Sicilian Expedition"; Parker, *Miasma*, 168–70; and Dover, "Freedom of the Intellectual." See also Thucydides 6.32.

45 This was the response of the intellectuals too and not just of the uneducated; see Powell, "Religion and the Sicilian Expedition," 20–21. On
a similar phenomenon in a different period, see Keith Thomas' classic
Religion and the Decline of Magic.

46 Dodds sees a shift here and a loss of faith in prophecy; see *Ancient
Concept of Progress*, 75–76.

47 See Douglas, *Natural Symbols*; Detienne, *Dionysos Slain*, chaps. 3, 4,
and esp. pp. 55–56, 88–94; and, on the role of pollution in maintaining

the separation of mortal and immortal, Parker, *Miasma*, 189–90, 256 (on the way disease was seen as reflecting the separation). See also Burkert, *Greek Religion*, 53, 56–59, 66, 255; and Vernant, *Myth and Society*, 135, 137, and chap. 8.

48 It is well known that during the war Delphi supported Sparta. See Powell, "Religion and the Sicilian Expedition," 17–18; and Dodds, *Ancient Concept of Progress*, 75–76. There were other oracles to which Athens turned during this period, notably Dodona and Ammon. Before undertaking the Sicilian expedition, the Athenians consulted the Oracle of Zeus at Dodona. Inscribed on a lead tablet, the question read: "Is it better for the Athenians to send an expedition to Sicily?" See Webster, *Everyday Life*, 76. There is some question about the authenticity of this oracle.

49 See Mikalson, *Athenian Popular Religion*, 11–12, esp. n. 17. Cf. Herodotus 9.36–39; Xenophon, *Anabasis* 6.4.12–5.2; Herodotus 9.33–6; and Burkert, *Greek Religion*, 113, 264–68. Also Herington, *Athena Parthenos*; and Webster, *Everyday Life*, 135–45, esp. 145. On Herodotus see the brief but excellent comments of G. E. R. Lloyd in *Magic, Reason, and Experience*, 29–32.

50 Dodds, *Greeks and the Irrational*, 193–95. As I have mentioned, this is not to deny the inherent openness of Greek religion and the changes of significance that occur throughout the fifth century. As Walter Burkert has pointed out to me, the prominence of Orphic themes and references in Pindar is an indication of continuing modification during this period, and, if Graf is right, there was an "orphic interpretation of Eleusis" that was established and widely accepted early in the fifth century.

51 I have in mind Lysander's deification in Samos in 404 (Plutarch *Lys.* 18); see St. Croix, *Origins of the Peloponnesian War*, 74. Also see Detienne, *Dionysos Slain*, 58–59; and Gernet, *Anthropology of Ancient Greece*, 6–8.

52 See Burkert, *Greek Religion*, 39, on sacred kingship in Knossos and Mycenae; n. 45 for references; p. 46 for Pylos; and pp. 203–08. See also Farnell's classic work *Greek Hero Cults*; and Griffin, *Homer on Life and Death*, 82, 167.

53 See Euripides *Heracles*. Pythagoras and Empedocles were also considered to be divine; see G. E. R. Lloyd's comments on Empedocles in *Magic, Reason, and Experience*, 33–37. See also Kahn, "Religion and Natural Philosophy." On Prodicus and the belief that gods are elevated human beings, see Henrichs, "Sophists and Hellenistic Religion," 139–45.

54 On writs of impiety for doing so illegally, see Mikalson, *Athenian Popular Religion*, 92–93.

55 On Asclepius see Parker, *Miasma*, 249–50, 252; see also *Ion* 530a. Parker reminds me that even though he was a recent import, Asclepius was a figure of "traditional genealogy and type."

56 Burkert, *Greek Religion*, 177–79. Kybele is an early import, but her significance increases during this period. Ammon's cult is established in Athens in the fourth century; Paus. 9.16.1.

57 This includes shamans and shamanic figures, like Empedocles. See Dodds, *Greeks and the Irrational*, 140ff.; and Lloyd-Jones, *Justice of Zeus*, 173.

58 In general see Dodds, *Greeks and the Irrational*, 193–95. Also see *Charmides* 156d3–6; and Guthrie, *Greeks and Their Gods*, 174ff. On Zalmoxis and his Thracian devotees see Herodotus iv. 93.

59 On Empedocles see Parker, *Miasma*, 304–05; on the influence of Empedocles on Socrates see Morgan, "Continuity Theory of Reality."

60 The best discussion of the religious dimension of the *Bacchae* is Dodds's edition and commentary, together with his paper "Maenadism in Euripides' *Bacchae*."

61 See Dodds on the *Ion*; and Burkert, *Greek Religion*, 109–11. See also Burkert, *Ancient Mystery Cults*, esp. chaps. 1, 2.

62 Jane Harrison's discussion of Durkheim's notion that such rituals as omophagy represent dramatically an attempt at total identification with the social group is discussed in Henrichs, "Loss of Self," 231 and n. 72.

63 See I. M. Lewis, *Ecstatic Religion*; Lienhardt, *Divinity and Experience*; Evans-Pritchard, *Witchcraft, Oracles, and Magic*; Evans-Pritchard, *Nuer Religion*; Geertz, *Islam Observed*; Geertz, *Religion of Java*; and Geertz, *Interpretation of Cultures*.

64 See Douglas, *Natural Symbols*; and Detienne, *Dionysos Slain*, 60–67, on the relation between cuisine among the Orphics and Pythagoreans and the way rules for eating reflect a certain view of cosmic structure (in both cases a rebellion against the traditional separation of the divine and the human). See also Detienne, *Gardens of Adonis*.

65 I refer of course to the profanations. The best treatment I know is in MacDowell, *Andokides*. One might note too the festivals of Dionysos and their performance.

66 See Mikalson, *Athenian Popular Religion*, 5–6; and den Boer, "Aspects of Religion."

67 But see Lloyd-Jones and Dodds, both of whom emphasize a uniformity in this period, Lloyd-Jones the traditional-retributive and Dodds the noncognitive and irrational. My brief sketch has been an attempt to respect the remarkable religious diversity of the years during and just after the Peloponnesian War.

68 The initial encounter in the *Republic* is between Socrates and Cephalus, a famous and wealthy metic. Neither wholly foreign nor wholly a citizen, such a person has a unique civil status in Athens, analogous to the ontological status of the soul and to the status of the philosophical

ruler, who as a quasi-divine being stands somewhere between ordinary humankind and the gods. These are all indications that the *Republic* concerns statuses that do not fit into normal, dichotomous classifications. See Mary Douglas' discussion of the pangolin in *Implicit Meanings*.

69 "Crito, we owe a cock to Asclepius: please pay the debt, and don't neglect it" (*Phaedo* 118a). See *Ion* 530a3–b3. On Heracles, Diaskouroi, and Asclepius as those who cross the boundary between divine and human see Burkert, *Greek Religion*, 208–15; and Burkert, *Structure and History*, 78–98. See also Pindar *Nem.* 3.22, *Pyth.* 3.7.

70 This is surely the case with Protagoras in the dialogue that bears his name and, I would argue, also applies to Parmenides in the dialogue that bears his.

71 *Ion* 533c1, 535c7–d7; *Apology* 40a2–c3.

72 See *Cratylus* 396c–e; see also Parker, *Miasma*, 221.

73 The conflict between old and new is not an uncommon trope; see Aristophanes *Clouds*. On *hosios*, *hieros*, see Burkert, *Greek Religion*, 269–70.

74 *Euthyphro* 4c1–3.

75 Walter Burkert has suggested to me that Euthyphro ought better be conceived as a *mantis* and a kind of Orphic himself rather than as a typical representative of polis religion. If Burkert is right, the *Euthyphro* already prefigures a Platonic attack on corrupt or degenerate versions of Orphic-Bacchic rites and practices that is developed in the *Republic* (see below). But I am not persuaded that Plato's portrayal of Euthyphro is that extreme.

76 For comments on the phenomenon of disciplinary distinctiveness see Wolf Lepenies, "'Interesting Questions' in the history of philosophy and elsewhere," in Rorty, Schneewind, and Skinner, *Philosophy in History*, 155–76. See too G. E. R. Lloyd's comments in *Magic, Reason, and Experience*, 100, on Plato's efforts to distinguish philosophical forms of elenchos from others; and Robinson, *Plato's Earlier Dialectic*, 85.

77 See *Euthydemus* 277d5–e3.

78 See *Euthydemus* 302b4–03a3 on Socrates' traditional piety.

79 Kraut, *Socrates and the State*, 245–309.

80 I try not to be rigid about expressing the relation between rational or philosophical inquiry and ecstatic ritual. See n. 7, above.

81 Cornford's felicitous phrase, the "Socratic Revolution," comes from *Before and after Socrates*; it is recalled appropriately by Allen in *Socrates and Legal Obligation*, 70.

82 Burnet, *Apology, Euthyphro, Crito*, 120.

83 See Sealey, *History of the Greek City States*, 315–16.

84 Possibly, to the Hyperborean Apollo? See Burkert, *Lore and Science*, 149–

50; and Dodds, *Greeks and the Irrational*, 144. On the identification of Apollo, Dionysos, and the Sun, see Burkert, *Ancient Mystery Cults*, 81–82.

85 I discuss these passages in chapter 4.

86 Mikalson, *Athenian Popular Religion*, 46, refers to Theophrastus; also n. 23. See also Demosthenes and Aristophanes.

87 Dodds, *Greeks and the Irrational*, 144, 165, and n. 60.

88 This passage influenced the later tradition on the dating of Pythagoras; see Burkert, *Lore and Science*, 109 n. 65.

89 Dodds, *Greeks and the Irrational*, 166 n. 61.

90 Stories about human sacrifices and underground caves were memorable to Herodotus. See Henrichs, "Two Doxographical Notes"; and Henrichs, "Sophists and Hellenistic Religion."

91 Notice the nominal association of one of the elderly interlocutors, Dionysodorus, with Dionysos. See Henrichs, "Loss of Self," 205, on the afterlife.

92 Dodds, *Greeks and the Irrational*, 96 n. 90.

93 See I. M. Lewis, *Ecstatic Religion*, 41ff.; and Linforth, "Corybantic Rites in Plato," esp. 155–56. See also Euripides' *Hippolytus*; Aristophanes; and Parker, *Miasma*, 245–48, 303–05, on initiation and purification rites. On the role of music in Corybantic rites, see Rouget, *Music and Trance*, 187–220.

94 Dodds, *Greeks and the Irrational*, 79, 99 n. 104; see also Linforth, "Corybantic Rites in Plato," 124–25.

95 For treatment of Socrates as a peripheral person see I. M. Lewis, *Ecstatic Religion*, 101, 126. See also Detienne for treatment of Orphics and Pythagoreans as rebels against traditional categories.

96 On divination see Mikalson, *Athenian Popular Religion*, chap. 6, esp. 39–40 and n. 4 (from Nilsson); see also Thomas, "History and Anthropology," 8–9, for the use of anthropology for history. In *Crito* 54d Socrates compares himself to the Corybantes. On Corybantic rites as a treatment for madness see Aristophanes *Vesp.* 118–24; Parker, *Miasma*, 245–46, and Rouget, *Music and Trance*, 192–213.

97 Dodds, *Greeks and the Irrational*, 79, 98 n. 102; see also Evans-Pritchard, *Witchcraft, Oracles, and Magic*. See *Ion* 531b on diviners and divination.

98 See the end of the *Meno* on virtue as divine disposition.

99 Dodds, *Greeks and the Irrational*, 98 n. 102; Linforth, "Corybantic Rites in Plato."

100 On women, peripheral persons, and such rites as revolutionary see I. M. Lewis, *Ecstatic Religion*, chap. 3; Detienne, *Dionysos Slain*; Detienne, *Gardens of Adonis*; and Douglas, *Implicit Meanings*, for marginal status and classifications. But see also Henrichs, "Changing Dionysiac Identities," 143–47.

101 Linforth, "Corybantic Rites in Plato," 132–33; Rohde, *Psyche*, 87–89; Burkert, *Greek Religion*, 173.

102 Anthesteria, rustic Dionysia, Great Dionysia; see Burkert, *Greek Religion*, 163. On Dionysos see Burkert, *Greek Religion*, 161–67. See also Webster, *Everyday Life*, 87–96; and Pickard-Cambridge, *Dramatic Festivals*.

103 See Dodds, "Maenadism in the *Bacchae*"; I. M. Lewis, *Ecstatic Religion*, 90; Nilsson, "Early Orphism," 203–04; and Henrichs, "Greek Maenadism." On the Mycenaean evidence for Dionysos see Burkert, *Greek Religion*, 45 and esp. n. 24.

104 See Euripides *Hippolytus* 141ff.; and Aristophanes *Wasps* 8. See also Linforth, "Corybantic Rites in Plato," 127, 133–34, 158; and Parker, *Miasma*, 208–09.

105 Evans-Pritchard, *Witchcraft, Oracles, and Magic*; I. M. Lewis, *Ecstatic Religion*, chap. 3; and Macfarlane, *Witchcraft in Tudor and Stuart England*.

106 See Guthrie, *Greeks and Their Gods*, chap. 6; and Rohde, *Psyche*.

107 Guthrie, *Greeks and Their Gods*, 149–50.

108 On Kybele, Phrygia, and others, see ibid., 154.

109 Ibid., 155.

110 Ibid., 165–82, esp. 172–73, 174 n. 1, discusses the historical context of Dionysos' domestication. Against the view that Dionysos was a Thracian import, see Burkert, *Greek Religion*, 45. This evidence does not contravene the suggestion that new Dyonysiac cults were imported from Thrace during this period.

111 Guthrie treats Zalmoxis as a god; see *Greeks and Their Gods*, 175, esp. n. 1.

112 Euripides *Bacchae* xi; Sophocles *Antigone* 1125ff. See also Guthrie, *Greeks and Their Gods*, 178. On the rural Dionysia see Pickard-Cambridge, *Dramatic Festivals*, 42–56; Parke, *Festivals of the Athenians*, 100–03; and Whitehead, *Demes of Attica*, 212–22.

113 See *Crito* 54d; and Linforth, "Corybantic Rites in Plato," 134–35.

114 For Socrates the soul is ill and inculcating virtue is the cure; wisdom is the cure for ignorance. See Parker, *Miasma*, 245–48; for a reference to Aristophanes *Vesp.*

115 Dionysiac rites generally involved some sense of identification with Dionysos; for a cautious assessment of how this identification occurred, see Henrichs, "Changing Dionysiac Identities," 159–60.

116 This Thracian religion is however not necessarily Dionysiac; see Henrichs, "Loss of Self," 225, where it is argued that Dionysos is not a Thracian import—which does not of course exclude the possibility that some versions of Thracian religion are Dionysiac. See Burkert, *Greek Religion*, 46.

117 This struggle takes place under the auspices of a daimon; see Eustathius
    On Dion. Pen. 819; Linforth, "Corybantic Rites in Plato," 123 and n. 5
    (for Linforth the Corybantes were *daimones*).
118 As Alcibiades, and Plato, seem to think; see *Symposium* 215c–e. Dodds
    portrays Euripides as advocating a nonrational version of such rites in
    Ancient Concept of Progress, 86–89; see also Dietrich's comment on
    Strepsiades, in Nilsson, "Early Orphism," 220 and n. 27: "Dietrich very
    ingeniously pointed out the similarity between the preparations which,
    according to Aristophanes, Strepsiades had to undergo when he wished
    to be initiated into the philosophical wisdom of Socrates and the ini-
    tiations into the mysteries."
119 Perhaps at least in part for this reason Plato sees Socrates as indicted,
    convicted, and ultimately executed. Was Socrates a *pharmakos*? See
    Burkert, *Greek Religion*, 82–83; and Taylor, *Socrates*, 115. The trial and
    execution took place in late spring or early summer; Brickhouse and
    Smith place the execution in May or June of 399 B.C.E. (*Socrates on
    Trial*, 13–14, n. 27). Could the time have been near the Thargelia? See
    Parker, *Miasma*, 23–29. Socrates was born on the sixth of Thargelion,
    when scapegoats were sent out, a time of cleansing; see too Lys. 6.53,
    where Andokides' exile is compared to "sending out a *pharmakos*"
    (quoted by Parker, 259). See Roberts, *City of Sokrates*, 124.
120 Someone who accepts this much for Socrates, that he believed in the
    centrality of an immaterial, immortal soul, is Bernard Williams; see
    Ethics and the Limits of Philosophy, 34. See also Williams, "Philoso-
    phy," 248.
121 On this view, *eudaimonia* involves this knowledge and the state of
    being properly possessed by a daimon. Immortality is not by itself eu-
    daimonia for Socrates, but the attainment of fully divine status would
    be—and that means the acquisition of knowledge sufficient to complete
    immortality. See Parker, *Miasma*, 247–48.
122 For example, Burkert, *Greek Religion*, 275.
123 Guthrie, *Greeks and Their Gods*, 176.
124 As Jaeger does, e.g., in "Greek Ideas of Immortality," 143.

CHAPTER TWO: RELIGION, POLITICS,
AND INQUIRY IN THE *MENO*

1 The current orthodoxy, to which I largely subscribe, holds that dialogues
  such as the *Euthyphro, Laches,* and *Lysis* portray Socrates outright, while
  passages in the *Meno* and the *Republic* only allude to him.
2 According to Cornford the shift occurs in the *Phaedo,* with the famous
  autobiographical passage. The famous thesis of Taylor-Burnet is even
  more robust in Socrates' favor. No decisive evidence is available. One is

forced to propose an interpretation based on philosophical issues and then to consider how persuasive an account of Socrates and Plato can be derived from it or made to suit it.

3 Bluck, *Plato's Meno*, 108–20.

4 Wickersham and Verbrugghe, *Greek Historical Documents*, 29; Sealey, *History of the Greek City States*, 396–99; Hornblower, *Greek World*, 198–201; Hammond, *History of Greece*, 457–65. See also Xen. *Hellenica* 5.1.25–36.

5 Wickersham and Verbrugghe, *Greek Historical Documents*, 6; Sealey, *History of the Greek City States*, 383–84; Bluck, *Plato's Meno*, 122; Hammond, *History of Greece*, 442–48; MacDowell, *Law in Classical Athens*, 47–48. See also Aristotle *Ath. Pol.* 39.

6 See Xen. *Hell.* 5.1; Sealey, *History of the Greek City States*, 392–98; Hornblower, *Greek World*, 198–201; and Hammond, *History of Greece*, 462–65.

7 Hammond, *History of Greece*, 463–64; Cawkwell, "Imperialism of Thrasybulus." See also Hornblower, *Mausolus*, 184–85; *Oxyrhynchus Historian (Oxyr. Hist.)*; Xen. *Hell.* 3.5.10; and Aristophanes *Plutus* (ca. 388).

8 As Lysander had done in 405! See Wickersham and Verbrugghe, *Greek Historical Documents*, 29; Hammond, *History of Greece*, 464; and Hornblower, *Greek World*, 198.

9 Xen. *Hell.* 5.1.31; Diod. Sic. 14.110.3. For problems see Sealey, *History of the Greek City States*, 397. See also Ryder, *Koine Eirene*.

10 Sealey, *History of the Greek City States*, 398; Hornblower, *Greek World*, 199.

11 Cawkwell, "King's Peace." See also Hornblower, *Greek World*, 198–99; Davies, *Democracy and Classical Greece*, 163; Xen. *Hell.* 5.1.35.

12 Hammond, *History of Greece*, 465.

13 On response to defeat see Christopher Hill, *The Experience of Defeat* (Harmondsworth: Penguin, 1984).

14 See Wickersham and Verbrugghe, *Greek Historical Documents*, 31.

15 Isocrates *Panegyrikos* 176, 106–07, 120–21, and Ninth Letter.

16 *Panegyrikos* 106; see the reference to Plutarch *Artae* 22 in Hammond, *History of Greece*, 466–67.

17 Demosthenes 15.29.

18 Hammond, *History of Greece*, 307, on the Treaty of Callias.

19 Especially after 447–446 and the conclusion of the Thirty Years Peace with Sparta (Sealey, *History of the Greek City States*, 291–94).

20 Hornblower, *Greek World*, 200.

21 Cephalus was a famous, wealthy Athenian metic; he plays an important role in Plato's *Republic*. Lysias, one of his sons, escaped from the Thirty Tyrants, supported Thrasybulus in exile, and was made a citizen on his return to Athens.

22 See Hammond, *History of Greece*, 464; and Xen. *Hell.* 5.1.26, 28.

23 See Davies, *Democracy and Classical Greece*, 168–69.

24 On the historical authenticity of the Seventh Letter see Morrow, *Plato's Epistles*, 44–45.

25 VII, 324b1–2.

26 VII, 324b6–7.

27 VII, 326a5–b4; cf. 328a6–b1.

28 Morrow, *Plato's Epistles*, 46.

29 Quoted in Morrow, *Plato's Epistles*, 47, from Diogenes Laertius III, 34.

30 Morrow, *Plato's Epistles*, 48–49; see Diodorus Sicilus XV.7.2.

31 See Plutarch *Dion.* 17; *Arist.* 1; and Morrow, *Plato's Epistles*, 49.

32 Morrow, *Plato's Epistles*, 58, 123–44.

33 VII, 338c. But when was the first meeting? See Burkert, *Lore and Science*, 27: "When Plato went to Magna Graecia for the first time, at the age of nearly forty, his intellectual attitudes must have been fairly well established"; see pp. 77–78 on Gorgias, Pythagoras, and Archytas.

34 See Burkert, *Lore and Science*, 92, and for sources n. 42.

35 Cicero *De Re Publica* I.X (Sabine, 115).

36 Burkert, *Lore and Science*; Burkert, *Orphism and Bacchic Mysteries*; Burkert, *Greek Religion*; Burkert, "Orpheus und die Vorsokratiker"; Burkert, "Craft versus Sect"; Zuntz, *Persephone*; Graf, *Eleusis und die orphische Dichtung Athens in vorhellenistischer Zeit*; West, *Orphic Poems*; Guthrie, *Orpheus and Greek Religion*; Linforth, *Arts of Orpheus*.

37 See West, *Orphic Poems*, 7–15. On Orphic tendencies and Greek art, with special reference to the funerary art of fourth-century Taras and the Derveni papyrus, see Martin Robertson, "Greek Art and Religion," in Easterling and Muir, *Greek Religion and Society*, 185–87.

38 Bluck, *Plato's Meno*, 274–76; see also 61–75.

39 Burkert, *Orphism and Bacchic Mysteries*, 7.

40 Herod. 2.81; Euripides *Hippolytus* 952–54; *Alc.* 967; Pindar frag. 133; *Pyth.* 4.176; Arist. *Birds* 693ff.

41 Later the issue of purification will arise in my discussion of the *Phaedo*, the *Republic* (364b–65a), and the *Phaedrus* (244d–e).

42 See Burkert, "Craft Versus Sect," 5, on the similar move in the Derveni papyrus, and 10–11, on Orphic vegetarianism.

43 See Burkert, *Orphism and Bacchic Mysteries*, 2–3 and notes.

44 Plato is of course our best source for Orphic materials before the Hellenistic period.

45 Herodotus 8.21; Euripides *Hippolytus* 952–54. See also Burkert, *Orphism and Bacchic Mysteries*, 4.

46 Cole, "New Evidence."

47 Ibid., 238.

48 The views of Caratelli, Zuntz, Burkert, and West. See Cole, "New Evidence," 226.

49 Ibid., 233–34; G. S. Kirk, J. E. Raven, and M. Schofield, *The Presocratic Philosophers*, 2d ed. (Cambridge: Cambridge University Press, 1983), 29–30.

50 West sees the tendencies as developments of a single strategy, to attribute to Orpheus, a shaman, poems that tell the truth of the nature and destiny of the soul and of the sacred history of the gods. See West, *Orphic Poems*, 7–24.

51 See ibid., esp. 2–3 on "Orphic" as a textual adjective.

52 See Kirk, Raven, and Schofield, *Presocratic Philosophers*, 21–33.

53 West, *Orphic Poems*, 111–13.

54 According to Burkert 330 B.C.E., with the commentary dating from ca. 400 and the text from the sixth century (p. 2). See also West, *Orphic Poems*, 75; Burkert, "Orpheus und die Vorsokratiker," 93–94; and Kirk, Raven, and Schofield, *Presocratic Philosophers*, 31–33.

55 West, *Orphic Poems*, 75–113.

56 For the dates see Burkert, "Orpheus und die Vorsokratiker," 93–100; and West, *Orphic Poems*, 81–82.

57 West, *Orphic Poems*, 78 and n. 13.

58 Ibid., 94, 98–101.

59 Ibid., 99; Empedocles B137, B115.

60 Recall the *Apology*'s testimony to Socrates' knowledge of Orpheus and Musaeus.

61 Burkert, *Orphism and Bacchic Mysteries*, 7; see also Detienne, *Dionysos Slain*, 68–94.

62 Detienne, *Dionysos Slain*, 70.

63 There is also good evidence for this experience in *Gorgias*, written around the same time; see Dodds, *Plato's Gorgias*, 18–30; Guthrie, *History of Greek Philosophy*, 4:284–85. See also *Gorgias* 493aff.; and Guthrie, *Orpheus and Greek Religion*, 161–63.

64 The members of Meno's family are *xenoi* of the Persian king. Later, in January 401, he will join an expedition of Cyrus as a mercenary; see Xenophon *Anabasis*.

65 On the problem of inferring intentions from actions, see A. Momigliano, "Marcel Mauss and the Quest for the Person in Greek Biography and Autobiography," in Michael Carrithers, Steven Collins, and Steven Lukes, eds., *The Concept of the Person* (Cambridge: Cambridge University Press, 1985), 83–92, esp. 88–91.

66 *Pan.* 16–100.

67 Ibid. 115.

68 Ibid. 115–26.

69 Ibid. 122–25.

70 Ibid. 150–53.

71 Ibid. 156.

72 Ibid. 170–76.

73 Ibid. 182–86.

74 It is interesting that Meno, like Isocrates, is a student of Gorgias; Anytus is of course one of Socrates' prosecutors.

75 See Field, *Plato and His Contemporaries*, 32, 34. On the *thiasos* form of organization for ecstatic cult communities see Burkert, *Ancient Mystery Cults*, 31, 44.

76 Field, in *Plato and His Contemporaries*, 126–27, gets the Platonic response wrong; see Hornblower, *Greek World*, 201, on fourth-century monarchism.

77 For example, that *arete* is something good (87d).

78 See Bluck, *Plato's Meno*, 435–36, for a correct critique of Berry on the role of theia moira and knowledge.

79 See Bluck, *Plato's Meno*, 427–28, 430–31; is it not more literal than he thinks?

80 Bluck notes that in the *Apology* (33c) Socrates attributes his mission to theia moira, perhaps trying to repudiate Aeschines' suggestion (fr. 110) that he was possessed, like a Bacchant. Pohlenz takes *Ion* 534a as such a repudiation.

81 Bluck notes the similarity between 99c2–3 and *Apology* 22a–c and *Ion* 534b–d, but does not develop this theme; see *Plato's Meno*, 524–25.

82 Both in *Meno* and in *Gorgias*; in the latter he compares *episteme* with *empeiria*.

83 For a full discussion of the paradox and how Plato solves it, see Michael L. Morgan, "How Does Plato Solve the Paradox of Inquiry in the *Meno*?" in J. Anton and A. Preus, eds., *Plato: Essays in Ancient Greek Philosophy* (Albany: State University of New York Press, 1989), 169–81.

84 The following discussion is indebted to these works: Bluck, *Plato's Meno*; Buchmann, *Die Stellung des Menon*; Ebert, "Plato's Theory of Recollection Reconsidered"; Ebert, *Meinung und Wissen*; Gulley, "Plato's Theory of Recollection"; Gulley, *Plato's Theory of Knowledge*, 4–23; Irwin, *Plato's Moral Theory*; Moravcsik, "Learning as Recollection"; Vlastos, "Anamnesis in the *Meno*"; N. P. White, *Plato on Knowledge and Reality*; and N. P. White, "Inquiry."

85 Bluck, *Plato's Meno*, 286, 81c5. *Oun* is inferential and discontinuous. Also, the Pindar text intercedes; a mere continuation would be awkward after it.

86 See Guthrie, *Orpheus and Greek Religion*, 164–65, 169; Dodds, *Greeks and the Irrational*, 155–56 and n. 131; Bluck, *Plato's Meno*, 277–86; and West, *Orphic Poems*, 112–13.

87 Dodds accepts it; see *Greeks and the Irrational*, 155–56 and n. 131.

88 See Bluck, *Plato's Meno*; and Burkert, *Greek Religion*, 290–301.

89 See Empedocles B115–46; see also Burkert, *Greek Religion*, 299–300.

90 This phrase must refer to some kind of *orpheotelestai*. See Bluck, *Plato's Meno*, 275–76, 290–93; Burkert, *Orphism and Bacchic Mysteries*, 3–4, 7; Burkert, "Craft versus Sect," 4–6; and Cole, "New Evidence."

91 There is ample evidence of Pindar's sympathy with Orphic teachings and his familiarity with Orphic texts, e.g., Olym. Ode 2:68–77; Pyth. 4:175–77; and fragments.

92 By means of Orphic myths and poems, I take it.

93 To Plato, I think that the comparison is a natural one. It is his intention that Socrates, like the *telestai*, should provide a *logos* of what he is doing, that is, of Socratic dialectical inquiry. The Orphic teachers are also practitioners, as Socrates is.

94 Does this prior acquaintance include particular events, persons, and places? Or does "all things" really mean 'all kinds of thing' but not necessarily all things per se? That is, does the doctrine incorporate a solution to the problem of all inquiry or only of something like non-empirical learning, say conceptual understanding and mathematical knowledge?

95 This deductive interpretation of the kinship of all things is defended by Allen and Moravcsik.

96 I take the dialogue with the slave boy to illustrate learning, and since the doctrine of learning as recollection makes such learning possible, the dialogue exemplifies it as well. But not all agree; some take the dialogue to prove the doctrine, and others take it to solve the paradox. See Irwin, White, and others.

97 Stanley Cavell distinguishes knowledge as a question of recognition from knowledge as a question of existence (*Claim of Reason*, 49–64, 76–77). In a sense Plato wants to keep the two kinds of knowledge together. But Cavell asserts that recognition (or acknowledgment) involves self-recognition; Plato wants recognition to involve the disposal of self-recognition and not the necessity of it (Cavell, *Must We Mean What We Say?* 273ff.). Thomas Nagel tries to show how the clash between objective and subjective perspectives is inevitable: "Humility falls between nihilistic detachment and blind self-importance" (*View from Nowhere*, 220, 223, and esp. 272). In the end Plato wants to retain a nondiscursive aspect of knowledge that is also not "personal" or "subjective."

98 The vehicles for such a transition are not made clear here; presumably they result in the *desmos*; that is, they are somehow associated with the process referred to by the phrase, *aitias logismo*.

99 I have given a detailed analysis of 85b8–86b4 in "How Does Plato Solve the Paradox of Inquiry in the *Meno*?"

100 At 86b6–c2 Plato has Socrates deny that he believes the whole business. But he is committed to vigorous inquiry—which requires inquiry,

which in turn requires recollection and immortality. What need not be accepted is the myth of the slaying of Dionysos, the guilt of the Titans, and so on.

101 The shift from truths in the soul to transcendent Forms is like the movement from spirit possession to soul flight in the career of the shaman; see I. M. Lewis, *Religion in Context*, chap. 5, 78–93.

CHAPTER THREE: PHILOSOPHY AND THE
LANGUAGE OF ECSTASY IN THE *PHAEDO*

1 See Hackforth, *Plato's Phaedo*, 7; Bluck, *Plato's Phaedo*, 144–45; Guthrie, *History of Greek Philosophy*, 4:225; and Bluck, *Plato's Meno*, 2.

2 In general on the Forms as the appropriate objects of knowledge, see Nagel, *View from Nowhere*, 69, for a description of Plato's as a *heroic theory of knowledge* and Plato's role concerning the rise of the objective point of view.

3 These features include, for example, being models or *paradeigmata* and being *aitiai*. My proposal is that the Forms arise first for religious-epistemological reasons and then come to take on metaphysical, linguistic, and moral significance.

4 It is clear that Plato takes the Orphic-Pythagorean conglomerate to be a pan-Hellenic phenomenon. Cebes and Simmias are Thebans; Echecrates is from Phlius, in northeast Peloponnese. See Hackforth, *Plato's Phaedo*, 29–31.

5 The best account of Plato's myths is still Frutiger, *Les mythes de Platon*. The most important myths are found in the *Gorgias*, *Phaedo*, *Republic*, *Phaedrus*, *Politicus*, and *Laws*.

6 See my discussion in chaps. 5 and 6 of the myth in Socrates' second speech in the *Phaedrus* and of the Sun, Line, and Cave in the *Republic*.

7 *Phaedo* 118; *Meno* 94e–95a, VII, 324e–25c; and *Republic*. See also *Gorgias* 486a–b, 508c–d, 521c–22e.

8 See Burkert, *Lore and Science*, 111 n. 12.

9 *Diogenes Laertius* VIII, 46; see Burkert, *Lore and Science*, 92 and n. 40. Also on the Theban-Pythagorean connection, see Pausanias IX.13.1 for evidence that Epaminondas studied with Lysis, a Pythagorean from Tarentum.

10 Bluck, *Plato's Phaedo*, 43 n. 2. Burkert, *Lore and Science*, 198, argues
. . . hree are among the *mathematici*; on Philolaus see 218–98, esp.

. . . *haedo* 61e6: had Philolaus by 399 already returned to Taren-

. . . *Greek Religion*, 165–67, with specific reference to Euripides'

Bacchae; see Burkert, *Greek Religion*, 178, concerning Semele in Thebes, and 281, on the Kabeiroi.

13 *Phaedo* 69e3–5: a new apology; see *Gorgias* 492c–d, 500c–d, 502e–03e, 511c–13c. See also Dodds, *Plato's Gorgias*, 19–34.

14 Thebes had precipitated the Corinthian War with her attack on Phokis in 395 (see Oxyr. Hist. xvi–xviii [Wickersham and Verbrugghe, *Greek Historical Documents*, 11–13], esp. xviii; and Sealey, *History of the Greek City States*, 389), later persuaded Athens to join her (Xenophon *Hellenica* 3.5.8–15; M. N. Tod, *A Selection of Greek Historical Inscriptions* (Oxford University Press: 1948), 2:101; Hammond, *History of Greece*, 455 and n. 27), and so drew Athens into a train of events that culminated in the embarrassment of the King's Peace (Hammond, *History of Greece*, 455–65; Hornblower, *Greek World*, chap. 14; Sealey, *History of the Greek City States*, chap. 15; Wickersham and Verbrugghe, *Greek Historical Documents*, 6–20).

15 On the division of the soul see *Phaedo* 91c8–d1, 94e5, 95c5, 63c2–3, 67a–b, 80a–84b.

16 In so doing, it establishes a theocentric model of knowledge; see Henry Allison, *Kant's Transcendental Idealism* (New Haven: Yale University Press, 1983), 19. Nagel, *View from Nowhere*, 74, gives a good description of self-transcendence as the "self-referential analogue of an external understanding." On this account, what Socrates and Plato really aim at in aspiring to the soul's divinity is an external conception of the world. The discovery of the Forms is an advance in objectivity. See Nagel, *View from Nowhere*, 75–77, 86–88; and Vlastos, "Degrees of Reality in Plato."

17 One might reasonably wonder to what degree Plato could have deepened his knowledge of Parmenides and Eleatic philosophy on his trip to Sicily.

18 For additional evidence see 77e–78a, 84e–85b, 114b–15a, and 74b–c.

19 Also, "lovers of riches and prestige" or "lovers of power and prestige" (67c, 82c).

20 See 63e9–64a2, 64a4–6, 64b8–9. See also Dodds, *Plato's Gorgias*, 296–99; and Guthrie, *Orpheus and Greek Religion*, 161–64. Guthrie attributes this teaching to the Orphic writings—perhaps it was passed on by a Sicilian or Italian. Dodds, following Linforth, is skeptical but takes the informant to be a Pythagorean; see Linforth, "Soul and Sieve," 312–13.

21 64d2ff.

22 65b7–d7; cf. *Gorgias* 493a–c (see above).

23 64e4–6.

24 66b7.

25 66e2–3, 67b4, 67b9–10, 68a1–2, 68a7, 68b2–3, 68b9–c1.

26 Later I shall discuss what this *truth* is—that is, what the Forms are.

The claim has a Socratic ring, as my discussion of the *Apology* has already shown.

27 See also *Republic* V for the treatment of the two as distinct types.

28 Compare the role of sense-perception in *anamnesis*. See also Morgan, "Sense-Perception and Recollection."

29 *Me akribes mede sapheis* (b5).

30 Burnet, *Plato's Phaedo*, 31, argues that Plato intends Epicharmus and Homer, not Parmenides and Empedocles as Olympiodoros suggests. But I disagree; Parmenides seems very plausible.

31 66d7–e4, 67b7–c3, 67e4–68b6.

32 68c5–69a5; cf. Irwin, *Plato's Moral Theory*, 160–64.

33 See an excellent discussion of how the Greek medical writers used the same terms for rational methods of healing as had previously been employed for magical methods, in G. E. R. Lloyd, *Magic, Reason, and Experience*, 37–49, esp. 45; cf. *Cratylus* 405a–b on *katharsis* by doctors and priests.

34 82d5–7.

35 See Parker, *Miasma*, chap. 10, esp. 281–83; and Burkert, *Lore and Science*, 213, contra Festugière and with Boyance.

36 *Phaedo* 62b2–5. See Burnet, *Plato's Phaedo*, 22–23; Burkert, *Orphism and Bacchic Mysteries*, 5; and *Cratylus* 400c4.

37 See Burnet, *Plato's Phaedo*, 17; and Burkert, *Lore and Science*, 212 n. 16.

38 *Phaedo* 83e2, 84b, 81a8–9; cf. 114b–115a.

39 According to Parker, magical purifications were common in the fourth century, especially to cure disease; see *Miasma*, chap. 7. The Pythagorean innovation was to turn temporary abstentions and other modes of purification into a total way of life, with salvation as its goal (*Miasma*, 297).

40 See 77d5–78a9 on such a person. Socrates, for example, was an *epodon*, a charmer. Burnet says that this recalls Thrace and Phrygia.

41 For example, 91c8–d1, 94e5, 95c5.

42 The best general accounts of the multiple functions of the Forms can be found in Cherniss' influential essay "The Philosophical Economy of the Theory of Ideas," and in the introduction to N. P. White, *Plato on Knowledge and Reality*. The other functions involve language, causality, and the role of Forms as universals and exemplars.

43 For example, 65c5–e5, 78c10–d7.

44 See 78b–80b.

45 The Forms as divine must also be causally influential in order to exemplify divine power.

46 See 78c7–8, 79c6–7, 80b4–5.

47 Irwin, "Plato's Heracleiteanism"; Vlastos, "Degrees of Reality"; Alexander Nehamas, "Predication and Forms of Opposites in the *Phaedo*," *Review of Metaphysics* 26 (1973): 461–91. See also 74b–c.

48 74b–c; cf. 103a–b.

49 67a–68a, 82e–83e.

50 He may not call the gap between the Forms and the physical world a *chorismos* very often, but he portrays the separation with unquestionable vivacity. For a contrary view see Fine, "Separation."

51 See Morgan, "Belief, Knowledge, and Learning."

52 See 76b, 66e, 67b.

53 On the discursive and intuitive intellect in Kant see Henry Allison, *Kant's Transcendental Idealism*, 65–68 and esp. n. 2 on intuitive intellect and the theocentric model. See also A. C. Lloyd, "Non-Discursive Thought"; and Sorabji, "Myths about Non-propositional Thought."

54 See Morgan, "Sense-Perception and Recollection."

55 See Morgan, "Belief, Knowledge, and Learning."

56 Further proofs are found in the *Republic* and *Phaedrus*.

57 There is no need to examine the arguments in detail; commentaries on them provide elaborate and helpful analysis. For recent treatments and useful bibliography see Gallop, *Plato Phaedo*; Dorter, *Plato's Phaedo*; and Bostock, *Plato's Phaedo*.

58 For general discussion see Jaeger, "Greek Ideas of Immortality"; and Farnell, *Greek Hero Cults*.

59 See Kahn, "Religion and Natural Philosophy," 436.

60 *Phaedo* 77a9–d5.

61 See *Phaedo* 84b. I think this interpretation can be supported by examining a passage that concludes the final argument, 105e10–107a1. This account suggests that the most Plato can mean by "immortality" is 'everlasting existence,' and in this sense soul is like the Forms. In the end Plato may not be wholly consistent about what "immortality" and "eternity" might come to. On the basis of the *Parmenides* and *Timaeus*, Richard Sorabji argues that Plato mixes together everlasting duration and timelessness, without resolving the issue; see *Time, Creation, and the Continuum*, chaps. 8 and 9, 98–136, esp. 108–112.

62 *Kai philochrematos kai philotimos*, 68c2; cf. 82c5–8.

63 Israel Scheffler discusses the "various roles of emotion in cognition," and particularly the ways emotion serves critical inquiry; see "In Praise of the Cognitive Emotions." R. S. Peters discusses the rational passions, the "obvious overriding one [being] the concern about truth," which expresses itself in a person's caring about correctness, clarity, and consistency, and abhorrence of irrelevance and arbitrariness; see "Reason and Passion," in *Education and the Development of Reason*, ed. R. F. Deardon, P. H. Hirst, and R. S. Peters (London, 1972), 225–27. See also Stocker, "Intellectual Desire, Emotion, and Action."

64 See *Meno* 83e11–84c9. The practical principle, of which this epistemological version is one application, is that one cannot want what one

already possesses. See Kenny, *Action, Emotion, and Will*, 115–16.

The same point might be formulated in terms of Alston's distinction between latent and aroused wants. Only aroused wants are motives for action, and "we might think of a want in the 'latent' sense as a disposition frequently to have the corresponding aroused want" ("Motives and Motivation," in *Encyclopedia of Philosophy*, ed. P. Edwards [New York: Macmillan, 1967], 5:402). For Plato in the *Meno*, then, the slave boy has a latent want for knowledge that is aroused when Socrates' questioning shows him that he does not presently grasp the truth. What I have called "releasing a desire" marks the transition between Alston's latent and aroused wants. Compare the similar distinction of wants or desires in Goldman, *Theory of Human Action*, 86–91; Goldman calls them "occurrent" and "standing" wants. My question is whether wanting to know is for Plato a standing want or desire that is natural and general for all human beings.

65 Perhaps Plato is more aware than I suggest that even a believer and inquirer, "purified" of his false beliefs, does not always and without further direction and motivation seek the truth. For in the *Meno* Meno himself, even after he is disabused of his false beliefs, is stubborn and recalcitrant, uninterested in pursuing the inquiry into the nature of virtue and continually pressing his original question. Meno's behavior is not atypical; Euthyphro seems uninterested in pursuing the inquiry once his false beliefs about piety are rejected.

Meno 77b6–78b2 may reveal something about whether the desire for moral knowledge is natural and inherent in everyone. For discussion see Gerismos Santas, "The Socratic Paradoxes," in *Plato's Meno: Text and Criticism*, ed. Alexander Sesonske and Noel Fleming (Belmont, Calif.: Wadsworth, 1965), 49–64, reprinted from *Philosophical Review* 73 (1964): 147–64; George Nakhnikian, "The First Socratic Paradox," *Journal of the History of Philosophy* 11, no. 1 (January 1973): 1–17; and Irwin, *Plato's Moral Theory*, 300 n. 51.

66 For valuable discussion of the argument from recollection in the *Phaedo*, see Gallop, *Plato Phaedo*, 115–19; Ackrill, "Anamnesis in the *Phaedo*"; and Gosling, "Similarity in *Phaedo* 73 seq."

67 Some might doubt that the perceiver approaches the observation with a desire to know what x is; rather he engages in a perception that "stimulates" or gives rise to such a question. This issue is raised again in *Republic* VII with regard to the role of arithmetic calculations and the propaedeutic nature of mathematics in the philosopher's education.

68 See *Phaedo* 81a5, 82b10–84b8, and esp. 83e1–3. On the philosopher's love of the Forms and the practice of *homoiosis theo* in Plato, see Rist, *Eros and Psyche*, 16–40.

69 *Phaedo* 64a, 65d11–67c3, and esp. 65c5–d2, 66e2–4.

70 In the *Phaedo* no distinction is indicated between *boulesis* and *epithumia*; both terms occur rarely (*boulesis* at 63e and 96a, *epithumia* at 66b3–7, 66c2–7, 66e2–3, 67e6–8, 68c9, 68e6, and 108a). Elsewhere in the dialogues Plato does observe a distinction between these two.

71 At 64d2–e7 Simmias takes for granted the philosopher's desire for the well-being of the soul; cf. 65a5–c9. Also, when Socrates portrays the true sentiments of the philosopher in his speech at 66b3–67b2, the desire for knowledge is a premise in the argument for the desirability of death and not in any way a conclusion. The same assumption is at work in an extremely important but neglected passage in which Plato describes how "the soul of the true philosopher abstains from pleasures and desires and pains" (83b5–7) in an effort to thwart the "cunning of the [bodily] prison" and ultimately to enter into communion with what is true and divine and not the object of belief (84a7–b1). In this passage (82d9–84b8) Plato explains the epistemological connection between the rejection of physical desires and the philosophical goal of wisdom: knowledge of what is real, pure, divine, and most clear. Not only does such an account assume that the philosopher has a desire for knowledge; it also assumes that such a desire is properly directed to the Forms. But although Plato does distinguish the philosopher who loves wisdom from others who desire everything from drunkenness to justice, from riches to honor and prestige (68c; 81e–82b), he does not account for the difference in their fundamental desires.

72 69c8–d1.

73 See Friedlander, *Plato*, vol. 1, chap. 9; and Frutiger, *Les mythes de Platon*.

74 The real novelty in Plato's use of myth and metaphor comes in the *Republic* and especially in the *Phaedrus*.

75 The *Gorgias* is probably written a bit earlier than the *Phaedo*, but the evidence for similarity of circumstance and other factors is transparent. See Dodds, *Gorgias*; and Irwin, *Plato Gorgias*.

76 *Gorgias* 522c–e.

77 *Phaedo* 107c–d.

78 Irwin, *Plato Gorgias*, 242.

79 See *Gorgias* 502e–03e, 511c–13c, 515a–19c.

80 For example, 524b–d.

81 At the same time, the myth in the *Gorgias* is a mixture of Orphic-Pythagorean materials and Platonic innovation; see Dodds, *Gorgias*, 372–86.

82 524d–26d.

83 527c6.

84 524a8–b2; cf 526d3–4, 527a5–8.

85 Dodds, *Gorgias*, 376–77.

86 Irwin, *Plato Gorgias*, 248–50.

87 Compare Simmias' views at 85c1–d4; the strategy prefigures James' famous proposals in "The Will to Believe."

88 Note Dodds's rather puritanical critique and his cautious conclusions in *Gorgias*, 373–76, esp. 376: "On the contrary, no single element of the present myth can be called 'Orphic' in the sense that it is known to have figured in a poem attributed in the classical age to Orpheus." But see Guthrie, *Orpheus and Greek Religion*, 168; and Guthrie, *History of Greek Philosophy*, 4:305–07.

89 Guthrie, *History of Greek Philosophy*, 4:339, 361.

90 Hackforth, *Plato's Phaedo*, 171–72.

91 The early antecedent of this procedure is the description in the *Apology* of posthumous inquiry and dialectic. See chap. 1.

92 65d–66b, 67e–68b, 69c–d; cf. Parker, *Miasma*, chap. 10.

93 79d, 80d–81a, and esp. 81a8–9, 84b.

94 *Paideias te kai trophes* (107d3–4); cf. 108a5–6 and Hackforth, *Plato's Phaedo*, 168 n. 3.

95 The *Gorgias* myth is less imaginative, more didactic; Dodds, *Gorgias*, 373, says that it has the vividness and directness of a folktale (see also p. 383, on 526c3–4). I am not saying that the mysteries *are* opposed to the polis tradition but rather that Plato used them in this way. Detienne and Vernant may be right, that the mysteries and similar rites are opposed, but surely there were domesticated versions that were integrated into polis life.

For an analogue: in seventeenth-century England the Levelers, Ranters, and others used biblical imagery and language to express their dissent from the national church; see Hill, *World Turned Upside Down*.

96 Hackforth, *Plato's Phaedo*, 174.

97 Hackforth, *Plato's Phaedo*, 175, is not at all clear; here he sees it as a temporary abode of good souls still to be reincarnated. See also p. 179; it symbolizes the *noetos topos* that is their true home.

98 110b1; cf. 114d7.

99 See Burkert, *Lore and Science*, 309 and references in n. 50; and Anaximander A11, A26.

100 Burkert, *Lore and Science*, 331, 342; see p. 344 on the impossibility of separating Ionian views from Pythagorean views.

101 Ibid., 320, 349 and n. 49, 342–44, 363–65.

102 See ibid., 365–66.

103 A23; cf. Burkert, *Lore and Science*, 346.

104 110d3–11b6.

105 Burkert, *Lore and Science*, 347–48.

106 69c2–3; cf. 82d5–6.

107 67a2–b2, 68b4, 79c–d, 80e–81d, 83d–e.

108 69c; cf. Parker, *Miasma*, 282–86.
109 Hackforth, *Plato's Phaedo*, 7.

CHAPTER FOUR: PHILOSOPHY, DESIRE,
AND THE MYSTERIES IN THE *SYMPOSIUM*

1 See Leon Robin, *Le Banquet* (Paris, 1938), xix–xxviii; Guthrie, *History of Greek Philosophy*, 4:365, 387–92; Dover, "Date of Plato's *Symposium*"; and W. Hamilton, trans., *Plato: The Symposium* (Harmondsworth: Penguin, 1951), 9 (but see also 116–17).
2 Guthrie, *History of Greek Philosophy*, 4:380–81.
3 Ibid., 4:381.
4 Ibid., 4:365–66.
5 Does this give the story the ring of authenticity? Perhaps, but it also distances it into the domain of something like *folktale*.
6 Agathon's only victory came at the Lenaia in 416; Athen. V.217a. See Pickard-Cambridge, *Dramatic Festivals of Athens*, 41. Held in the month of Gamelion (roughly January), the Lenaia was a festival for Dionysos Lenaias, for the maenads of Dionysos (*Dramatic Festivals of Athens*, 30); it was administered by the *archon basileus* associated with officials of the Eleusinian mysteries. See Burkert, *Greek Religion*, 290–91; and Parke, *Festivals of Athens*, 104–06.
7 Hornblower, *Greek World*, 142. See also Mylonas, *Eleusis and the Eleusinian Mysteries*, 225–26; MacDowell, *Andokides*, introduction; Plutarch *Alkibiades* 19–22; Thucydides VI.27–29, 53, 61; and Xenophon I.4.14.
8 The two speeches are really a complementary pair; Socrates discusses his own love for truth and the ritual ascent to knowledge of the beautiful, while Alcibiades portrays Socrates himself as the paradigm of the philosopher devoted to knowledge and truth. Moreover, although both are presented as rhetorical pieces, in fact Alcibiades' speech is a panegyric whereas Socrates includes a dialectical conversation with Agathon and a reported one with Diotima. In the *Phaedo* Socrates is represented wholly through dialectical encounter; in the *Gorgias* the method breaks down when Callicles becomes uncooperative. Here the Socratic portrait is a double one, executed in complementary styles. We see in the *Symposium* the superhuman Socrates of Alcibiades set alongside the probing, relentless, aspiring Socrates of Plato.
9 Irwin has discussed the *Symposium* and the education of desire in the context of Plato's moral theory. See *Plato's Moral Theory*, 164–72; and "Recollection and Plato's Moral Theory."
10 See Robin, *Le Banquet*, lxxii–cviii; Nussbaum, *The Fragility of Goodness*, 176–84 and in general chap. 6; and Rosen, *Plato's Symposium*, chap. 7.
11 One can desire what one does not have *or* one can desire to keep what

one already has; see Descartes, *The Passions of the Soul*, in *The Philosophical Works of Descartes*, trans. John Cottingham, Robert Stoothoof, and D. Murdoch (Cambridge: Cambridge University Press, 1985), 1:358.

12 Later in the *Symposium* Plato uses *boulesis* as a synonym as well.

13 See 195a3–5 and 199c4–5; note the change of terminology to *ta erga*.

14 See *Meno* and *Republic*, although the distinction here is not identical with the one drawn in either.

15 203b1–04c6.

16 204d4–05a4.

17 Here, *boulesis*: 205a5–b3.

18 206c6–8, 206e7–07a4.

19 Plato is not really clear about the nature of this relationship between what one desires to do and the immortality that one ultimately desires for oneself, that is, divine existence.

20 207b6–7, 208c1–d2; cf. *ek logismou* (b6–7) with *tes alogias* (c3).

21 See Cornford, "Doctrine of Eros"; Markus, "Dialectic of Eros"; and Moravcsik, "Reason and Eros."

22 For example, 205d4–5.

23 See 212a.

24 211a1–b5; cf. Vlastos, "Degrees of Reality."

25 210b6–c2.

26 210c3–6.

27 See 211b7, 211b5, 210e3.

28 For example, 206a11–12, 207a2, 204d4–05a4.

29 See Guthrie, *History of Greek Philosophy*, 4:387–92, and the articles cited in n. 21 above.

30 Guthrie, *History of Greek Philosophy*, 4:392.

31 In this regard my interpretation of the *Symposium*, the *Republic*, and *Phaedrus*, is opposed to the account that Nussbaum gives in *Fragility of Goodness*.

32 Guthrie, *History of Greek Philosophy*, 4:390.

33 What can *entautha auto monachou* (a2–3) mean?

34 See Bluck, *Plato's Phaedo*, 28–29 n. 1.

35 A case of the Heraclitean view about the physical world; see 207d4–08b2.

36 Especially 208d6–e1.

37 208e5–09e4.

38 Luce, "Immortality in Plato's *Symposium*," 139; cf. Guthrie, *History of Greek Philosophy*, 4:388–89.

39 *Timaeus* 37c–38b; cf. Sorabji, *Time, Creation, and the Continuum*, 108–12.

40 See esp. 206c2–3, 206c4, 206c5, 206c7, 206e8, 207b6, 207d1; cf. 207e1–2.

41 Guthrie, *History of Greek Philosophy*, 4:389.

42 This point has not been appreciated.

43 206c2–3, 207e1–2, and esp. 210b6–c2 for an image of the figures of Silenus in Alcibiades' speech.

44 For example, *bioton anthropo* (211d2); cf. 212a1. Is there a shift at 211d8–e3 with the rejection of human flesh? But see 212a1.

45 See Dover, "Date of Plato's *Symposium*," 19–20; Luce, "Immortality in Plato's *Symposium*," 139–40; but I disagree with Luce about the relevance of the argument from Forms and Recollection (also the final argument), which presumes too much and is unnecessary. See also Bluck, *Plato's Phaedo*, 28 n. 1.

46 Parke, *Festivals of the Athenians*, 104–06; cf. Burkert, *Greek Religion*, 290–91.

47 See 175e9.

48 And Alcibiades' reference to Socrates' remarkable capacity; see 176a–e.

49 174d4–75b3.

50 Parke, *Festivals of the Athenians*, 105.

51 Perhaps it is also significant that this month's major festival is the Anthesteria, a great festival of Dionysos.

52 174d4–75b3.

53 McGinty, *Interpretation and Dionysos*, 110–11; Oskar Seyffert, *Dictionary of Classical Antiquities*, ed. Henry Nettleship and J. E. Sandys (Cleveland: Meridian, 1956), 380, 386–87. In the *De Musica* (Pseudo-Plutarch) not only is Marsyas the prototypical *aulete*, as here, but he is said to come from Phrygia and to have been the teacher of Olympus, the aulete who composed nomoi and introduced those played at Greek festivals. Andrew Barker notes that the story of the contest between Apollo, symbolizing what is rational, and Marsyas and Dionysos, symbolizing what is foreign, emotional, and irrational, is a "Hellenistic fancy, presumably based on Plato" (esp. *Rep*. 399e). See Barker, *Greek Musical Writings*, 22 n. 9, 92 n. 197, 210–19. See Aristotle *Pol*. 1340a13–14 on the capacity of Olympus' music to cause ecstasy in the soul. On Aristotle see Anderson, *Ethos and Education*, 186–88. On the encounter between Marsyas and Apollo see Xen. *Anab*. I.2.18; Herodotus 7.26; and *Euthydemus* 285c–d. See also Anderson, *Ethos and Education*, 67 and 238 n. 11.

54 That is, like the daimon Eros in man striving for immortality.

55 215c5–d1 (see preceding note).

56 215e1–3.

57 216a4–6.

58 216d7, 216e7–17a1.

59 See 221d–22a, 219b7–c1, where the phrase *daimonio hos alethos* is used.

60 Or better, he is the god's surrogate, like a satyr. See Dodds, *Bacchae*, 82f.; Henrichs, "Male Intruders," 72. Is Socrates *the one* male celebrant? Is he the god himself? Henrichs' criticism is germane (see esp. pp. 85ff.). See also Dodds, "Maenadism in the *Bacchae*," 170 n. 71.

61 On divinity as loss of self and as the goal of human aspiration, see Henrichs, "Loss of Self."

62 See esp. Henrichs, "Changing Dionysiac Identities"; Cole, "New Evidence"; Burkert, *Orphism and Bacchic Mysteries*; Burkert, *Greek Religion*, 290–95; and Burkert, *Ancient Mystery Cults*.

63 Cole, "New Evidence," 236–37; Dem. 18.259, 19.199. See also Henrichs, "Changing Dionysiac Identities," 150–51.

64 Cole, "New Evidence," 224ff. From the Hipponion tablet, 1.16: *mystai kai bacchoi*. This term refers centrally to a devotee of Dionysos (p. 231), but later it refers generally to a kind of madness or frenzy. Men can be called *bacchos* (p. 230).

65 Heraclitus B14 (= Markovich 87a). See Kahn, *Art and Thought of Heraclitus*, 262–63; Herodotus 2.51; and Cole, "New Evidence," 232–33.

66 But see Henrichs, "Changing Dionysiac Identities," 223 n. 91.

67 Cole, "New Evidence for the Mysteries of Dionysos," 234, refers to *Phaedo* 69c. See Henrichs, "Changing Dionysiac Identities," 228 n. 137.

68 Henrichs, "Changing Dionysiac Identities," 139; maenadism for women, wine-drinking for men. But initiation is catharsis for all! On satyrs and wine see 140–43; on wine as a *pharmakon* see 141. See also Otto, *Dionysus*, 149–51, on wine as a social vehicle.

69 Henrichs, "Changing Dionysiac Identities," 147; Burkert, *Greek Religion*, 291.

70 Burkert, *Ancient Mystery Cults*, chaps. 1, 2.

71 Henrichs, "Changing Dionysiac Identities," 151–55.

72 Burkert, *Greek Religion*, 291.

73 Henrichs, "Changing Dionysiac Identities," 153. See also Burkert, *Ancient Mystery Cults*.

74 Henrichs, "Changing Dionysiac Identities," 154.

75 Henrichs, "Changing Dionysiac Identities," 158 and n. 192, with references to Nietzsche and Rohde. See also Burkert, *Greek Religion*, 293–95.

76 Henrichs, "Changing Dionysiac Identities," 160.

77 219e6–20c1. See Heraclitus on drunkenness (B36, B117, B118) and how bad it is for the soul; a dry soul is wisest and best. See also M. C. Nussbaum, "*Psyche* in Heraclitus," *Phronesis* 17 (1972): 1–16, 153–70; and Kahn, *Art and Thought of Heraclitus*.

78 220c3–d5; note *dzeton* (c5).

79 Dodds, *Greeks and the Irrational*, 140–42, 210, 225 n. 6, and on the Pythia, 72, 73–74, 87 n. 41. See *Ion* 553e on Corybantic trance; see also Lewis, *Ecstatic Religion*.

80 E. des Places, "Platon et la langue des mystères," *Etudes Platon* (1981), 83–98; Cornford, "Doctrine of Eros," 75–78; Guthrie, *History of Greek Philosophy*, 4:377.

81 Burkert, *Greek Religion*, 323–34. But see p. 276, where they are simply

called *ta mysteia*; see also pp. 285–90. In *Ancient Mystery Cults*, Burkert is more explicit. He says the distinction between "preliminary initiation" on the one hand and "perfect and epoptic mysteries" on the other "clearly refers to Eleusis" (p. 92).

82 *Myetheies* at 210a1; *epoptika*, too, but nowhere else.

83 Mylonas, *Eleusis and the Eleusinian Mysteries*, 247–85; Burkert, *Homo Necans*, 248–97.

84 This fits the text at 209e5–10a4 (*men . . . de* and *isos, already*). See Mylonas, *Eleusis and the Eleusinian Mysteries*, 237, 274–78.

85 It is unlikely that the early part refers to the Lesser Mysteries held in Anthesterion, for the Lenaia is in Gemalion and the pattern fits (see Mylonas, *Eleusis and the Eleusinian Mysteries*, 239, 240–43).

CHAPTER FIVE: EDUCATION, PHILOSOPHY, AND
HISTORY IN THE *REPUBLIC*

1 On metics as peripheral people, sometimes treated as *pharmakoi*, and on the attack on them in 404, see Parker, *Miasma*, 262 and n. 30. See also Xenophon; and Whitehead, *Ideology of the Athenian Metic*, 129, 155.

2 As I shall try to show, the *Republic* coordinates an otherworldly contemplative ideal with a this-worldly realism. My interpretation opposes those of Nussbaum, *Fragility of Goodness*, chap. 5; and Leo Strauss, *City and Man*, 50–138.

3 See *Rep.* II, 364–65; *Theaet.* 176a–b; *Rep.* 500d; and Burkert, *Greek Religion*, 149, on Apollo as the sun, and 175, on Helios. See also *Symp.* 220d; and Burkert, *Greek Religion*, 335–36.

4 Dies in Bude edition, cxxii–cxxxviii; Guthrie, *History of Greek Philosophy*, 4:437; see Hackforth, *Phaedrus*, 7 and n. 1. The dramatic date is much less certain. Alternatives include 411, 421, 409, 456, among others. Most likely the conversation was intended to have occurred at some unspecified time during the war. See Guthrie, *History of Greek Philosophy*, 438 n. 1. As I showed in chapter 1, the Peloponnesian War was the setting for many imported cults. See Dodds, *Greeks and the Irrational*, 204 n. 89; the public cult of Bendis was established in the plague year 430–429. Dodds follows Ferguson, *Hesperia*, suppl. 8 (1949): 131ff. See also Parke, *Oracles of Zeus*, 149, who notes that the cult is established under the guidance of Dodona. But see also Dover, *Lysias and the Corpus Lysiacum*, 131 and n. 3.

5 See Hornblower, *Greek World*, 202–22; Sealey, *History of the Greek City States*, 405–22; Hammond, *History of Greece*, 466–70, 482–98; Wickersham and Verbrugghe, *Greek Historical Documents*, 34–59; and Xenophon *Hellenica* V.4, VI.2–4.

6 Hornblower, *Greek World*, 219.

7 See Cawkwell's introduction to Xenophon *Hellenica* 35; see also Hornblower, *Greek World*, 209, on Xenophon's neglect of the confederacy, which is a pro-Spartan response.

8 Wickersham and Verbrugghe, *Greek Historical Documents*, sec. 22. See also Hornblower, *Greek World*, 210–15; Sealey, *History of the Greek City States*, 411–12; Cawkwell, "Foundation of the Second Athenian Confederacy," and Cawkwell, "Notes on the Failure of the Second Athenian Confederacy."

9 Wickersham and Verbrugghe, *Greek Historical Documents*, sec. 22, pp. 39–40.

10 See Hornblower, *Greek World*, 210–15; Sealey, *History of the Greek City States*, 410–14; and Hammond, *History of Greece*, 485–90.

11 *Rep.* I, 332e–33a; cf. 331d–36a, 351b–52c.

12 Hammond, *History of Greece*, 488–92.

13 Ibid., 491; Hornblower, *Greek World*, 215–16; Cawkwell, "Notes on the Peace of 375/4"; Sealey, *History of the Greek City States*, 414–19; Aeschines 3.243.

14 Hammond, *History of Greece*, 491–94; Sealey, *History of the Greek City States*, 419–21; Hornblower, *Greek World*, 217.

15 This is part of the point of *Rep.* II, 369b–74e.

16 This strategy is hinted in the *Republic*, 427b–c, and fully elaborated in the *Laws*.

17 I do not mean to suggest that Plato's treatment of ecstatic rites and practitioners in the *Republic* is completely new. Even in earlier dialogues Plato lampoons inspiration and inspired poets, mantics, and so forth. This is a pattern that will continue in the account of *mania* in the *Phaedrus*. What is surprising in the *Republic* are the special features of the attack on ecstatic practitioners and its juxtaposition with Plato's own account of paideia and philosophical knowledge.

18 Fontenrose, *Delphic Oracle*, 42–43.

19 Ibid., 247–48; the date of the inscription is ca. 420. See *Laws* 738b–c, 828a; and Xenophon *Memorabilia* 1.3.1.

20 469a–b, 469e–70a.

21 *Rep.* 590c–d.

22 In this same tradition, compare the philosophical religion of Spinoza's *Ethica* with the scriptural religion in his *Tractatus Theologico-Politicus*; also the role of religion in the state according to Machiavelli in the *Discoursi* and Rousseau in *The Social Contract*.

23 470e.

24 Perhaps Plato is setting the stage for a critique of the *Euthyphro* here; the terms *therapenein* and *theophilesteron* are reminiscent of the proposals in the *Euthyphro* that *to hosion* is what is dear to the gods, or that it is service to the gods and care of them.

25 See Jones, *Athenian Democracy*; M. I. Finley, *Economy and Society in Ancient Greece* (New York: Viking Penguin, 1982); and Austin and Vidal-Naquet, *Economic and Social History*, 121–22, 131–55, 334–83. See also Xenophon *Oeconomicus* 2:5–8; Demosthenes *On the Crown* 257–65; and Demosthenes *Against Aristocrates* 206–09.

26 Does this refer to Eumolpus or to Orpheus? Or to someone else altogether? We shall come back to this later.

27 Notice here the recurrence of the Heraclitean motif, that the best soul is driest and the worst like a drunken man.

28 358b–d.

29 365b–c.

30 Linforth, *Arts of Orpheus*, 75–77.

31 365d–66b.

32 These rites are part of the background for the *Meno*, *Phaedo*, and *Symposium*, as has been shown; cf. esp. Burkert and Cole.

33 365d, 493a–c.

34 West, *Orphic Poems*, 23–24; Nilsson, "Early Orphism," 208–09; Linforth, *Arts of Orpheus*, 85–89; Guthrie, *Orpheus and Greek Religion*, 158–59. See Pausanias 10.25–31 on Polygnotos' paintings on the Lesche (clubhouse) at Delphi.

35 Nilsson, "Early Orphism," 209; Guthrie, *Orpheus and Greek Religion*, 191 n. 2; Rohde, *Psyche*, 2, 359 n. 70.

36 West, *Orphic Poems*, 23–24. See also Dodds, *Greeks and the Irrational*, 234 n. 82; and Linforth, *Arts of Orpheus*, 96–97.

37 Linforth, *Arts of Orpheus*, 86.

38 Burkert, "Craft versus Cult," 4–5; Evans-Pritchard, *Witchcraft, Magic, and Oracles*.

39 390d–e; see G. E. R. Lloyd's discussion of the attack on magic and other practices in *Magic, Reason, and Experience*, 15–29.

40 366a–b. See Linforth, *Arts of Orpheus*, 92–95; Thomas, *Religion and the Decline of Magic*; and Macfarlane, *Witchcraft in Tudor and Stuart England*. For a portrait of the victim of such practitioners, see Theophrastus' account of the superstitious man (*The Characters*, sec. 16).

41 376e; cf. Marrou, *History of Education*.

42 411e–12a.

43 377d–78e; cf. Xenophanes B11, B14, B16, B15.

44 In defending (1), for example, Socrates argues that the divine cannot be the cause of bad or harmful things, since it is good (379c2, 380b6–7) and the good is beneficial and the cause only of well-being. But if "the good" refers to goodness itself, surely the divine is not identical with it, and if it refers to whatever is good, it is false that it causes only well-being. And if "the good" refers to things only insofar as they are called "good," then although it may be true that the divine qua good

only brings about good things, this result does not make it impossible for the divine to bring about evils as well. In short, the argument as it stands is a muddle or at least incomplete, and Glaucon's agreement is too easily got. Either that, or he is sympathetic to its spirit if not its letter.

45 See Cherniss' important paper "The Sources of Evil"; note my discussion of the antinomian forces in human nature later in this chapter. The divine is related to law, order, rationality, in sum to all that harnesses chaos and evil desire to good purposes.

46 Cf. Descartes *Mediations on First Philosophy* III.

47 See esp. 381c7–9, and Parmenides B8. Sorabji discusses the changelessness of the divine and the justification that what is best can change only to being worse than it is (*Time, Creation, and the Continuum*, 239ff.). See Aristotle *De Phil.* fr. 16 (Ross); and Sorabji, *Time, Creation, and the Continuum*, 281 n. 56.

48 If Plato ever achieves such a goal, he does so in the *Timaeus* and the *Laws*.

49 The key text is 396b10–97b5; the pure style of diction involves imitation of good men in good circumstances or the use of third-person narration.

50 See Annas, *Introduction to Plato's Republic*, 336–44; Moravcsik and Temko, *Plato on Beauty, Wisdom, and the Arts*, chaps. 1–3, 5–6; Murphy, *Interpretation of Plato's Republic*; Cross and Woozley, *Plato's Republic*; and Nehamas, "Plato on Imitation and Poetry," for excellent bibliography.

51 See 607b–08b, a kind of epilogue on the ancient quarrel between poetry and philosophy.

52 As a critique of imitative painting and poetry, Plato's is aimed at innovative tendencies in Greek art of the late fifth century and the early fourth. These tendencies were marked by the increased use of representational techniques, such as proportion, perspective, and foreshortening, as well as of shading. In part Plato attacks imitation for attempting to represent nature (the objects of perceptual experience) and deceiving in order to do so. On proportion see Erwin Panofsky, "The History of the Theory of Human Proportions as a Reflection of the Theory of Styles," *Meaning and the Visual Arts* (Garden City, N.Y.: Doubleday, 1955), 55–107, esp. 62–72. See Diod. Sic. I.98; Pliny *Nat. Hist.* XXXV.81–83. Among the painters central to the movement toward greater representational realism are Polyclitus, Polygnotos, and Nicias of Athens.

53 That Plato focuses on shaded painting is not inappropriate, because his goal is to discuss tragic poetry. Oddly, Grube translates "scene-painting" (*schenographia*) rather than "shaded painting" (*skiagraphia*; 602d2), as do Shorey and Lee. Annas also gets it wrong (*Introduction to Plato's Republic*, 338); cf. *Republic* 365c, 523b. See Pollitt, *Ancient*

View of Greek Art, 217–24; but cf. 240. See Henychius, s.v. *skia* (Pollitt, *Ancient View of Greek Art*, 232). Gallop gets it right at *Phaedo* 69b (*Plato Phaedo*).

54 See Nehamas, "Plato on Imitation and Poetry," 55–58; see above. See also Gombrich, *Art and Illusion*, 116–45.

55 Pollitt, *Ancient View of Greek Art*, 240.

56 Ibid., 192–93. See also Pollitt, *Art and Experience in Classical Greece*, 54–56, 162.

57 Light and shade would have been more appropriate, but color will do.

58 If Gombrich is right, what it elicits is perceptual reception and imaginative completion.

59 602c–03b; see 603b9–c2.

60 This is Nehamas' point; cf. Marrou, *History of Education*. On the restricted role of painting see Pollitt, *Art and Experience*.

61 602d6–03a5. Is this the same division? See Annas, *Introduction to Plato's Republic*.

62 605b8–c2. The soul is persuaded by the appearance and by its own imaginative involvement in the completion of it.

63 605b7–c4.

64 On hymns as songs of praise to gods or heroes see Barker, *Greek Musical Writings*, 1:33–34 n. 1, 39, 58.

65 One might compare Plato's critique of the representational painting of his day, and its use of foreshortening and perspective, to his critique of the "new" music of Timotheus, so ornamental, emotional, and dramatic (397a–401b). See Barker, *Greek Musical Writings*, vol. 1, chaps. 7, 8. For Timotheus' style see Arist. *Meter*. 993b, and Ps.-Plut. 1135c–d. See also Anderson, *Ethos and Education*, 50–53, 58–62, 65. Plato's critique is indebted to Damon (see Anderson, *Ethos and Education*, 74–81; and Barker, *Greek Musical Writings*, 1:130–35, 168–69). See also Morgan, "Plato, Inquiry, and Painting," *Apeiron* (forthcoming Spring 1990).

66 See Festugière, *Contemplation et vie contemplative selon Platon*.

67 521c5–8; from a day that is night to a true day.

68 Hermann Fraenkel, "A Thought Pattern in Heraclitus," in *The Presocratics*, ed. A. P. D. Mourelatos (Garden City, N.Y.: Doubleday, 1974), 214–28 (article orig. pub. 1938).

69 Adam 2:141, refers to 363d, which does *not* seem appropriate. But see *Phaedo* 69c.

70 Glaucus was thrown mad into the sea; he prophesied and bemoaned that he could not die.

71 Immortality is here not a status but discarnate, everlasting existence.

72 498c.

73 See 383c, 499b–c, 589c–d, and 589e.

74 Notice Heraclitus B14 on the bacchants.

75 On mud see Guthrie, *Orpheus and Greek Religion*, 160–64; on night see West, *Orphic Poems*; on darkness and death see Burkert, *Greek Religion*, 288–89. On gold leaf and hope of an afterlife see Burkert, *Greek Religion*, 293–95; and Zuntz, *Persephone*, 277–393. See also Cole, "New Evidence," on Hipponion.

76 As Plato goes on to show at 500d–01c.

77 490b.

78 For the notion of "referential access" to the Forms, see below.

79 Plato also employs a sexual vocabulary of love and desire, especially early in *Rep*. VI. I have already discussed such language to a degree in chapter 4, on the *Symposium*, and return to it in chapter 6, on the *Phaedrus*.

80 Plato suggests that the Dionysiac festivals are part of the background for his account at 475dff., where the philosopher is contrasted with a "lover of spectacles"; cf. 476b6–8, 484c–d, 501a–c, 507b–41b.

81 612b–c.

82 608c5–7.

83 The soul's immortality should come as no surprise to Glaucon. See *Rep*. III, 386b–87d; IX, 585b–c.

84 Annas, *Introduction to Plato's Republic*, 344–46. See also Bluck, *Phaedo*, 28–29; and N. P. White, *A Companion to Plato's Republic*, 259–60.

85 In addition to those that Annas itemizes, notice the equivocation on death, or alternatively the slide from destruction to death. See esp. 609d: Is destruction of the soul death? Or is destruction of the soul destruction of the person?

86 612a5–6.

87 This is a Pythagorean motif, one akin to the Empedoclean principle that like attracts like.

88 611b9–10.

89 612e8–13b1. Note the expression *homoiousthai theo*.

90 But see Annas, *Introduction to Plato's Republic*, 346, who claims simplicity. This is an error; cf. Guthrie, *History of Greek Philosophy*, 4:476–78, 556–57.

91 This epistemological problem of continuity is the philosophical analogue of the question of how genuine ecstasy is possible.

92 Strauss and Nussbaum of course exaggerate the transcendence of the philosophical life.

93 475c–80, 506c–d, 533e–34a, 601e–02a.

94 On logoi see 531e, 534b; visual language is present everywhere.

95 I originally called this a "referential component" of knowing and believing; what I have in mind is the psychological aspect of referring, whereby some thing is had before the mind's eye, as it were. Hector-

Nerî Castañeda suggested the phrase "referential access," and I have adopted it. Sorabji has an excellent discussion of nonpropositional thought in Greek philosophy. See "Myths about Non-Propositional Thought," 295–314, esp. 299–301 and n. 12; also *Time, Creation, and the Continuum*, 137–56, esp. 140–44. For Sorabji, Plotinus is the real hero of the story of nonpropositional thought in antiquity, for he takes with complete seriousness the metaphor of mental contact. But the only Platonic dialogue that Sorabji deals with is the *Republic*; his account is too sketchy and is based on other accounts that simply ignore the framework elaborated in this chapter, like that of Annas. See Annas, *Introduction to Plato's Republic*, 280–84, for a discussion that Sorabji finds congenial but that strikes me as typically one-sided.

96 I think that characterizing Plato's conception of knowledge in this way is in effect to agree with Moravcsik and Burnyeat that what Plato means by knowledge is really a kind of understanding. See Moravcsik, "Understanding and Knowledge"; and Burnyeat, "Aristotle on Understanding Knowledge."

97 The second step is absolutely necessary. In his excellent discussion in *Plato on Knowledge and Reality*, White considers how the discursive and nondiscursive elements work together, and considers the propositional component as providing increasingly better specifications or identifying descriptions. But this fails to distinguish two issues, or questions: Why this particular object? And why this *type* of object? White overlooks the key problem of the type of object and hence does not adequately appreciate the role of mathematics. The metaphysical fact is the ontological difference between Forms and physical things and properties; see Nehamas, "Plato on the Imperfection of the Sensible World."

98 The methods involve the famous upward and downward paths; see 510c–11d, 531d–34e, 537c–d. Also see Annas, *Introduction to Plato's Republic*; Cross and Woozley, *Plato's Republic*; Crombie, *Examination of Plato's Doctrines*; and Richard Robinson, *Plato's Earlier Dialectic*.

99 See esp. 533d–e. *Dianoia* as *symperiagogois* is clearer than *doxa* and more obscure than *episteme*; cf. 511d.

100 See Gallop, "Dreaming and Waking in Plato"; and Paul Shorey, trans., *Plato: The Republic* (Cambridge: Harvard University Press, 1930), 2:143 n. g (note to VII, 520c). See 576b for the imagery of dreaming and waking in a different context.

101 *Republic* VI, 509d9.

102 Of course the term *dianoia* later takes on a precise, narrowly defined meaning as *mathematical thinking*. Here it has a generic sense, as it does, e.g., at *Phaedo* 65e7 and 79a3.

103 Later this judgment is either qualified or retracted, as it must be if

learning or education is to take place. If learning is a matter of coming to apprehend and understand the timeless order or structure of the moral and natural world, the Forms, it must be possible for *some* to learn. But others may be intransigent or wholly uneducable. See my discussion of the *Phaedrus*.

104 Notice that the imagery of dreaming and waking is dependent, for Plato's application of it, on the introduction of the Forms. Hence dreaming and waking do not apply to the dialogue between Socrates and Glaucon at V, 477–80, precisely because for dialectical reasons Forms cannot be introduced into the discussion. But they do apply in *Republic* VI–VII, when the Forms are reintroduced to develop the philosophical curriculum and its goals.

105 See, e.g., Irwin, *Plato's Moral Theory*; Malcolm, "Line and the Cave"; J. E. Raven, "Sun, Divided Line, and Cave," *Classical Quarterly*, new ser., 3 (1953): 22–32; Ferguson, "Plato's Simile of Light"; and Tanner, "*Dianoia* and Plato's Cave."

106 Among them, Murphy, "The 'Simile of Light'"; and Ferguson, "Plato's Simile of Light."

107 For this description see V, 475e and following, and *Phaedo* 83a–b.

108 Tanner, "*Dianoia* and Plato's Cave," 85–86, identifies the whole cave and its inhabitants with nonphilosophical human life in order to view the chained prisoners in a restricted way, as the "contemporary methods of Greek education" operating within that everyday life (p. 86). Tanner is misled into making this distinction because he views the Cave as a critique of Greek education rather than as part of an attempt to clarify what genuine education is. Context shows that *paideias te peri kai apaideusias* (VII, 514a2) does not mean that the Cave has a critical purpose but rather that it has an elucidatory one.

It is interesting to note that Malcolm, like Tanner, divides the cave experience, but in a way diametrically opposed to Tanner he takes the original position to represent "the uneducated state of the common man" (Malcolm, "Line and the Cave," 43). But notice Malcolm's facile defense of the parallel with *eikasia* (p. 44), which wrecks his account.

109 See Richard Robinson, *Plato's Earlier Dialectic*, 197–201; and Morrison, "Two Unresolved Difficulties."

110 At VII, 533d, Plato uses Orphic imagery to suggest that mathematical thinking serves dialectic in the same way as the auxiliaries serve the guardians of the ideal state.

111 This claim is of course quite controversial, and runs counter to those "parallelists" like Irwin, Ferguson, Malcolm, and Raven who are convinced that Plato's "architectonic" pronouncements require a strict isomorphism between the Line and the Cave. I am not sure that any view will satisfy fully all the evidence, but I believe that those like Murphy,

Joseph, and Robinson who deny the parallel and appreciate the historical or developmental factor in the passage are worth a serious hearing.
No attempt to identify eikasia with the experience of the chained prisoners can succeed.

112 On this change of terminology see Ferguson, "Plato's Simile of Light";
Murphy, *Interpretation of Plato's Republic*; and Raven, "Sun, Divided
Line, and Cave."

Some commentators have appreciated that the two lower sections of
the Line ramify the domain of the dreamlike believer of *Republic* V but
have failed to notice that they also ramify the prisoner's situation. This
has led to some extreme views about the nature of eikasia. I have in
mind, among others, Gallop ("Image and Reality") and Paton ("Plato's
Theory of Eikasia"). Any view that treats eikasia as sensing sense-data,
e.g., I take to be extreme.

The centrality of the account of eikasia is widely appreciated. See
Malcolm, "Line and the Cave," 42; Joseph, *Knowledge and the Good*,
34; Paton, "Plato's Theory of Eikasia"; Richard Robinson, *Plato's Earlier Dialectic*, 190–91; and Hamlyn, "Eikasia in Plato's *Republic*."
Clearly, eikasia plays an important role in the Line, but that role is no
longer needed in the Cave.

113 See VII, 534a5, where Plato directs Glaucon to compare dianoia with
eikasia.

114 Eikasia is both a genuine cognitive state and an illustration of dianoia.
The two functions are surely compatible, although Irwin fails to see
this (*Plato's Moral Theory*, 335 n. 44, sect. 2). On the illustrative nature
of the primary role of eikasia see Raven, "Sun, Divided Line, and Cave,"
26.

115 In my view eikasia is presented by Plato as a matter of apprehending x
through an image of x and not of mistaking that image for x itself.
Eikasia is described as an accurate way of perceiving. Hence it cannot
be identical with the prisoner's state of mind, which is described as
erroneous. Compare Robinson, Paton, Hamlyn, Cooper, and Tanner for
valuable discussion of the nature of eikasia (see bibliography).

It is important to keep in mind that in describing the Sun, the Line,
and the Cave, Plato does not sharply distinguish the point of view of
the cognitive state being described and that of the describer, one like
him who has attained philosophical knowledge of the Forms, but he
does appreciate the distinction. The question of error and eikasia is
whether the nonphilosophical believer is in error when he engages in
eikasia, not whether he is in error in general. Vis-à-vis the upper part
of the Line, the entire lower part is in error, but vis-à-vis pistis, eikasia
is not.

116 Plato has continual problems with mediating what seem to be exhaus-

tive dichotomies. For example, what is the precise nature of the soul that is intermediate between physical bodies and Forms (*Timaeus* 35a–b)? What exactly is the role and nature of the *thumos* in *Republic* IV? Are the auxiliaries a genuine, distinct class, separate from the guardians and the general citizenry?

117 For the relation between the Good and unity see VI, 511b3–d2; and VII, 532a1–b2, 532d8–35a2. See also N. P. White, *Plato on Knowledge and Reality*, 95–104, 109–15.

118 A more thorough account of dialectical study must here be deferred. The main features are these: the dialectician deals only with Forms (VI, 510b8–10, 511c1–2); his goal is a completely satisfactory, perfectly true definition of every Form (VII, 532a6–7, 533b1–3, 534b3–4); this definitional knowledge depends on a completely satisfactory and true definition of the Good, the acquisition of which is the pinnacle of dialectical study (VI, 508b9–11; VII, 532b1, 533c7–d1, 534b8–d1); the method of dialectic is akin to the Socratic elenchos, a process of asking and answering questions that results in more and more well-certified knowledge until completely perfect knowledge is achieved (VII, 533b6–c5, 533c7–d1, 534b8–d1, 534d8–10); it incorporates too a cognitive ascent from "hypothesis" to "an unhypothesized starting-point" and a descent down again (VI, 510b6–9, 511b3–c2; VII, 533c7–d1). Although the details of these processes can be neglected here, I take them to be part of the elenctic procedure and aimed at completely true definitions. For discussion of the nature of dialectical inquiry and its relation to elenctic questioning, see Cornford, "Mathematics and Dialectic"; Harold Cherniss, "Plato as Mathematician," *Review of Metaphysics* 4 (1951): 395–425; Harold Cherniss, "Some War-Time Publications Concerning Plato," *American Journal of Philology* 68 (1942): 113–46, 225–65; and Irwin, *Plato's Moral Theory*, 223, 336.

119 At VI, 507d12, Plato notes that the object of vision is a "colored" object.

120 The analogy with the intelligible world would look like this: (1) soul with nous; (2) Forms with intelligibility; (3) Truth and Reality; and (4) the Good. Compare VI, 508c–09c. One must admit that here Plato's description becomes increasingly obscure. On (1) and (2), Plato suggests in the *Sophist* while discussing the doctrine of the "friends of the Forms" that dunamis is the essence of being and that this comes to the capacity to act and be acted on.

121 The situation does not prevail before this, for the prisoner's eyes are still dazzled and he can bear to look only at shadows and reflections; his capacity for vision is not yet fully actualized.

122 Yet at VII, 532b–c, Plato explicitly identifies these conversionary steps with mathematical thinking, *he pragmateia ton technon*.

123 The search for mathematicals as objects of dianoia, ontologically in-

termediate between physical objects and Forms, is perennial. See Adam, *Republic of Plato*, 2:159–63; Wedberg, *Plato's Philosophy of Mathematics*, 99–111; Annas, "On the 'Intermediates'"; and Hackforth, "Plato's Divided Line"; and Hardie, *Study in Plato*, chap. 6. For a refutation of attempts to find mathematicals in the *Republic* see Morgan, "Belief, Knowledge, and Learning." For an unusual attempt to find a type of object different from Forms and physical objects, see Tanner, "*Dianoia* and Plato's Cave."

124 See Morrison, "Two Unresolved Difficulties," 223–25, on the relation between the objects of pistis and those of dianoia. Morrison emphasizes that the two middle sections of the Line are equivalent in length, a point mentioned by several commentators and one worth remembering.

125 Tanner argues that the hypotheseis of dianoia are ontologically distinct, like the *skiai* of eikasia (Tanner, "*Dianoia* and Plato's Cave," 81–83). Tanner is moved by VI, 509d6–8, and similar passages to find *four* orders of objects. He concludes that "the *hypotheseis* of Segment B in the Divided Line of *Republic* 6 [the objects of dianoia] are to be defined as *mental images implanted in the memory . . .* the *recollection* (*anamnesis*) of these mental images is stimulated by the perception of similar objects occurring in the world of sense or 'solar realm.' Further this recollection is to be clarified by the application of dianoia either to *eidonlonti en logois* or to an actual diagram or model prepared for the purpose" (p. 84). Dianoia is the process of "deducing the Form which caused" a recollected "memory image" (p. 85). I think Tanner is right that (a) dianoia is akin to recollection, (b) it is initiated by sense experience of a model or verbal "image," and (c) it leads to knowledge of Forms but does not yet contain it. Nonetheless, the interposition of mental memory-images as the ontologically distinct objects of dianoia is gratuitous and unwarranted by the text.

Irwin, *Plato's Moral Theory*, 221–22, describes the stages of the Line in terms of Socratic elenchoi on moral beliefs. He does not directly address the relations among the confident beliefs of pistis, which have withstood a certain degree of elenctic interrogation, the hypothetical definitions of dianoia, defended by an assessment of their consequences, and the fully certified hypotheses of *noesis*, with their complete teleological explanations. He does claim that the hypotheses are different from the ordinary beliefs of pistis (p. 223) and that they are also different from the diagrams (p. 335 n. 44, sect. 6). But if Cooper is right, some images, verbal ones, can be hypothetical. Overall, however, Irwin's account is ontologically neutral on the present question.

Doubtless one reason for seeking a distinct object for dianoia and for rejecting a bipolar interpretation, such as the one I am proposing, is the principle of "one dunamis–one object" embodied in V, 477c6–d5. If in this passage Plato requires that one kind of object belong to each dunamis, of which doxa and episteme are two, does this not mandate an ontologically distinct object for dianoia? First, even if the principle were valid and dianoia should be conceived as a dunamis with a unique kind of object, there is nothing to forbid our taking dianoia's pair of objects as unique to it, insofar as it alone takes X to be an image of a Form without our yet having a firm grasp of that of which it is an image. Second, since the principle of one dunamis, one object occurs in a dialectical argument with Glaucon, who is playing the part of a nonphilosopher, it is not clear that Plato himself would have to agree with Glaucon and himself adhere to the rule. On this see Morgan, "Belief, Knowledge, and Learning." For an early version of the bipolarity of mathematical thinking, see Stocks, "The Divided Line."

126 Irwin seems to agree that while mathematical thinking is about the Forms, "the mathematician need not explicitly recognize Forms" (Plato's Moral Theory, 336 n. 44, sect. 6). I would of course argue that "need not" be replaced by "does not," if the mathematician is acting qua mathematician.

127 Murphy, " 'Simile of Light,' " 96–97, doubts whether "the mathematical level is symbolized in the Cave by the whole series of pictures . . . from the conversion to the looking at the theia phantasmata." But Murphy takes Plato's architectonic too seriously; the dichotomous Cave makes an intermediate stage impossible to picture. Murphy fails to appreciate that knowledge of Forms is prepared for by an "indirect awareness" that precedes a direct awareness of them. Hence he has trouble with VII, 532b, and VII, 526e, for in the former Plato groups the puppets with the theia phantasmata and in the latter he speaks of recognition of the puppets as already a turn to what is more real (from genesis to ousia; see VII, 515d, pros mallon onta tetrammenos orthoteron blepoi). Clearly, the puppets are only onta relative to eikones, but seeing this is the beginning of realizing that there is something "more real" than they.

128 Plato then uses this notion of being an image of an image in Republic X, for rather a different purpose.

129 For an epistemological account of the constituents of this single act and the notion of the agent's referential access that is the key to it, see Morgan, "Belief, Knowledge, and Learning."

130 I agree with much of Neil Cooper's excellent account of the objects of dianoia as eidola, both physical objects and logoi (e.g., the accounts of the just state and the just man in Republic IV), and his account of the process of dianoia as "a stepping-stone to the direct apprehension of a Form" ("Importance of Dianoia," 66). I also agree with Cooper that there are only three orders of objects in the Line and that dianoia

is an "indirect knowledge of the Forms," but I try to explain exactly how this is so. See Cooper's accurate diagram (p. 69) and Tanner's inaccurate revision ("*Dianoia* and Plato's Cave," 90). For a similar account of the objects of dianoia as logoi see Gallop, "Image and Reality," 121–23.

131 I agree with Irwin that this is a case of recollection; see *Plato's Moral Theory* and "Recollection and Plato's Moral Theory." For an interesting discussion of anamnesis in the Cave see Tanner, "*Dianoia* and Plato's Cave."

132 Raven helpfully notices that in the images there is an initial use of sight as an analogy of intelligence and then, in the Cave, a contrast of belief with knowledge. Hence, Plato moves from "temporary analogy back to habitual contrast" ("Sun, Divided Line, and Cave," 32). My interpretation suggests a further development, for mathematics is introduced to overcome the contrast and make education possible.

133 My account suggests that the rational ascent depicted in the Cave and facilitated by mathematical thinking is a Platonic "substitution" for the Eleusinian mysteries. I have also tried to show how Plato conceived of rational inquiry as ecstatic in some broad sense, but Burkert doubts that Eleusis involved ecstasy (*Ancient Mystery Cults*, 113).

134 Mylonas, *Eleusis and the Eleusinian Mysteries*, 226, 243–44; cf. Burkert, *Greek Religion*, 278, 285–90.

135 See Mylonas, *Eleusis and the Eleusinian Mysteries*, chap. 9.

136 On the trials of Alcibiades and Andokides see Mylonas, *Eleusis and the Eleusinian Mysteries*, 224, 225; see also MacDowell, *On Andokides*, introduction and notes. That the effect was to guarantee a better afterlife is clear; see Burkert, *Greek Religion*, 289, who cites the relevant texts— Hym. Dem. 280–82, Pindar Frag. 137a, Soph. Frag. 837, and Isocrates 4.28.

137 See, e.g., Mylonas, *Eleusis and the Eleusinian Mysteries*; and Parke, *Greek Festivals*.

138 See Mylonas, *Eleusis and the Eleusinian Mysteries*; Richardson, *Homeric Hymn*; and Burkert, *Greek Religion*, 285–90.

139 Mylonas, *Eleusis and the Eleusinian Mysteries*, 237 and n. 66; see also 252ff. On the role of procession see Burkert, *Greek Religion*, 99–101.

140 Mylonas, *Eleusis and the Eleusinian Mysteries*, 261; see also 261–79.

141 Ibid., 261–64.

142 Ibid., 264–69.

143 Ibid., 270–71. On Plato's use of the terminology of the mysteries see E. des Places, "Platon et la langue des mystères," *Etudes platoniciennes* (1981): 83–98; and Burkert, *Greek Religion*, 324.

144 Mylonas, *Eleusis and the Eleusinian Mysteries*, 273–74; see also 275–76. Burkert believes, after Hippolytus (*Ref.* 5.8.39), that it is an ear of corn cut in silence (*Greek Religion*, 288).

145 Mylonas, *Eleusis and the Eleusinian Mysteries*, 274. Cavell notes that profound changes in a form of life are often presented as revelations, a point well known to students of religion (*Must We Mean What We Say?* 118–19).

146 376c4–5.

147 539a–c.

148 410c–12a.

149 See *Rep.* 491d7, 495b, 519c8–9; see also 491e, 494a, 497b.

150 At V, 475e4, the philosopher is called *tous tes aletheias . . . philotheamonas*; see also V, 476b4–d6.

151 The argument occurs at V, 474c8–75c8, and is based on the principle that one who desires something (*philein ti*, 474c9; *tinos epithumetikon*, 475b4) desires all of it and not only some of it. This principle is ambiguous between (1) and (2):

   (1) One is a desirer of x-things only if there is no kind of x-thing, K, such that one does not desire K-things. For example, a real food-lover loves all kinds of food.

   (2) One is a desirer of x-things only if there is no x-thing such that one does not desire that x-thing. For example, a real food-lover loves all food; he is never sated.

As a general principle, (1) is plausible, while (2) seems preposterous. Yet in the case of the philosopher and the lover of wisdom, both (1) and (2) seem reasonable and accurate.

152 We need not explore here the nature or methods of that corruption, the core of which lies in a sophistical education; see VI, 492a–93e.

153 To understand how a person's love of truth is *realized* as a love of the Forms, one should examine the Cave and the passage about "contradictory" perception, propaedeutic to the philosophical curriculum (523a1–24d5).

154 This is the point of *Rep.* VII, 523a1–24d5.

155 588b–92a.

156 580d–81c.

157 586c–87a.

158 577c–d.

159 558d–59d.

160 571a–80a.

161 571c–d.

162 573b–c.

163 See Immanuel Kant on radical evil and the evil will in *Religion within the Limits of Reason Alone*, trans. T. H. Greene and H. H. Hudson (New York: Harper, 1960), 15–39. See also Allen W. Wood, *Kant's Moral Religion* (Ithaca: Cornell University Press, 1970), chap. 6; E. L. Fackenheim, "Kant and Radical Evil," *University of Toronto Quarterly* 23

(1954): 339–53; and Hannah Arendt, *The Origins of Totalitarianism* (New York: Harcourt Brace Jovanovich, 1951), 437–59. Parker (*Miasma*, app. 4 and esp. p. 360) discusses the Greeks' abstinence from food and particularly from the most offensive things. Eating dung and human flesh were the most disgusting practices imaginable to the Greeks.

164 How is this wellspring of antinomian desires related to the sources of evil in Plato's thought? See Cherniss, "Sources of Evil." Does it depend on the role of soul as self-motion?

165 571b–c.

166 See *Phaedo* 113c.

167 487c–89a.

168 For example, 543a.

169 See Andokides 1.111; and Demosthenes 22.27, 35.48. See also MacDowell, *Law in Classical Athens*, 24–27. He also leased sacred lands; see Rhodes, *Athenian Boule*, 97.

170 On Andokides, see Rhodes, *Athenian Boule*, 160.

171 MacDowell, *Law in Classical Athens*, 117–18; MacDowell, *Athenian Homicide Law*, 33–38.

172 *Athenaion Politeia* 57.1; see Burkert, *Greek Religion*, 95. The Panatheneia and the Dionysia are conducted by the archon and not the basileus.

173 Burkert, *Greek Religion*, 256; see also Rhodes, *Athenian Boule*, 122–34; and Mikalson, *Sacred and Civil Calendar*.

174 Consider Plato's criticism in *Rep.* II of conjurers, magicians, and Bacchic "hacks." If Burkert is right, such zealots and charlatans are already being lampooned in the *Euthyphro*. See the discussion above.

175 375b–c.

176 376a–c.

177 485a–b.

178 485c–87a.

179 490a–d, 494b, 503c–d, 535a–36c.

180 469a–b, 540b–c. See Plato's amazement with Euripides, who calls the tyrant *isotheon* at 568b. In the language of the *Symposium*, the philosopher has within the daimon Eros, a striving for the good, the beautiful, wisdom, and immortality.

181 It provides a single goal for public and private actions (519c).

182 See 498b–c.

183 520b–d.

184 See Heraclitus B114.

185 The importance of this passage and the passage itself are easily missed. My attention was drawn to it many years ago by Gregory Vlastos, "Slavery in Plato's Thought," *Platonic Studies* (Princeton: Princeton University Press, 1973), 151 n. 17; see also 13 n. 34. Although Vlastos' use of it and mine differ, they are not unrelated.

186 The identification of rational subordination and freedom has a long history in Western philosophy: Hobbes, Spinoza, Locke, Rousseau, and Kant are among the central figures in this tradition.

187 The republic does have nomoi, some identified by Socrates and his interlocutors, some to be fixed by its eventual legislators. The nomoi fixed in the *Republic* do not make up a comprehensive list; they are generally constitutional, procedural, or programmatic. The key nomos is that periodically the philosopher must rule.

188 Here we have a Platonic version of Socrates' argument in the *Crito*, that not to rule would be destructive of himself and of the best polis. As Allen has argued, the argument for legal obligation in the *Crito* is primarily delictual. It is therefore not surprising that Plato's primary argument for philosophical rule should also be delictual.

189 See *Symposium* and *Timaeus*. The Demiourgos is ungrudging; creation is part of divine perfection; the desire for immortality in the *Symposium*, while the soul is incarnate, yields "procreation in beauty."

190 Could the mention of Pythagoras (600b) be too distant in the reader's mind? The association with reincarnation is obvious.

191 377b–c, 377d, 378e.

192 The parable of the ship and its pilot in *Republic* VI, for example, is called an *eikon* (487e), as is the parable of the Cave (517a8). See 517d1.

193 See Adam, *Republic of Plato*, 2:434; at 508b11 the Sun is called an analogue of the Good.

194 *Sophist* 234d–36c. See Pollitt, *Ancient View of Greek Art*, 46–47.

195 But see Annas, *Introduction to Plato's Republic*, 350–53. One ought to take the story seriously as one dealing with the importance of any given life for the soul's future—overall—and not just in *this* life.

196 See Guthrie, *History of Greek Philosophy*, 4:557–60; F. M. Cornford, *The Republic of Plato* (Oxford: Oxford University Press, 1941), 346–59; Guthrie, *Orpheus and Greek Religion*, chap. 5; and Adam, *Republic of Plato*, 2:434–63.

197 See Hilda Richardson, "The Myth of Er," *Classical Quarterly* 20 (1926); F. M. Cornford, *Plato's Cosmology* (London: Routledge, 1937), 74–75; and Sir Thomas Heath, *Aristarchus of Samos* (Oxford: Oxford University Press, 1913; repr. New York: Dover, 1981), 148–58.

198 Do only the righteous reap rewards for justice and piety?

199 The daughter of Necessity.

200 621c3–d3.

201 See Kraut on Socrates' acceptance of democracy as second-best for just this reason (*Socrates and the State*, 194–244). For a defense of Socrates' democratic sympathies see Gregory Vlastos, "The Historical Socrates and Athenian Democracy," *Political Theory* 11 (1983): 495–516; and Reeve, *Socrates in the Apology*, 97–105.

202 See Dover, "Freedom of the Intellectual."
203 561a7–8: *me pera ekbaccheuthe.*
204 Recall *Rep.* 496d–e, quoted above.

CHAPTER SIX: PHILOSOPHICAL MADNESS AND
POLITICAL RHETORIC IN THE *PHAEDRUS*

1 Plato's intoxication with defining the philosophical enterprise has a
long subsequent history. For stimulating modern examples see Cavell,
Claim of Reason; and Cavell, *Must We Mean What We Say?* chaps. 1,
2, 4. See too G. E. R. Lloyd, *Magic, Reason, and Experience*, 100, on
the ancient setting.
2 Hackforth, *Plato's Phaedrus*, 3–7, esp. 7. There is further evidence for
this dating, although it is somewhat indirect. The mention of the temple of Zeus at Dodona (275b5–6; see also 244b) stands out as a modest
reminder of the landslide of 373 that devastated Delphi and led the
Greeks to use oracles at Dodona and Ammon during the forty-three
years when Delphi was being rebuilt (Parke, *Greek Oracles*, 114–17).
Indeed, Cicero records an oracle submitted by Sparta in 371 B.C.E. concerning war with Thebes (Cicero *De Divinatione* 1, 34, 76 and 2, 32,
69), and Demosthenes mentions several later Athenian inquiries at Dodona (e.g., Demosthenes 21, 51). Parke notes too that in the same period
Athens escalates her involvement with Ammon. Situated at the oasis
of Siwa in the Libyan Desert—see J. Boardman, *Greeks Overseas* (London: Thames and Hudson, 1980), 110—Ammon was distant but nonetheless available, having been used by Athens at least from the period
of the Peloponnesian War (Parke, *Greek Oracles*, 109–10, 117). And not
only by Athens, we can surmise; as Pausanias tells us, a shrine of Ammon stood on the Theban acropolis, not far from the statue of Epaminondas; see Pausanias IX.16.1. (On the connection between Ammon
and Thebes see Parke, *Oracles of Zeus*, 206–07. Robert Parker notes that
the Spartans were Greece's leading worshipers of Ammon [Pausanias
III.18.3], but this serves only to underline the special character of
Thebes's commitment to Ammon in this period.) Plato couched the
story of Theuth and the invention of writing in a setting that included
the Egyptian Thebes and its ruler, Thamus, who was called Ammon.
Could he not have expected that at that historic moment his reader's
attention would be drawn to the Greek Thebes and *her* "ruler" Epaminondas? (See 242b for a comparison of Phaedrus, colleague of Alcibiades, with Simmias of Thebes, countryman of Epaminondas and
friend of Philolaus.) That the shrine of Ammon on the Theban acropolis
then stood near the great statue of Epaminondas seems likely.
3 Hackforth, *Plato's Phaedrus*. I of course do not mean that the *Phaedrus*

has only a political character. But what I shall try to show is that at least part of its purpose is political, to oppose the political character and role of professional rhetoric.

4 See Jebb, *Attic Orators*, 2:10–11.

5 Xenophon *Hellenica* 35–36; see also Cawkwell, "Epaminondas and Thebes." To appreciate something about Epaminondas' reputation, one ought to recall the themes of liberation and freedom expressed in the treaty and juxtapose them with Pausanias' reminder from the statue of Epaminondas in Thebes that he was viewed as the one who brought freedom and independence to Greece (IX.15.4). As for Epaminondas' religious and artistic character, Aristoxenus tells us that he was an aulete, taught by Olympiadorus and Orthagoras. See Barker, *Greek Musical Writings*, 1:271–72; and Athenaeus *Deipnosophistae* 184d–e. See also Arist. Quint. 91.27–92.3; and Anderson, *Ethos and Education*, 218 n. 33, 250 n. 61.

6 Xenophon *Hellenica* 36–37.

7 Xenophon *Anabasis* 15–16; see also Pausanias IX.15.3.

8 Davies, *Democracy and Classical Greece*, 215.

9 Ibid., 222, 221–27.

10 Xenophon *Hellenica* 6.5.1; Tod 135 (Wickersham and Verbrugghe, *Greek Historical Documents*, 37). On the alliance with Dionysius see Tod 136 (Wickersham and Verbrugghe, *Greek Historical Documents*, 38); and Sealey, *History of the Greek City States*, 423–26.

11 Xenophon *Hellenica* 6.4.19–20; 6.5.1–3.

12 Sealey, *History of the Greek City States*, 414–19, 425. See Pausanias I.29.3, IX.15.2 on Chabrias, IX.14.3 on Iphicrates, and I.24.7. See also Xenophon *Hellenica* 6.2.39; and Hornblower, *Greek World*, 225, 229–30.

13 Pausanias I.29.14, I.24.3, I.3.2.

14 Jonathan Swift, *A Tale of a Tub* (1706), sect. 9, "A Digression Concerning Madness." For excellent historical and literary discussion see Victor Ehrenpreis, *Swift: The Man, His Works, and the Age*, vol. 1 (Cambridge: Harvard University Press, 1967).

15 See Simon, *Mind and Madness*. Of course madness, like any disease, may be thought to be both natural and divine. On the distinction between disease as divine punishment and as natural event, especially in Herodotus, see Parker, *Miasma*, 242–43. Following Lewis (*Ecstatic Religion*, chap. 3 and 79–85), Parker also discusses madness as caused by peripheral spirits and their effects on peripheral people, the cultic responses, and so on (pp. 246–47).

16 571c3–72b1. See Simon, *Mind and Madness*, 169–70; Parker, *Miasma*, 360; and Nussbaum, *Fragility of Goodness*, 200–33.

17 573d–76b.

18 266a. See Hackforth, *Plato's Phaedrus*, 133 n. 1, on problems in describing the divisions; see also Parker, *Miasma*, 242–43.

19 241e1–5.

20 242b8–43a2.

21 Hackforth, *Plato's Phaedrus*, 54–55.

22 228d, 234d. See Linforth, "Corybantic Rites," 134–35; and Parker, *Miasma*, 288 and n. 38.

23 See Nussbaum, *Fragility of Goodness*, chap. 7; on the old quarrel between philosophy and poetry see Martha Nussbaum, "'This story isn't true': Poetry, Goodness and Understanding in Plato's *Phaedrus*," in *Plato on Beauty, Wisdom and the Arts*, ed. Moravcsik and Temko, 79–124; cf. 257a, 265c. Also see Charles L. Griswold, Jr., *Self-Knowledge in Plato's Phaedrus* (New Haven: Yale University Press, 1986); and G. R. F. Ferrari, *Listening to the Cicadas: A Study of Plato's Phaedrus* (Cambridge: Cambridge University Press, 1987).

24 244a3–8.

25 Dodds shapes his excellent chapter on "the blessings of madness" around Plato's account of the first three kinds of divine madness. Since we are not interested in the historical issues concerning the antiquity in Greece of ecstatic prophecy and divination, rites of initiation and purification, and poetry (especially lyric poetry), we need not summarize his discussion or revise or supplement it. See *Greeks and the Irrational*, 64–101; Burkert, *Greek Religion*, 109–18, 276–304; and Parke, *Greek Oracles*. What we want to understand is precisely how Plato describes each of these phenomena in the *Phaedrus* and hence how philosophy is distinguished from them.

26 245b1–c2.

27 265a–b is simply inaccurate as a report of what had earlier been intended—or of what had been achieved.

28 But see Gurthrie, *History of Greek Philosophy*, 4:417–19. For brief discussion see Griswold, *Self-Knowledge*, 74–78.

29 See 248d–e, where the order would not fit.

30 Parke denies the similarity of the priestess at Dodona; see *Greek Oracles*, 93; and *Oracles of Zeus*, 81–83.

31 See 244b4: *mantike entheo*.

32 See *Republic* 364b for the lesser kind and *Timaeus* 71a–72b for the heftier.

33 265b.

34 Dodds, *Greeks and the Irrational*, 70–74.

35 In addition to Dodds see Parke, *Greek Oracles*, 74–85; and Fontenrose, *Delphic Oracle*, chap. 7, for the most conservative view.

36 Fontenrose, *Delphic Oracle*, 204.

37 See I. M. Lewis, *Ecstatic Religion*, 58.

38 244d5–45a1. See Linforth, "Telestic Madness"; Linforth, "Corybantic Rites"; Dodds, *Greeks and the Irrational*, 75–80; and Parker, *Miasma*, 286–91, esp. n. 38. See also Rouget, *Music and Trance*, 188–201.

39 See *Euthydemus* 277d; Hackforth, *Plato's Phaedrus*, 59–60, thinks they are Orphic.

40 Linforth, "Telestic Madness," 171.

41 Guthrie, *History of Greek Philosophy*, 4:418.

42 245a5–8.

43 Hackforth, *Plato's Phaedrus*, 60 and n. 1. See *Apology* 22b; and Dodds, *Greeks and the Irrational*, 82.

44 The subtle and deep character of the philosopher's interpersonal love is one of the themes of Ferrari's brilliant study; see Ferrari, *Listening to the Cicadas*, chap. 6.

45 Hackforth, *Plato's Phaedrus*, 68 and n. 2. On the argument see Griswold, *Self-Knowledge*, 78–87.

46 Hackforth, *Plato's Phaedrus*, 68. Skemp, *Theory of Motion*, 7–10, differs about the thrust of the change from one argument to the other.

47 Skemp, *Theory of Motion*, 5; Hackforth, *Plato's Phaedrus*, 68; Guthrie, *History of Greek Philosophy*, 4:420; Burkert, *Lore and Science*, 296 and n. 97.

48 *De Anima* 405a30.

49 Diels and Krantz, 24A12. See G. S. Kirk, J. E. Raven, and M. Schofield, *The Presocratic Philosophers*, 2d ed. (Cambridge: Cambridge University Press, 1983), 347; and Guthrie, *History of Greek Philosophy*, 1:350–51.

50 Guthrie, *History of Greek Philosophy*, 4:420–21; see also Skemp, *Theory of Motion*, 8–9 n. 2, on Bury's reference to Anaxagoras and to the *deuteros plous* in the *Phaedo*.

51 376e–83c.

52 Guthrie, following Hermeias, gives him too much credit by reading the *Laws* back into the *Phaedrus*; see *History of Greek Philosophy*, 4:420–21. Hackforth provides a helpful reading of the argument, although he tends to gloss over problems rather than face them; see *Plato's Phaedrus*, 66–67. See also Griswold, *Self-Knowledge*, 82–85.

53 245c5–46a2.

54 245c3. On the superiority in Plato and Aristotle of contemplating the truth to seeking it, see Sorabji, *Time, Creation, and the Continuum*, 148–49; see also *Symp.* 204a.

55 245c2–4, 246a3–4.

56 The eschatological myths of the *Gorgias*, *Phaedo*, and *Republic*.

57 See Kirk, *Nature of Greek Myths*, 22–23, 108 (although what he says here is not very helpful), and chap. 3, on the five theories of myth. See Kirk, *Myth*, esp. 259.

58 On strategic grounds Plato may feel that others are ill-equipped to appreciate a philosophical defense of philosophy, so he casts his apologia in more traditional form. Alternatively, he may think that in principle no philosophical defense of philosophy can be more than question beg-

ging. Insofar as philosophy is not merely a way of thinking but rather a way of living that incorporates a way of thinking, Plato may have come to believe that no grounding or justification of philosophy can be philosophical without there being a threat of regress.

59 See Burkert's excellent *Structure and History*, chap. 1, esp. 18–29.

60 Ibid., 27.

61 Ibid., chap. 2, esp. 35–36, with very full references. The key figures in the ritualist school are Robertson-Smith, Harrison, Murray, and Cornford. See Kirk, *Myth*, 8–31, for a critique.

62 For a list of parallels between Orphic and Pythagorean motifs in Platonic myths see Frutiger, *Les mythes de Platon*, 254–60.

63 253a3: *enthousiontes*.

64 250e1: *neoteles*; 251a2: *artiteles*.

65 250c5–6: *aseimantoi toutou ho nun de soma peripherontes onomadzomen*. See Hackforth, *Plato's Phaedrus*, 95; and Burkert, *Ancient Mystery Cults*, 92–93.

66 255b5–7: *ton entheon philon*.

67 Guthrie, *History of Greek Philosophy*, 4:426.

68 248a1–b5. See Thompson, *Phaedrus of Plato*, 51. The last category is hard to make out, but this identification seems right (see 248a6–b5).

69 248c2–5.

70 The causes of the incarnation of such souls are *lethe* and *kakia* (248c6–7). These are the aitiai of the soul's losing its wings (246d3–5).

71 *Phaedrus* 248c5–e3, 249a1–2. Hackforth comments that this 'order of merit' of lives, which represents nine degrees of prenatal awareness of the Forms, "seems to be one of decreasing worth to society" (Hackforth, *Plato's Phaedrus*, 83), with the last place taken by the tyrant, as "every reader of *Rep*. IX would expect" (p. 84). See Thompson, *Phaedrus of Plato*, 52–53. On the highest form of incarnation as a single type, called by any one of these four designations, see G. J. de Vries, *Commentary on the Phaedrus*, 143, 248d3–4. Of the various kinds of human life, only this one allows the soul an early exit from physical life and renewed community with the divine souls (248e5–49d3). On philosophy and music in Plato see Anderson, *Ethos and Education*, chap. 3; and Barker, *Greek Musical Writings*, vol. 1, chap. 10.

72 At *Phaedrus* 246a4–7 the charioteer with his pair of horses is specifically called a "likeness" of the idea of the soul. Since the soul in question has just been shown to be immortal, a matter hardly in dispute with regard to divine, disembodied souls, the soul depicted by the likeness of the charioteer and his horses must be nondivine. T. B. L. Webster, *Art and Literature in Fourth-Century Athens* (London: Batsford, 1956), 7, 33–34, 41–42, suggests that Heracles and his chariot are the model for Plato's myth (see plate 4a, an Attic bell-krater, Heracles in a chariot, ca. 370–360 B.C.E.).

73 At 247c3–d1 Socrates refers to *ton huperouranion topon* as the place
where *he achromatos te kai aschematistos kai anaphes ousia ontos
ousa, psyches kubernete mono theate no*. That is, it is seen only by
nous, "the soul's pilot" (Hackforth, *Plato's Phaedrus*, 79).

74 Socrates is in the process of defining the fourth kind of madness (*mania*); one who shares in this madness is one who loves beautiful things
and is called a "lover" (249d4–e4). Hence the relevant knowledge is
knowledge of the Form of the Beautiful. See Hackforth, *Plato's Phaedrus*, 93–94.

75 Compare *Phaedrus* 250b5–c6 with *Republic* VI, 500c–d, and *Timaeus*
90a–c.

76 The expression "primary reason" is used by Donald Davidson in a sense
both different from mine and more technical. See "Actions, Reasons,
and Causes," reprinted in D. Davidson, *Essays on Actions and Events*
(Oxford: Oxford University Press, 1980), 3–19. For Davidson, a primary
reason why an agent S. performs the act A is: (a) S.'s want or desire to
achieve or gain some end; and (b) S.'s belief that A is of a certain kind,
viz., a kind that will bring that end about. What I mean by "primary
reason" is a dominant, overriding pro-attitude. For a discussion of the
strength of reasons and the nature of overriding reasons see Joseph Raz,
Practical Reason and Norms (London: Hutchinson, 1971), 25–28.

77 To use Goldman's term, intellectual desire in such a case is a standing
want. See Alvin I. Goldman, *A Theory of Human Action* (Princeton:
Princeton University Press, 1970), 86–91.

78 On the principle of the attraction of like by like see *Lysis* 214a–b.

79 On this element of chance (or grace!) in the viewing of Forms by rec-
ollection see Sorabji's discussion of Augustine and Plotinus in *Time,
Creation, and the Continuum*, 171–72; cf. 157–58. See also Aug. *Conf.*
VII.21; and Plot. *Enn.* 5.5.8 (3–7), 5.8.10 (43), 5.8.11 (2).

80 Richard Robinson, *Plato's Earlier Dialectic*; Vlastos, "Socratic Elen-
chus"; Vlastos, "Afterthoughts on the Socratic Elenchus"; N. P. White,
Plato on Knowledge and Reality; Irwin, *Plato's Moral Theory*; Allen,
Plato's Euthyphro; Kraut, *Socrates and the State*, chap. 8; and Kraut,
"Comments on Gregory Vlastos." This is only a small sample of dis-
cussion.

81 N. P. White, *Plato on Knowledge and Reality*, 70–74, however, ascribes
too much to the *Phaedo*.

82 There are two possible mistakes or confusions, both about identity or
identification: (1) mistaking a physical state, property, or whatever for
what *x* really is—for a Form; and (2) mistaking one Form for another.
The two are not unrelated. See N. P. White, *Plato on Knowledge and
Reality*, 94–95, on *Republic* VII, 523ff. In White's words, "The effort to
gain knowledge involves more than simply the training of the mind's

eye on them so as to be able blankly to view them. It also involves, in some sense or other, the recognition or correct identification of, and the avoidance of certain sorts of confusion about, the Forms that one has in one's ken" (p. 95) I disagree of course with the words "simply" and "blankly," as if the referential access to the Forms were not of any real importance.

83 See Ferrari, *Listening to the Cicadas*, chap. 6.

84 See 261a–b.

85 One might usefully compare this relationship to the notion of revelation in such modern thinkers as Kierkegaard, Buber, and Rosenzweig. Of special interest is Kierkegaard's conception of revelation as an "immediacy after reflection" and Rosenzweig's view that revelation is an event of which all accounts are human interpretations—that revelation is already a human response.

86 Thompson, *Phaedrus of Plato*, 107, cites Xenophon (*Memorabilia* iv.5.12) on Socrates and division but calls it a novelty. See Hackforth, *Plato's Phaedrus*, 134; and Guthrie, *History of Greek Philosophy*, 4:431 and n. 1.

87 See 277b–c.

88 For discussion of the details of the method see N. P. White, *Plato on Knowledge and Reality*, 120–23; Moline, *Plato's Theory of Understanding*, 172–73; and Griswold, *Self-Knowledge*, 173–86.

89 Field, *Plato and His Contemporaries*, 112.

90 Jebb, *Attic Orators*, 2:369–70.

91 See Thompson, *Phaedrus of Plato*, 181 n. 8, on Lysias' *Against Eratosthenes*, ca. 403 (see Jebb, *Attic Orators*, 1:153). The *Olympiakos* too was delivered in person.

92 One should not ignore the political, social, and legal importance of forensic oratory; see Dover, *Lysias and the Corpus Lysiacum*, 55–56 and chap. 4; cf. 261b3–5.

93 Dover places it earlier, 418–16, and surveys all the conflicting evidence; *Lysias and the Corpus Lysiacum*, chap. 2.

94 278e–79b; see Thompson, *Phaedrus of Plato*, app. 2, pp. 170–83; cf. pp. 147–48.

95 The two sections of the argument are 259e–74b and 274b–78b.

96 See 260e. As Hackforth notes, *atechnos tribe* (e5) recalls *Gorgias* 463b (*Plato's Phaedrus*, 160).

97 Also, more briefly, at 273d8–e4.

98 See 260c6–d1; cf. *Republic* 493a–c.

99 See 261a and following.

100 To press for the plausible or the probable (*to eikos*); cf. 272d–73a.

101 The examples Socrates gives in the two speeches concern ambiguity. The real rhetorician should divide disputed from undisputed terms and define key disputed terms to avoid equivocation; see 263a–66c.

102 268a–69c, esp. 269c1–5. The comparison with Plato's treatment of painting, music, and poetry in the *Republic* is telling.

103 269d–70a.

104 270b–72b.

105 At 270c–d Socrates presents a two-step method for understanding the
nature of anything. One should ask: (1) is x simple or complex?; and
(2a) if simple, how is it acted on and how does it act on another, or
(2b) if complex, what are its parts and how do they act and how are
they acted on?

106 See 271c10–72b2.

107 275d–e; it cannot reply to questions and it addresses many people. See
G. E. R. Lloyd, *Magic, Reason, and Experience*, 86–98, esp. 98, on literacy and the role of face-to-face encounters in medical and biological
learning.

108 A Semitic import, the cult of the dying god Adonis was restricted to
women and was marked by a midsummer festival with two features:
the sowing of quickly germinating seeds in pots (gardens of Adonis) on
flat roofs, and the carrying through the streets of biers containing small
silhouettes of the god. See Burkert, *Structure and History*, 105–08,
esp. 107 and nn. 23, 24. In the end both the pots and the biers were
thrown into the sea. As Burkert puts it, "In Greece, the special function
of the Adonis cult is as an opportunity for the unbridled expression of
emotion in the strictly circumscribed life of women, in contrast to the
rigid order of polis and family with the official women's festivals in
honor of Demeter" (*Greek Religion*, 176–77). One might add the un-
settling fact that according to tradition it was on the evening of the
Adonia that the Hermes were mutilated, just before the disastrous Sicilian expedition (Plutarch *Alcibiades* 18). See Nussbaum, " 'This story
isn't true,' " 96 and n. 23.

   Detienne's *Gardens of Adonis* treats comprehensively and ambi-
tiously the rituals of the Adonia and their connections with myth,
social life, and economics.

109 276c.

110 277d10–e2; cf. *Republic* V, 477.

111 See Hackforth, *Plato's Phaedrus*, 164, for a comparison with *Symposium*
209b.

112 I am reminded of Franz Rosenzweig's comment in "The New Thinking"
that Platonic dialogues are boring and tedious. They are not, by Rosenzweig's standards, genuine dialogues that have a sense of time and
development. Rosenzweig's reasons for giving such a biased and narrow
reading to the dialogues can only be surmised, but they must surely
have something to do with the dialogues' lack of a center, of revelation
on the biblical model, and thus of access to whatever truth can be
known.

113 Hackforth, *Plato's Phaedrus*, 162–63; Friedlander, *Plato*, vol. 1, chap. 5, "The Written Work."

114 Jebb, *Attic Orators*, 2, 47.

115 *Antid.* sect. 40.

116 Friedlander, *Plato*, 1:111.

117 See *Phaedrus* 276a.

118 Again, the outstanding discussion of the phenomenology of such loving relationships is in Ferrari, *Listening to the Cicadas*.

119 The phrase is Martin Buber's; he uses it to refer not to Plato's rulers but to the biblical prophets. To both, reality is timeless and eternal, but for Plato it involves knowledge of the Forms, for Buber an encounter with the Divine Presence.

CONCLUSION

1 See Glenn Morrow, *Plato's Cretan City* (Princeton: Princeton University Press, 1960); Reverdin, *La religion de la cité platonicienne*; Burkert, *Greek Religion*, 332–37; and Guthrie, *History of Greek Philosophy*, 5:357–67.

2 I omit the *Timaeus* and *Critias*. Personally I prefer a later reading, of course before the *Laws* but after the *Philebus*.

3 See Guthrie, *History of Greek Philosophy*, 5:63; and Field, *Plato and His Contemporaries*, 36–48. See also Cherniss, *Riddle of the Early Academy*.

4 See Field, *Plato and His Contemporaries*, 45–46.

5 Field, *Plato and His Contemporaries*, 36–37.

6 Morrow, *Plato's Epistles*, 158; see 158–59, for Morrow's argument that this is not necessarily the plan of the *Republic*.

7 See Morrow, *Plato's Epistles*, 137–44.

8 Hornblower, *Greek World*, 224–38; see also Cawkwell, "Epaminondas and Thebes."

9 Xenophon *Hellenica* 6.5.1–7.1.32; Diodorus 15.59, 66. See also Sealey, *History of the Greek City States*, 423–26; and Hornblower, *Greek World*, 224–26.

10 Hornblower, *Greek World*, 226–28.

11 Diodorus 15.62.3; cf. Hornblower, *Greek World*, 225.

12 Diodorus 15.76.3; Hornblower, *Greek World*, 230. See also Cawkwell, "The Common Peace of 366–65"; Sealey, *History of the Greek City States*, 426–27; and Hammond, *History of Greece*, 502. But see Ryder, *Koine Eirene*, 137–39; and *Classical Quarterly* 7 (1957): 199ff.

13 Sealey, *History of the Greek City States*, 432; Hammond, *History of Greece*, 503; Hornblower, *Greek World*, 230–32.

14 Hornblower, *Mausolus*, 197–201. The failures occur not only in foreign policy. Whitehead, *Demes of Attica*, 270–90, 291, points to a realignment

of the boundaries between local and central government involving changes in the role of *demes* in the sortition for magistrates. In part, the change was the result of abuses and corruption at the level of the deme. Whitehead also notices the fourth-century development of private financing for liturgies to replace financing by the deme, the result of a "chronic fiscal shortfall" in the demes themselves (pp. 173–75; but see Dow, "Six Athenian Sacrificial Calendars").

15 Ostwald, introduction to J. B. Skemp, trans., *Statesman* (Indianapolis: Bobbs-Merrill, 1957), xx.

16 Cornford, *Plato's Theory of Knowledge*, 168–69; cf. *Politicus* 258a.

Ackrill, J. L. "Anamnesis in the *Phaedo*: Remarks on 73c–75c." In *Exegesis and Argument*, ed. E. N. Lee, A. P. D. Mourelatos, and R. Rorty, 177–95. Assen: Van Gorcum, 1974.

Adam, James, ed. *The Republic of Plato*. Cambridge: Cambridge University Press, 1965 (orig. pub. 1901).

Adkins, Arthur W. H. "Greek Religion." In *Historia Religionum*, ed. Claas J. Bleeker and Geo Widengren, 1:377–441. Leiden: E. J. Brill, 1969.

Allen, R. E. "The Argument from Opposites in *Republic* V." *Review of Metaphysics* 15 (1961): 325–35.

———. *Plato's Euthyphro and the Earlier Theory of Forms*. London: Routledge and Kegan Paul, 1970.

———. *Socrates and Legal Obligation*. Minneapolis: University of Minnesota Press, 1980.

———, ed. *Studies in Plato's Metaphysics*. London: Routledge and Kegan Paul, 1965.

Anderson, Warren. *Ethos and Education in Greek Music*. Cambridge: Harvard University Press, 1966.

Andrewes, A. *The Greek Tyrants*. London: Hutchinson, 1956.

Annas, Julia. *An Introduction to Plato's Republic*. Oxford: Oxford University Press, 1981.

———. "On the 'Intermediates.'" *Archiv für Geschichte der Philosophie* 57 (1975): 146–66.

Aristotle. *The Athenian Constitution*, trans. P. J. Rhodes. Harmondsworth: Penguin, 1984.

———. *Constitution of Athens*, trans. Kurt von Fritz and Ernst Kapp. New York: Hafner, 1950.

Austin, M. M., and P. Vidal-Naquet. *Economic and Social History of Ancient Greece: An Introduction*. Berkeley: University of California Press, 1977.

Bambrough, R., ed. *New Essays on Plato and Aristotle*. London: Routledge and Kegan Paul, 1965.

Barker, Andrew. *Greek Musical Writings*, vol. 1. Cambridge: Cambridge University Press, 1984.

Beckman, James. *The Religious Dimension of Socrates' Thought*. Waterloo, Ontario: Wilfred Laurier University Press, 1979.

Belknap, George N. "Religion in Plato's States." *Studies in the Humanities*, vol. 1, bulletin 2, *Studies in Greek Religion*. n.d.

Bluck, R. S. *Plato's Meno*. Cambridge: Cambridge University Press, 1961.

———. *Plato's Phaedo*. London: Routledge and Kegan Paul, 1955.

Bos, A. P. *Providentia Divina: The Theme of Divine Pronoia in Plato and Aristotle.* Amsterdam: Van Gorcum, 1976.

Bostock, David. *Plato's Phaedo.* Oxford: Oxford University Press, 1986.

Bremmer, Jan. *The Early Greek Concept of the Soul.* Princeton: Princeton University Press, 1983.

——, ed. *Interpretations of Greek Mythology.* Totowa, N.J.: Barnes and Noble, 1986.

Brickhouse, Thomas C., and Nicholas D. Smith. *Socrates on Trial.* Princeton: Princeton University Press, 1989.

Bruno, Vincent. *Form and Color in Greek Painting.* New York: W. W. Norton, 1977.

Buchmann, Klara. *Die Stellung des Menon in der Platonischen Philosophie.* Leipzig: Dieterich'sche Verlagsbuchhandlung, 1936.

Burger, R. *Plato's Phaedrus: A Defense of a Philosophical Art of Writing.* University: University of Alabama Press, 1980.

Burkert, Walter. *Ancient Mystery Cults.* Cambridge: Harvard University Press, 1987.

——. "Craft versus Sect: The Problem of Orphics and Pythagoreans." In *Jewish and Christian Self-Definition,* vol. 3, *Self-Definition in the Graeco-Roman World,* ed. Ben F. Meyer and E. P. Sanders. Philadelphia: SCM Press, 1982.

——. *Homo Necans: The Anthropology of Ancient Greek Sacrificial Ritual and Myth.* Berkeley: University of California Press, 1983.

——. *Greek Religion,* trans. John Raffan. Cambridge: Harvard University Press, 1985.

——. "Greek Tragedy and Sacrificial Ritual." *Greek, Roman and Byzantine Studies* 7 (1966): 87–121.

——. "Herodot über die Namen der Gotter: Polytheismus als historisches Problem." *Museum Helveticum* 42 (1985): 121–32.

——. *Lore and Science in Ancient Pythagoreanism.* Cambridge: Harvard University Press, 1972.

——. "Orpheus und die Vorsokratiker." *Antike und Abenland* 14 (1968): 93–114.

——. *Orphism and Bacchic Mysteries: New Evidence and Old Problems of Interpretation.* Berkeley: Center for Hermeneutical Studies in Hellenistic and Modern Culture, 1977.

——. *Structure and History in Greek Mythology and Ritual.* Berkeley: University of California Press, 1979.

Burnet, John. *Apology, Euthyphro, Crito.* Oxford: Oxford University Press, 1924.

——. "The Socratic Doctrine of the Soul." In *Essays and Addresses,* 126–62. New York: Macmillan, 1930.

——. *Plato's Phaedo.* Oxford: Oxford University Press, 1911.

Burnyeat, Myles F. "Aristotle on Understanding Knowledge." In *Aristotle on Science: The "Posterior Analytics,"* ed. Enrico Berti. Padua: Antenore, 1981.

——. "Socratic Midwifery, Platonic Inspiration." *Bulletin of the Institute of Classical Studies, University of London* 24 (1977): 7–15.

Cassirer, Ernst. *Kant's Life and Thought*. New Haven: Yale University Press, 1981 (orig. Ger. ed. pub. 1918).

Cavell, Stanley. *The Claim of Reason*. Oxford: Oxford University Press, 1979.

————. *Must We Mean What We Say?* Cambridge: Cambridge University Press, 1969.

Cawkwell, G. L. "The Common Peace of 366–65 B.C." *Classical Quarterly* 11 (1961): 80–86.

————. "Epaminondas and Thebes." *Classical Quarterly* 22 (1972): 254–78.

————. "The Foundation of the Second Athenian Confederacy." *Classical Quarterly* 23, no. 1 (1973): 47–60.

————. "The Imperialism of Thrasybulus." *Classical Quarterly* 26, no. 2 (1976): 270–77.

————. "The King's Peace." *Classical Quarterly* 31 (1981): 64–83.

————. "Notes on the Failure of the Second Athenian Confederacy." *Journal of Hellenic Studies* 101 (1981): 40–55.

————. "Notes on the Peace of 375/4." *Historia* 12 (1963): 84–95.

Cherniss, Harold F. "The Philosophical Economy of the Theory of Ideas." In *Studies in Plato's Metaphysics*, ed. R. E. Allen. London: Routledge and Kegan Paul, 1965.

————. *The Riddle of the Early Academy*. Berkeley: University of California Press, 1945. Reprint, 1962.

————. "The Sources of Evil according to Plato." In *Plato*, ed. Gregory Vlastos, vol. 2. Garden City, N.Y.: Doubleday, 1971.

Claus, D. B. *Toward the Soul: An Inquiry into the Meaning of Psyche before Plato*. New Haven: Yale University Press, 1981.

Clinton, K. *The Sacred Officials of the Eleusinian Mysteries*. Philadelphia: American Philosophical Society, 1974.

Cole, Susan Guettel. "New Evidence for the Mysteries of Dionysos." *Greek, Roman and Byzantine Studies* 21, no. 3 (1980): 223–38.

Connor, W. R. *The New Politicians of Fifth-Century Athens*. Princeton: Princeton University Press, 1971.

Cooper, Neil. "The Importance of *Dianoia* in Plato's Theory of Forms." *Classical Quarterly* 16 (1966): 65–69.

Cornford, Francis M. *Before and after Socrates*. Cambridge: Cambridge University Press, 1932.

————. "The Doctrine of Eros in Plato's *Symposium*." In *The Unwritten Philosophy*, ed. W. K. C. Guthrie. Cambridge: Cambridge University Press, 1967.

————. "Mathematics and Dialectic in the *Republic* VI–VII." *Mind* (1932). Reprinted in R. E. Allen, *Studies in Plato's Metaphysics*. London: Routledge and Kegan Paul, 1965.

————. *Principium Sapientiae*, ed. W. K. C. Guthrie. New York: Harper and Row, 1965 (orig. pub. 1952).

————. *The Unwritten Philosophy and Other Essays*, ed. W. K. C. Guthrie. Cambridge: Cambridge University Press, 1967.

Crombie, I. M. *An Examination of Plato's Doctrines*. London: Routledge and Kegan Paul, 1963.

Cross, R. C., and A. D. Woozley. *Plato's Republic: A Philosophical Commentary*. London: Macmillan, 1964.

Davies, J. K. *Democracy and Classical Greece*. Glasgow: Fontana, 1978.

den Boer, W. "Aspects of Religion in Classical Greece." *Harvard Studies in Classical Philology* 77 (1973): 1–21.

Despland, Michel. *The Education of Desire: Plato and the Philosophy of Religion*. Toronto: University of Toronto Press, 1985.

Detienne, Marcel. *Dionysos mis à mort*. Paris: Gallimard, 1977. Eng. trans. *Dionysos Slain*. Baltimore: Johns Hopkins University Press, 1979.

———. *Les jardins d'Adonis*. Paris: Gallimard, 1972. Eng. trans. *The Gardens of Adonis: Spices in Greek Mythology*. Atlantic Highlands, N.J.: Humanities Press, 1977.

Deubner, L. *Attische Feste*. Berlin, 1932. Reprint, 1966.

de Vries, G. J. *A Commentary on the Phaedrus of Plato*. Amsterdam: Hakkert, 1969.

Dietrich, B. C. *Death, Fate and the Gods*. London: University of London, 1965.

Dodds, E. R. *The Ancient Concept of Progress and Other Essays*. Oxford: Oxford University Press, 1973.

———. *The Greeks and the Irrational*. Berkeley: University of California Press, 1951.

———. "Maenadism in the Bacchae." *Harvard Theological Review* 33 (1940): 155–76.

———. "Plato and the Irrational." *Journal of Hellenic Studies* 65 (1945): 16–25.

———. *Plato Gorgias*. Oxford: Oxford University Press, 1959.

———, ed. *Euripides' Bacchae*. 2d ed. Oxford: Oxford University Press, 1960.

Dorter, Kenneth. *Plato's Phaedo: An Interpretation*. Toronto: University of Toronto Press, 1982.

Douglas, Mary. *Implicit Meanings*. London: Routledge and Kegan Paul, 1975.

———. *Natural Symbols*. New York: Pantheon, 1982.

———. *Purity and Danger: An Analysis of the Concepts of Pollution and Taboo*. London: Routledge and Kegan Paul, 1966.

Dover, K. J. "The Date of Plato's *Symposium*." *Phronesis* 10 (1965): 2–20.

———. "The Freedom of the Intellectual in Greek Society." *Talanta* 7 (1976): 24–54.

———. *Greek Popular Morality*. Berkeley: University of California Press, 1974.

———. *Lysias and the Corpus Lysiacum*. Berkeley: University of California Press, 1968.

Dow, Sterling. "Six Athenian Sacrificial Calendars." *Bulletin de correspondance hellénique* 92 (1968): 170–86.

Drachman, A. B. *Atheism in Pagan Antiquity*. London: Gyldendal, 1922.

Easterling, P. E., and J. V. Muir, eds. *Greek Religion and Society*. Cambridge: Cambridge University Press, 1985.

Ebert, T. *Meinung und Wissen in der Philosophie Platons*, 83–104. Berlin: Walter de Gruyter, 1974.

———. "Plato's Theory of Recollection Reconsidered: An Interpretation of *Meno* 80a–86c." *Man and World* 6, no. 2 (1973): 163–81.

Edelstein, Ludwig. "The Function of the Myth in Plato's Philosophy." *Journal of the History of Ideas* 10 (1949): 463–81.

Ehnmark, Erland. "Socrates and the Immortality of the Soul." *Eranos* 44 (1946): 105–22.

———. "Some Remarks on the Idea of Immortality in Greek Religion." *Eranos* 46 (1948): 1–21.

Evans-Pritchard, E. E. *Nuer Religion*. Oxford: Oxford University Press, 1956.

———. *Witchcraft, Oracles, and Magic among the Azande*. Oxford: Oxford University Press, 1937.

Farnell, L. R. *The Cults of the Greek States*. 4 vols. Oxford: Oxford University Press, 1896–1909.

———. *Greek Hero Cults and Ideas of Immortality*. Oxford: Oxford University Press, 1921.

Feibleman, James K. *Religious Platonism*. London: George Allen and Unwin, 1959.

Ferguson, A. S. "The Impiety of Socrates." *Classical Quarterly* 7 (1913): 157–75.

———. "Plato's Simile of Light." *Classical Quarterly* 15 (1921): 131–52; 16 (1922): 15–28.

———. "Plato's Simile of Light Again." *Classical Quarterly* 28 (1934–35): 190–210.

Ferrari, G. R. F. *Listening to the Cicadas: A Study of Plato's Phaedrus*. Cambridge: Cambridge University Press, 1987.

Festugière, A. J. *Contemplation et vie contemplative selon Platon*. Paris: Vrin, 1967 (orig. pub. 1935).

Field, G. C. *Plato and His Contemporaries*. London: Methuen, 1930.

Fine, Gail. "Knowledge and Belief in *Republic* V." *Archiv für Geschichte der Philosophie* 60 (1978): 121–39.

———. "Separation." *Oxford Studies in Ancient Philosophy* 2 (1984): 31–87.

Fontenrose, Joseph. *The Delphic Oracle: Its Responses and Operation*. Berkeley: University of California Press, 1978.

Frankfurt, H. *The Importance of What We Care About*. Cambridge: Cambridge University Press, 1988.

Freeman, Kenneth J. *Schools of Hellas*. New York: Teachers College Press, 1969.

Friedlander, Paul. *Plato*. 3 vols. Princeton: Princeton University Press, 1958.

Frutiger, Perceval. *Les mythes de Platon*. Paris: Alcan, 1930.

Fustel de Coulanges, Numa D. *The Ancient City*. Paris, 1864. Eng. trans., 1873.

Gallop, David. "Dreaming and Waking in Plato." In *Essays in Ancient Greek Philosophy*, ed. John P. Anton and George L. Kustas. Albany: State University of New York Press, 1971, 187–210.

———. "Image and Reality in Plato's *Republic*." *Archiv für Geschichte der Philosophie* 47 (1965): 113–31.

———. *Plato Phaedo*. Oxford: Oxford University Press, 1975.

Geertz, Clifford. *The Interpretation of Cultures*. New York: Basic Books, 1973.

———. *Islam Observed*. New Haven: Yale University Press, 1968.

———. *The Religion of Java*. Glencoe, Ill.: Free Press, 1960.

Gernet, Louis. *The Anthropology of Ancient Greece*, trans. J. Hamilton and B. Nagy. Baltimore: Johns Hopkins University Press, 1981.

Goldman, Alvin I. "Discrimination and Perceptual Knowledge." *Journal of Philosophy* 73 (1976): 771–91.

———. *A Theory of Human Action*. Princeton: Princeton University Press, 1970.

Gombrich, E. H. *Art and Illusion*. Princeton: Princeton University Press, 1969.

Goody, Jack, and Ian Watt. "The Consequences of Literacy." *Comparative Studies in Society and History* 5 (1963): 304–45.

Gordon, R. L., ed. *Myth, Religion and Society*. Cambridge: Cambridge University Press, 1981.

Gosling, Justin. "*Doxa* and *Dunamis* in Plato's *Republic*." *Phronesis* 13 (1968): 119–30.

———. "*Republic* Book V: *ta polla kala* etc." *Phronesis* 5 (1960): 116–28.

———. "Similarity in *Phaedo* 73 seq." *Phronesis* 10 (1965): 151–61.

Graf, Fritz. *Eleusis und die orphische Dichtung Athens in vorhellenistischer Zeit*. Berlin: Walter de Gruyter, 1974.

Griffin, Jasper. *Homer on Life and Death*. Oxford: Oxford University Press, 1980.

Griswold, Charles, Jr. *Platonic Writings, Platonic Readings*. New York: Routledge and Kegan Paul, 1988.

———. *Self-Knowledge in Plato's Phaedrus*. New Haven: Yale University Press, 1986.

Grube, G. M. A. "Euripides and the Gods." In *Euripides*, ed. Erich Segal. Englewood Cliffs, N.J.: Prentice-Hall, 1968.

Gulley, Norman. *The Philosophy of Socrates*. London: Macmillan, 1968.

———. *Plato's Theory of Knowledge*. London: Macmillan, 1962.

———. "Plato's Theory of Recollection." *Classical Quarterly* 3–4 (1954): 194–97.

Guthrie, W. K. C. *The Greeks and Their Gods*. London: Methuen, 1950.

———. *A History of Greek Philosophy*. 4 vols. Cambridge: Cambridge University Press, 1967–75.

———. *In the Beginning*. Ithaca: Cornell University Press, 1957.

———. *Orpheus and Greek Religion*. 2d ed. London: Methuen, 1952.

Hackforth, R. "Immortality in Plato's *Symposium*." *Classical Review* 64 (1950): 43–45.

————. "Plato's Divided Line and Dialectic." *Classical Quarterly* 36 (1942): 1–9.

————. *Plato's Phaedo*. Cambridge: Cambridge University Press, 1955.

————. *Plato's Phaedrus*. Cambridge: Cambridge University Press, 1952.

Hamlyn, D. W. "Eikasia in Plato's *Republic*." *Philosophical Quarterly* 8 (1958): 14–23.

Hammond, N. G. L. *A History of Greece to 322 B.C.* 2d ed. Oxford: Oxford University Press, 1967.

Hansen, Mogens Herman. "The Athenian 'Politicians,' 403–322 B.C." *Greek, Roman and Byzantine Studies* 24 (1983): 33–55.

————. "Political Activity and the Organization of Attica in the Fourth Century B.C." *Greek, Roman and Byzantine Studies* 24 (1983): 227–38.

Hardie, W. F. R. *A Study in Plato*. Oxford: Oxford University Press, 1936.

Harrison, J. E. *Prolegomena to the Study of Greek Religion*. 3d ed. Cambridge: Cambridge University Press, 1922.

————. *Themis: A Study of the Social Origins of Greek Religion*. 2d ed. Cambridge: Cambridge University Press, 1927.

Henrichs, Albert. "Changing Dionysiac Identities." In *Jewish and Christian Self-Definition*, vol. 3, *Self-Definition in the Graeco-Roman World*, ed. Ben F. Meyer and E. P. Sanders. London: SCM Press, 1982.

————. "Greek Maenadism from Olympias to Messinia." *Harvard Studies in Classical Philology* 82 (1978): 121–60.

————. "Male Intruders among the Maenads: The So-Called Male Celebrant." In *Mnemai: Classical Studies in Memory of Karl K. Hulley*, ed. H. D. Evjen, 69–91. Chico, Calif.: Scholars Press, 1984.

————. "Loss of Self, Suffering, Violence: The Modern View of Dionysus from Nietzsche to Girard." *Harvard Studies in Classical Philology* 88 (1984): 205–40.

————. "The Sophists and Hellenistic Religion: Prodicus as the Spiritual Father of the Isis Aretalogies." *Harvard Studies in Classical Philology* 88 (1984): 139–58.

————. "Two Doxographical Notes: Democritus and Prodicus on Religion." *Harvard Studies in Classical Philology* 79 (1975): 93–123.

Herington, C. J. *Athena Parthenos and Athena Polias*. Manchester: Manchester University Press, 1955.

Hignett, C. *A History of the Athenian Constitution to the End of the Fifth Century*. Oxford: Oxford University Press, 1952.

Hill, Christopher. *The World Turned Upside Down*. New York: Viking Penguin, 1975.

Hornblower, Simon. *The Greek World, 479–323 B.C.* London: Methuen, 1983.

————. *Mausolus*. Oxford: Oxford University Press, 1982.

Humphreys, S. C. *Anthropology and the Greeks*. London: Routledge and Kegan Paul, 1978.

Irwin, Terence H. *Plato Gorgias*. Oxford: Oxford University Press, 1979.

————. "Plato's Heracleiteanism." *Philosophical Quarterly* 27 (1977): 1–13.

———. *Plato's Moral Theory*. Oxford: Oxford University Press, 1977.

———. "Recollection and Plato's Moral Theory." *Review of Metaphysics* 27 (1974): 752–72.

———. "Socrates and Athenian Democracy." *Philosophy and Public Affairs* 18 (Spring 1989): 184–205.

Jaeger, Werner. "The Greek Ideas of Immortality." *Harvard Theological Review* 52, no. 3 (1959): 135–47.

———. *Paideia: The Ideals of Greek Culture*. 3 vols. New York: Oxford University Press, 1939–44.

———. *The Theology of the Early Greek Philosophers*. Oxford: Oxford University Press, 1947.

Jeanmaire, H. *Couroi et Courètes*. Avesnes-sur-Helpe, France: G. Deloffre, 1939.

———. *Dionysos: Histoire du culte de Bacchus*. Paris: Payot, 1951.

Jebb, R. C. *The Attic Orators*. 2 vols. London: Macmillan, 1893.

Joint Association of Classical Teachers. *The World of Athens: An Introduction to Classical Athenian Culture*. Cambridge: Cambridge University Press, 1984.

Jones, A. H. M. *Athenian Democracy*. Oxford: Oxford University Press, 1957.

Jordan, B. *Servants of the Gods*. Göttingen: Vandenhoeck und Ruprecht, 1979.

Joseph, H. W. B. *Knowledge and the Good in Plato's Republic*. Oxford: Oxford University Press, 1948.

Kahn, Charles H. *The Art and Thought of Heraclitus*. Cambridge: Cambridge University Press, 1979.

———. "Religion and Natural Philosophy in Empedocles' Doctrine of the Soul." *Archiv für Geschichte der Philosophie* 42 (1981): 3–35. Suppl. In *The Pre-Socratics*, ed. A. P. D. Mourelatos, 426–56. Garden City, N.Y.: Doubleday, 1974.

Kennedy, George. *The Art of Persuasion in Greece*. Princeton: Princeton University Press, 1963.

Kenny, Anthony. *Action, Emotion and Will*. London: Routledge and Kegan Paul, 1963.

Kerferd, G. B. *The Sophistic Movement*. Cambridge: Cambridge University Press, 1981.

Kirk, G. S. *Myth: Its Meaning and Functions in Ancient and Other Cultures*. Berkeley: University of California Press, 1970.

———. *The Nature of Greek Myths*. Harmondsworth: Penguin, 1974.

Kosman, L. A. "Platonic Love." In *Facets of Plato's Philosophy*, ed. W. H. Werkmeister, 53–69. Assen: Van Gorcum, 1976.

Kraut, Richard. "Comments on Gregory Vlastos, 'The Socratic Elenchus.'" *Oxford Studies in Ancient Philosophy* 1 (1983): 59–70.

———. "Egoism, Love, and Political Office in Plato." *Philosophical Review* 82, no. 3 (1973): 330–44.

———. *Socrates and the State*. Princeton: Princeton University Press, 1984.

Krentz, Peter. *The Thirty at Athens*. Ithaca: Cornell University Press, 1982.

Kuels, Eva C. *Plato and Greek Painting*. Leiden: E. J. Brill, 1978.

Kurtz, D. C., and J. Boardman. *Greek Burial Customs*. Ithaca: Cornell University Press, 1971.

Lacey, W. K. *The Family in Classical Greece*. Ithaca: Cornell University Press, 1968.

Lattimore, Richmond A. *Themes in Greek and Latin Epitaphs*. Urbana: University of Illinois Press, 1962.

Lewis, David M. *Sparta and Persia*. Leiden: E. J. Brill, 1977.

Lewis, I. M. *Ecstatic Religion: An Anthropological Study of Spirit Possession and Shamanism*. Harmondsworth: Penguin, 1971.

———. *Religion in Context*. Cambridge: Cambridge University Press, 1986.

Lienhardt, G. *Divinity and Experience*. Oxford: Oxford University Press, 1961.

Linforth, Ivan M. *The Arts of Orpheus*. Berkeley: University of California Press, 1941.

———. "The Corybantic Rites in Plato." *University of California Publications in Classical Philology* 13 (1946): 121–62.

———. "Soul and Sieve in Plato's *Gorgias*." *University of California Publications in Classical Philology* 12 (1944): 295–313.

———. "Telestic Madness in Plato, Phaedrus 244 DE." *University of California Publications in Classical Philology* 13 (1950): 163–72.

Lloyd, A. C. "Non-Discursive Thought: An Enigma of Greek Philosophy." *Proceedings of the Aristotelian Society* 70 (1969–70): 261–75.

———. "Non-Propositional Thought in Plotinus." *Phronesis* 31 (1986): 258–65.

Lloyd, G. E. R. *Magic, Reason, and Experience: Studies in the Origins and Development of Greek Science*. Cambridge: Cambridge University Press, 1979.

———. *Polarity and Analogy*. Cambridge: Cambridge University Press, 1966.

Lloyd-Jones, Hugh. *The Justice of Zeus*. Rev. ed. Berkeley: University of California Press, 1971, 1983.

Loraux, Nicole. *The Invention of Athens: The Funeral Oration in the Classical City*, trans. Alan Sheridan. Cambridge: Harvard University Press, 1986.

Luce, J. V. "Immortality in Plato's *Symposium*: A Reply." *Classical Review* 2 (1952): 137–41.

MacDowell, D. *Andokides: On the Mysteries*. Oxford: Oxford University Press, 1962.

———. *Athenian Homicide Law in the Age of the Orators*. Manchester: Manchester University Press, 1963.

———. *The Law in Classical Athens*. London: Thames and Hudson, 1978.

Macfarlane, A. D. J. *Witchcraft in Tudor and Stuart England*. London: Routledge and Kegan Paul, 1970.

McGinty, Peter. *Interpretation and Dionysos: Method in the Study of a God.* The Hague: Mouton, 1978.

Malcolm, John. "The Line and the Cave." *Phronesis* 7 (1962): 38–45.

Marcovich, M. "The Gold Leaf from Hipponion." *Zeitschrift für Papyrologie und Epigraphik* 23 (1976): 221–24.

Markus, R. A. "The Dialectic of Eros in Plato's *Symposium.*" In *Plato*, ed. Gregory Vlastos, vol. 2.

Marrou, H. I. *A History of Education in Antiquity*, trans. G. Lamb. New York: Sheed and Ward, 1956.

Mattingly, Harold B. "The Date of Plato's *Symposium.*" *Phronesis* 3 (1958): 31–39.

Meiggs, R. *The Athenian Empire.* Oxford: Oxford University Press, 1975.

Meuli, K. "Griechische Opferbrauche." In *Phyllobolia Festschrift P. Von der Muhll*, 185–288; *Gesammelt Schriften*, 2: 907–1021. Basel: 1946.

Mikalson, Jon D. *Athenian Popular Religion.* Chapel Hill: University of North Carolina Press, 1983.

———. "Religion in the Attic Demes." *American Journal of Philology* 98 (1977): 424–35.

———. *The Sacred and Civil Calendar of the Athenian Year.* Princeton: Princeton University Press, 1975.

Mills, K. W. "Plato's 'Non-Hypothetical Starting Point,'" *Durham University Journal* (n.d.): 152–59.

Moline, Jon. *Plato's Theory of Understanding.* Madison: University of Wisconsin Press, 1981.

Moore, J. M., trans. *Aristotle and Xenophon on Democracy and Oligarchy.* London: Chatto and Windus, 1975.

Moravcsik, Julius. "Learning as Recollection." In *Plato*, ed. Gregory Vlastos, vol. 1, *Metaphysics and Epistemology*, 53–69. Garden City, N.Y.: Doubleday, 1971.

———. "Reason and Eros in the 'Ascent'-Passage of the *Symposium.*" In *Essays in Ancient Greek Philosophy*, ed. John Anton and G. Kustas. Albany: State University of New York Press, 1971.

———. "Understanding and Knowledge in Plato's Philosophy," *Neue Hefte für Philosophie* 15–16 (1978): 53–69.

Moravcsik, Julius M. E., and Philip Temko, eds. *Plato on Beauty, Wisdom, and the Arts.* Totowa, N.J.: Rowman and Littlefield, 1982.

More, Paul Elmer. *The Religion of Plato.* Princeton: Princeton University Press, 1921.

Morgan, Michael L. "Authorship and the History of Philosophy." *Review of Metaphysics* 42 (1988): 327–55.

———. "Belief, Knowledge, and Learning in Plato's Middle Dialogues." *Canadian Journal of Philosophy*, suppl. vol. 9 (1983): 63–100.

———. "The Continuity Theory of Reality in Plato's *Hippias Major.*" *Journal of the History of Philosophy* 21 (April 1983): 133–58.

———. "The Goals and Methods of the History of Philosophy." *Review of Metaphysics* 40 (1987): 717–32.

———. "How Does Plato Solve the Paradox of Inquiry in the *Meno?*" In

Essays in Ancient Greek Philosophy: Plato, ed. J. Anton and A. Preus. Albany: State University of New York Press, 1989.

——. "Plato, Inquiry, and Painting." *Apeiron* (forthcoming, Spring 1990).

——. "Sense-Perception and Recollection in the *Phaedo*." *Phronesis* 29, no. 3 (1984): 237–51.

Morrison, J. S. "Two Unresolved Difficulties in the Line and Cave." *Phronesis* 22 (1977): 212–31.

Morrow, Glenn R., trans. *Plato's Epistles*. Indianapolis: Bobbs-Merrill, 1962.

Mossé, C. *Athens in Decline, 403–386 B.C.* London: Routledge and Kegan Paul, 1973.

Murdoch, Iris. *The Fire and the Sun: Why Plato Banished the Artists*. Oxford: Oxford University Press, 1977.

Murphy, N. R. "Back to the Cave." *Classical Quarterly* 28 (1934–35): 211–13.

——. *The Interpretation of Plato's Republic*. Oxford: Oxford University Press, 1951.

——. "The 'Simile of Light' in Plato's *Republic*." *Classical Quarterly* 26 (1932): 93–102.

Murray, Gilbert. *Five Stages of Greek Religion*. Garden City, N.Y.: Doubleday, 1955.

Mylonas, G. *Eleusis and the Eleusinian Mysteries*. Princeton: Princeton University Press, 1961.

Nagel, Thomas. *The View from Nowhere*. Oxford: Oxford University Press, 1986.

Nehamas, Alexander. "Plato on Imitation and Poetry in *Republic* 10." In *Plato on Beauty, Wisdom, and the Arts*, ed. Julius M. E. Moravcsik and Philip Temko, 47–78. Totowa, N.J.: Rowman and Littlefield, 1982.

——. "Plato on the Imperfection of the Sensible World." *American Philosophical Quarterly* 12 (1975): 105–17.

Nilsson, Martin P. "Early Orphism and Kindred Religious Movements." *Harvard Theological Review* 28 (1935): 181–230.

——. *Greek Folk Religion*. New York: Columbia University Press, 1940.

——. *Greek Piety*. Oxford: Oxford University Press, 1948.

——. *A History of Greek Religion*. 2d ed. Oxford: Oxford University Press, 1952.

——. *The Minoan-Mycenaean Religion and Its Survival in Greek Religion*. 2d ed. Lund: 1950.

——. *The Mycenaean Origin of Greek Mythology*. Berkeley: University of California Press, 1932.

Nock, Arthur D. "The Cult of Heroes." *Harvard Theological Review* 37 (1944): 141–74.

——. "Religious Attitudes of the Ancient Greeks." *Proceedings of the American Philosophical Society* 85 (1942): 472–82.

Nussbaum, Martha C. *The Fragility of Goodness: Luck and Ethics in Greek Tragedy and Philosophy*. Cambridge: Cambridge University Press, 1986.

Oliver, James H. *The Athenian Expounders of the Sacred and Ancestral Law.* Baltimore: Johns Hopkins University Press, 1950.

Otto, Walter F. *Dionysus: Myth and Cult,* trans. Robert B. Palmer. Bloomington: Indiana University Press, 1965.

———. *The Homeric Gods: The Spiritual Significance of Greek Religion,* trans. Moses Hadas. New York: Pantheon, 1954.

Owen, G. E. L. "A Proof in the *Peri Ideon.*" In *Studies in Plato's Metaphysics,* ed. R. E. Allen, 293–312. London: Routledge and Kegan Paul, 1965.

Panofsky, Erwin. *Meaning and the Visual Arts.* Garden City, N.Y.: Doubleday, 1955.

Parke, H. W. *Festivals of the Athenians.* Ithaca: Cornell University Press, 1977.

———. *Greek Oracles.* London: Hutchinson, 1967.

———. *The Oracles of Zeus.* Cambridge: Harvard University Press, 1967.

Parke, H. W., and D. E. W. Wormell. *The Delphic Oracle.* 2 vols. Oxford: Oxford University Press, 1956.

Parker, Robert. *Miasma: Pollution and Purification in Early Greek Religion.* Oxford: Oxford University Press, 1983.

Paton, H. J. "Plato's Theory of Eikasia." *Proceedings of the Aristotelian Society* 22 (1921–22): 69–104.

Penner, T. "Thought and Desire in Plato." In *Plato,* ed. Gregory Vlastos, 2: 96–118.

Pickard-Cambridge, A. *The Dramatic Festivals of Athens.* 2d ed. Oxford: Oxford University Press, 1968.

Plato. *Statesman,* trans. J. B. Skemp. Indianapolis: Bobbs-Merrill, 1957.

———. *Symposium,* ed. K. J. Dover. Cambridge: Cambridge University Press, 1980.

Pollitt, J. J. *The Ancient View of Greek Art: Criticism, History, and Terminology.* New Haven: Yale University Press, 1974.

———. *Art and Experience in Classical Greece.* Cambridge: Cambridge University Press, 1972.

———. *The Art of Greece, 1400–31 B.C.: Sources and Documents.* Englewood Cliffs, N.J.: Prentice-Hall, 1965.

Pomeroy, Sarah B. *Goddesses, Whores, Wives, and Slaves: Women in Classical Antiquity.* New York: Schocken, 1975.

Powell, C. "Religion and the Sicilian Expedition." *Historia* 28 (1979): 15–31.

Pritchett, W. K. *The Greek State at War.* Vol. 3, *Religion.* Berkeley: University of California Press, 1979.

Reeve, C. D. C. *Philosopher-Kings: The Argument of Plato's Republic.* Princeton: Princeton University Press, 1988.

———. *Socrates in the Apology.* Indianapolis: Hackett, 1989.

Reverdin, O. *La religion de la cité platonicienne.* Paris: Ecole Française d'Athènes, 1945.

Rhodes, P. J. *The Athenian Boule.* Oxford: Oxford University Press, 1972.

Rice, David G., and John E. Stambaugh, eds. *Sources for the Study of Greek Religion.* Missoula, Mont.: Scholars Press, 1979.

Richardson, N. J. *The Homeric Hymn to Demeter*. Oxford: Oxford University Press, 1974.

Richter, G. M. A. *Perspective in Greek and Roman Art*. London: Phaidon, 1970.

Rist, John M. *Eros and Psyche*. Toronto: University of Toronto Press, 1964.

Roberts, J. W. *City of Sokrates: An Introduction to Classical Athens*. London: Routledge and Kegan Paul, 1984.

Robinson, Richard. *Plato's Earlier Dialectic*. 2d ed. Oxford: Oxford University Press, 1953.

Robinson, T. M. *Plato's Psychology*. Toronto: University of Toronto Press, 1970.

Rohde, Erwin. *Psyche: The Cult of Souls and Belief in Immortality among the Greeks*, trans. W. K. C. Guthrie. 2 vols. New York: Harper and Row, 1966.

Rorty, Richard, J. B. Schneewind, and Quentin Skinner, eds. *Philosophy in History*. Cambridge: Cambridge University Press, 1984.

Rose, H. J. *Religion in Greece and Rome*. New York: Harper and Row, 1959.

Rosen, Stanley. *Plato's Symposium*. 2d ed. New Haven: Yale University Press, 1987.

Rosenmeyer, Thomas G. "Tragedy and Religion: The *Bacchae*." In *Euripides*, ed. Erich Segal. Englewood Cliffs, N.J.: Prentice-Hall, 1968.

Rouget, Gilbert. *Music and Trance*. Chicago: University of Chicago Press, 1985.

Rowe, Christopher. "One and Many in Greek Religion." *Eranos Yearbook* 45 (1980): 37–67.

Rutenber, Culbert G. *The Doctrine of the Imitation of God in Plato*. New York: King's Crown, 1946.

Ryder, T. T. B. *Koine Eirene: General Peace and Local Independence in Ancient Greece*. Oxford: Oxford University Press, 1965.

Ste. Croix, G. E. M. de. *The Origins of the Peloponnesian War*. Ithaca: Cornell University Press, 1972.

Scheffler, Israel. "In Praise of the Cognitive Emotions." *Teachers College Record* 79, no. 2 (1977): 171–86.

Scully, Vincent. *The Earth, the Temple, and the Gods: Greek Sacred Architecture*. Rev. ed. New Haven: Yale University Press, 1979.

Seager, R. "Thrasybulus, Conon and Athenian Imperialism, 396–386 B.C." *Journal of Hellenic Studies* 87 (1967): 95–115.

Sealey, Raphael. *A History of the Greek City States, ca. 700–338 B.C.* Berkeley: University of California Press, 1976.

Simon, Bennett. *Mind and Madness in Ancient Greece: The Classical Roots of Modern Psychiatry*. Ithaca: Cornell University Press, 1978.

Skemp, J. B. *The Theory of Motion in Plato's Later Dialogues*. Enlarged ed. Amsterdam: Hakkert, 1967.

Snell, Bruno. *The Discovery of the Mind*, trans. T. Rosenmeyer. Cambridge: Harvard University Press, 1953. Reprint, New York: Harper, 1960.

Snodgrass, Anthony. *Archaic Greece: The Age of Experiment*. Berkeley: University of California Press, 1980.

Solmsen, Friedrich. *Plato's Theology*. Ithaca, N.Y.: Cornell University Press, 1942.

Sorabji, Richard. "Myths about Non-Propositional Thought." In *Language and Logos*, ed. Malcolm Schofield and Martha Nussbaum. Cambridge: Cambridge University Press, 1982.

———. *Time, Creation, and the Continuum*. Ithaca, N.Y.: Cornell University Press, 1983.

Sprute, J. *Der Begriff der Doxa in der Platonischen Philosophie*. Göttingen: Vandenhoeck und Ruprecht, 1962.

Starr, Chester G. "Religion and Patriotism in Fifth-Century Athens." In *Panathenaia: Studies in Athenian Life and Thought in the Classical Age*, ed. T. E. Gregory and A. J. Podlecki. Lawrence, Kans.: Coronado, 1979.

Stocker, Michael. "Intellectual Desire, Emotion, and Action." In *Explaining Emotions*, ed. Amelie Rorty, 323–38. Berkeley: University of California Press, 1980.

Stocks, J. L. "The Divided Line of Plato *Rep.* VI." *Classical Quarterly* 5 (1911): 73–88.

Strauss, Barry S. *Athens after the Peloponnesian War: Class, Faction and Policy, 403–386 BC*. Ithaca, N.Y.: Cornell University Press, 1986.

———. "Thrasybulus and Conon: A Rivalry in Athenian Politics in the 390s B.C." *American Journal of Philology* 105 (1984): 37–48.

Strauss, Leo. *The City and Man*. Chicago: Rand McNally, 1964.

Tanner, R. G. "*Dianoia* and Plato's Cave." *Classical Quarterly* 20 (1970): 81–91.

Taylor, A. E. *Socrates: The Man and His Thought*. Garden City, N.Y.: Doubleday, 1952 (orig. pub. 1933).

Thomas, Keith. "History and Anthropology." *Past and Present* 24 (1963): 3–24.

———. *Religion and the Decline of Magic*. New York: Charles Scribner's Sons, 1971.

Thompson, W. H. *The Phaedrus of Plato*. London: Whittaker, 1868.

Turner, V. W. *The Ritual Process*. London: Routledge and Kegan Paul, 1969.

Vermeule, Emily. *Aspects of Death in Early Greek Art and Poetry*. Berkeley: University of California Press, 1979.

Vernant, Jean-Pierre. *Myth and Society in Ancient Greece*, trans. Janet Lloyd. Atlantic Highlands, N.J.: Humanities Press, 1980.

Vlastos, Gregory. "Afterthoughts on the Socratic Elenchus." *Oxford Studies in Ancient Philosophy* 1 (1983): 71–74.

———. "Anamnesis in the *Meno*." *Dialogue* 4 (1965): 143–67.

———. "Degrees of Reality in Plato." In *New Essays in Plato and Aristotle*, ed. R. Bambrough. London: Routledge and Kegan Paul, 1965. Reprinted in *Platonic Studies*, 2d ed. Princeton: Princeton University Press, 1981.

———. "The Historical Socrates and Athenian Democracy." *Political Theory* 11 (1983): 495–516.

———. "A Metaphysical Paradox." In *Platonic Studies*, 43–57. 2d ed. Princeton: Princeton University Press, 1981.

———. "The Paradox of Socrates." In *The Philosophy of Socrates*. Garden City, N.Y.: Doubleday, 1971.

———. *Platonic Studies*. 2d ed. Princeton: Princeton University Press, 1981.

———. "Religion and Medicine in the Cult of Asclepius: A Review Article." *Review of Religion* 13 (1949): 269–90.

———. "Socrates' Disavowal of Knowledge." *Philosophical Quarterly* 35 (1985): 1–31.

———. "The Socratic Elenchus." *Oxford Studies in Ancient Philosophy* 1 (1983): 25–58.

Vlastos, Gregory, ed. *The Philosophy of Socrates*. Garden City, N.Y.: Doubleday, 1971.

———. *Plato*. 2 vols. Garden City, N.Y.: Doubleday, 1971.

von Fritz, Kurt. "Greek Prayers." *Review of Religion* 10 (1945): 5–39.

Webster, T. B. L. *Everyday Life in Classical Athens*. London: Batsford, 1969.

Wedberg, A. *Plato's Philosophy of Mathematics*. Stockholm: Almquist och Wiksell, 1955.

West, M. L. *The Orphic Poems*. Oxford: Oxford University Press, 1983.

White, John. *The Birth and Rebirth of Pictorial Space*. 2d ed. London: Faber and Faber, 1967.

White, Nicholas P. *A Companion to Plato's Republic*. Indianapolis: Hackett, 1979.

———. "Inquiry." *Review of Metaphysics* 28 (1974–75): 289–310.

———. *Plato on Knowledge and Reality*. Indianapolis: Hackett, 1976.

Whitehead, David. *The Demes of Attica*. Princeton: Princeton University Press, 1986.

———. *The Ideology of the Athenian Metic*. Cambridge: Cambridge University Press, 1977.

Wickersham, John, and Gerald Verbrugghe. *Greek Historical Documents: The Fourth Century B.C.* Amsterdam: Hakkert, 1973.

Wilamowitz-Moellendorff, U. v. *Der Glaube der Hellenen*. 2 vols. Berlin, 1931–32.

Williams, Bernard. *Ethics and the Limits of Philosophy*. Cambridge: Harvard University Press, 1985.

———. "Philosophy." In *The Legacy of Greece*, ed. M. I. Finley. Oxford: Oxford University Press, 1984.

Wollheim, Richard. *The Thread of Life*. Cambridge: Harvard University Press, 1984.

Xenophon. *Anabasis*, ed. G. L. Cawkwell. Harmondsworth: Penguin, 1973.

———. *Hellenica (A History of My Times)*, ed. G. L. Cawkwell. Harmondsworth: Penguin, 1979.

Zuntz, G. *Persephone*. Oxford: Oxford University Press, 1971.

pp. 145-146. Context of philosopher king in
traditional office of Athenian archon-basileus
- basically a religious leader, a mystes,

168. Change and immortality
" What is always changing is immortal."
(Cf. Gregory of Nyssa).

173-4. Apocatastasis & reunion of souls
with divinity (Cf. Origen).